Politics

Editor

PROFESSOR W. A. ROBSON
B.SC (ECON), PH.D., LL.M

Professor Emeritus of Public Administration
in the University of London

THE GOVERNMENT AND
POLITICS OF INDIA

W. H. Morris-Jones
Director of the Institute of Commonwealth Studies
University of London

HUTCHINSON UNIVERSITY LIBRARY
LONDON

HUTCHINSON & CO *(Publishers)* LTD
178–202 Great Portland Street, London W1

London Melbourne Sydney
Auckland Johannesburg Cape Town
and agencies throughout the world

First published 1964
Second edition 1967
Third (revised) edition 1971

The cover of the paperback edition shows the
voting symbols of some Indian political parties
round the symbol of independent India.

This book has been set in Times type, printed in Great Britain
on smooth wove paper by Anchor Press, and
bound by Wm. Brendon, both of Tiptree, Essex

ISBN 0 09 106910 6 (cased)
0 09 106911 4 (paper)

To Graziella

CONTENTS

MAPS

ABBREVIATIONS

India is fond of abbreviations and many of the following (marked *) are in very common use. A few, however, have been included solely because they are employed to save space in this text.

*AICC	All-India Congress Committee
AIKS	All-India Kisan Sabha
*AITUC	All-India Trades Union Congress
*BDO	Block Development Officer
*BKD	Bharatiya Kranti Dal
CD	Community Development
*CPI	Communist Party of India
CPI(M)	Communist Party (Marxist)
*DCC	District Congress Committee
*DMK	Dravida Munnetra Kazhagam [Party]
*IAS	Indian Administrative Service
*ICS	Indian Civil Service
IPS	Indian Police Service
*KMP	Kisan Mazdoor Praja [Party]
LS	Lok Sabha (House of the People)
MCC	Mandal Congress Committee
*MLA	Member of [a State] Legislative Assembly
*NDC	National Development Council
*PAC	Public Accounts Committee
PC	Planning Commission
*PCC	Pradesh (State) Congress Committee
PM	Prime Minister

*PSP	Praja Socialist Party
PR	Panchayat Raj
PWP	Peasants and Workers Party
RRP	Ram Rajya Parishad [Party]
RS	Rajya Sabha (Council of States)
*RSS	Rashtriya Swayamsevak Sangh
*SSP	Samyukta Socialist Party
SRC	States Reorganization Commission
*VLW	Village Level Worker

PREFACE TO THIRD (REVISED) EDITION

When the first edition was sent to press, India had scarcely recovered from the death of Nehru. In the last half-dozen years the political scene has witnessed many changes. In particular the Congress Party which had presided over the country's political stability for two decades after independence suffered several defeats in the general elections of 1967 and scarcely improved its position in the mini-general election in five states in 1968–9. The harmony in the top leadership which had been secured during Shastri's period as Prime Minister did not long survive the second succession, and its erosion was an important factor in the election failure. That failure, so far from producing consolidation, seemed only to make matters worse and by the autumn of 1969 Congress, already weakened by earlier defections, split into two warring segments each claiming the tarnished mantle.

This series of events clearly modified the nature of the party system. Moreover it also emphasised and accentuated the changing relations between the central government and the states. From both viewpoints it seemed to those who had been speaking since Nehru's death of the disintegration of Indian democracy that their predictions were coming true. In these circumstances it might have been expected that this book, which took a less alarmist view, might by the start of the seventies stand in need of substantial revision. I have certainly added a good deal about the years since 1964. There has also been some re-writing of certain passages, mainly to accommodate new material. Beyond that, however, I have not felt obliged to go: there has been little to retract and the terms and tone of my analysis remain unaltered.

It is no doubt true that if one were writing the book now for the first time it would differ more than any revision can do. One never steps into the same river twice because both the person and the river change. But the water that has flowed in the meantime consists not only of fresh events to be studied but also of the studies of others. I hope I have included the more important of these in my note on further reading. (This makes the note even longer than before. In trusting that this will maintain its usefulness I am taking a risk: one American student complained frankly that my reading lists were, as he put it, interfering with his outside business activities.) I have taken some account of the fresh insights lately provided by fellow scholars; to have done more would have entailed altering the framework and scale of the book. My justification for leaving these alone is that the call for a new edition suggests that the present form retains its value.

Calm efficiency and tactful patience were required to ensure that my scribbled revisions became translated into a form acceptable for presentation to the publishers; I am most grateful to Mrs Anne Barnes for displaying both qualities.

London, August 1970

PREFACE TO FIRST EDITION

A full treatment of the subject is not claimed for a book of this size. While I have tried not to omit any matter of importance, I have been unable to avoid some selection of themes for elaboration. Moreover, I have allowed my emphasis on certain aspects to be influenced not only by my views on their intrinsic significance but also by my own interests and my assessment as to which areas of the subject stood most in need of exposition. In this sense the book may be regarded as a group of essays.

I naturally hope that readers already conversant with the subject will find the presentation helpful. The main purpose of the book, however, is to serve as an introductory guide. If it makes it easier for students of politics to extend their general understanding towards the most important of the 'new states', I shall be content. If a few students are encouraged to make modern Indian politics a subject of special study, this would be most rewarding.

The book is less the outcome of particular periods of research than the product of continuing study of the Indian political scene. I must nevertheless record my gratitude to the Rockefeller Foundation for again making it possible for me to spend some months in India collecting information. I wish to thank the University of Chicago whose invitation to conduct a graduate course in this subject gave me a valued opportunity of trying out my ideas on an unusually lively group of students. To El Colegio de Mexico I am indebted for offering me the interesting experience of talking about one developing polity to students for another. My own university has been most understanding and generous in its granting of leave of absence. A limited version of Chapter 2 appeared as 'India's political idioms' in C. H. Philips (Ed.), *Politics and Society in India* (1963).

I have received help from Mr S. Waddell, who located lost items of information and wrestled with election statistics on my behalf, and from Mrs Joan Hepburn, who in the midst of other duties produced presentable typescript from often untidy handwriting.

My fellow workers in this field are not many in number but it is to them that I owe most. Their own researches and stimulating interpretations, as well as their encouragement to my own efforts, have made the present enterprise possible and enjoyable. My debt is especially to Lloyd and Susanne Rudolph who read the typescript.

I

SOME LEGACIES

Introduction

The political systems of modern states are usually developments from earlier, sometimes much earlier, times. The systems undergo change in response to changes in other aspects of human behaviour and thought; they also have the capacity to exert independent influence on these other aspects. If, in haste, we speak of a political system 'reflecting' social conditions, we would recognize that the process of reflection is one which changes both the instrument and the subject. Parliament, monarchy, political parties and the arrangement of law courts have throughout their history in British life reflected in some measure the patterns of thought, the social and economic forces at work in and through the people. In doing so they have changed in structure and role; in doing so they have also changed and moulded the character of those non-political ideas and actions. The transformation of the British monarchy from the effective to the 'dignified' head of the constitution; the parallel development of parliament from royal court to sovereign forum; the very different evolution of the American presidency—no one can doubt that these changes of political institutions have served not only to express but to shape the conduct and thinking of men outside their political relations. The independent influence of political institutions on the lives of human beings is surely subject to great variations, but is never wholly absent. For that reason it was poor advice that was implied in saying 'for forms of government, let fools contest'. To argue and debate about political systems is not likely to be everybody's business, but it would be a sad error to leave it to fools.

The pattern and style of the interaction between political institutions and the rest of human life has varied from time to time and also from country to country. Sometimes the interaction can be seen as a steady movement over a period. Sometimes the nature of the interaction seems to be dominated by some great revolutionary changes. Cases of the latter kind—we may call them changes of regime—fall into three main categories according as they are brought about by internal upheaval, by the imposition of alien rule or, thirdly, by its withdrawal or overthrow. We then have what are frequently referred to as new states. In the modern world numerous examples of all three kinds are to be found—more easily indeed than are old-established states. India is a leading member of the third group.

New states usually like to believe that they are in some respects much newer—and in other respects much older—than in fact they can be. The newness is exaggerated out of loyalty and excessive faith in the revolution. The new rulers, makers of the new regimes, who come into possession of power after what often seems and sometimes is a long and difficult struggle, seek to put their predecessors firmly behind them. The slate is imagined as wiped clean, the future to be created anew. And sometimes this notion will be expressed and reinforced by an ideology. In such circumstances men come to believe contradictory things about the power of political institutions: those of the new 'political kingdom' can achieve wonders in the moulding of all aspects of life, while those of yesterday's regime shrink in significance or even vanish without trace and become as if they never were. They will see only with difficulty and resentment the extent to which the new political system bears at least some of the marks of its distrusted forerunner. The fact that the former institutions often carry on *faute de mieux*, into the brave new world, shaped by it but also shaping, is suppressed. (Of course, the view of the revolutionaries is not unchallenged. Such men beget fresh revolutionaries who see too little changed. These fall into the opposite error, attributing strange feebleness to the new and weirdly satanic power to the old surviving institutions.) The contradictions entailed in the dream of novelty are rendered more digestible by being joined to a dream of antiquity. It happens particularly in former colonial or imperial territories that the new regime is thought of as a manifestation of some original indigenous ways of life long concealed and of national aspirations long frustrated. The new state is then at once a rejection of yesterday and a re-creation of the day before. This convenient but dubious belief in leap-frog history serves to dispel the contradictions: the reason why the immediate past can be so easily escaped from is that it was alien and the explanation of the potency of the new institutions is that they are 'ours' of yore, belonging to the 'genius of the people'. There is something of all this in India but less than elsewhere—she is inured to the mixing of continuity and change, too sophisticated to be deceived by either of the dreams. It is the business of this chapter to explore the nature of modern India's political inheritance from the past. In August 1947 British rule came to an end in the sub-continent and power was transferred to two independent Dominions, India and Pakistan. In January 1950 India adopted a new Constitution and became a republic. The momentous events are easily put in the two sentences. But we have to ask: how new was the new republic and what was handed over along with 'power'? The main legacies of relevance to our present enquiry can be conveniently considered under four heads: Government; Movement; Mediating institutions; Problems and promises.

Government

It is in more than one sense that the new India inherited government. In the first place it inherited a widely held sentiment regarding the importance of there being a government. This is not as usual as it sounds; it is not difficult to think of new states which have suffered grievously by the absence of such sentiment. It is probably true that rural India—the several hundred thousand scattered villages, made of earth and hardly rising out of it, connected with each other and with towns only by the merest rutted tracks—this India was not intimately acquainted with British rule. Government was numerically tiny and even the most conscientious district officer on horse or jeep would leave many villages rarely visited. But in every village there would be the headman and the *patwari* (accountant, for land revenue purposes), men of the village who in these capacities represented the government. Government itself was far away in a capital seldom or never seen and its remoteness only increased its imposing stature; the power and authority were awesome; it was Government, *Raj*, *Sarkar*. Yet its little finger was a continuous presence in the alleyways between the huts. Like a great god it had its contrasting aspects, giver and taker of all, protector and tax-collector. What is important is that it was respected and that the necessity for its existence and strength was accepted and perhaps even understood.

Nor was this feeling restricted to the illiterate tiller of the fields. Urban attitudes towards government were, of course, more varied, as urban society is more varied; clerk, factory worker, shopkeeper and lawyer would perhaps have their own special ways of looking on government. All of them, by virtue of education or urban living, would share certain feelings towards government that would be different from those of the villager; it would be less remote, more subject to criticism and influence, less mysterious, more bitterly detested as alien (for to the villager all government from outside itself is alien). Yet even among such people there would be respect for government, a respect probably supported by the capacity of government service to attract so much of the country's educational cream. (Security, salary and satisfying work, together with the absence of significant competition from industry, largely explain the prestige of government service. But something must also be allowed for the status of government itself; to serve such respected authority would have enhanced a person's prestige even if other factors had been absent.) Men in cities, less close to the vicissitudes of nature and, until lately at least, less directly aware of the government as gatherer of taxes than the cultivators, would scarcely have the latter's clear double view of the *Raj* as destroyer and protector. But in sophisticated circles no less than among the simple people there would be an importance attached to government, a regard, albeit resentful at times, for the *Raj*, a disposition in a significantly common Indian phrase to 'look to government'.

Much of this has been carried forward in the transfer of power, though not without modifications. For several reasons, government is less remote and awesome: it is no longer alien to the country; it is numerically vastly larger; it is less bureaucratically anonymous. The presence of government is felt on a new increased scale and in fresh areas of activity; government controls and regulates, it establishes bodies for the actual undertaking of industrial enterprises, it reaches down through its Community Development organization to the villages and does so not merely as policemen and tax-collector but as agent for the improvement of agriculture and the transformation of rural society. The little finger has become the whole hand. Government is everywhere and inescapable. It is true that some people—especially perhaps Indian civil servants who worked under both regimes—consider that government is now less respected than formerly in spite of its increased activity. It is also true that the expansion of government is not peculiar to India but common to all modern states. It remains the case, however, that the observer from outside discovers in India an awareness of government, a sense of its importance and a feeling of the need for its stability and strength which is found in few other countries.

This psychological fact of Indian political life was evidenced frequently during the discussions in the Constituent Assembly during 1947–9 when the new Constitution was being hammered out. It played an important part, for instance, in the rejection of proportional representation, in the insertion of emergency provisions, in the resistance against elected state governors and in the qualifications attached to fundamental rights. The need for government, so many seemed to say, is where we start from, the indispensable centre around which political forces must play. It is not fanciful to see the same sentiment at work in some features of post-independence politics such as the concern that elections should return effective governments (I am not suggesting that such concern was a factor of dominating importance in the minds of voters, but it had some force) and the reluctance to see imposed on government procedures which go so far beyond ensuring full criticism that they hamper the vitality of rule.

India's political leaders inherited under this heading of government still more than the accumulated sum of psychological capital; they received the more tangible equipment and machinery of government. These may be considered first as organization, structure and procedures, and, secondly, as personnel.

If it is fair to describe India's present Constitution as federal but with important unitary features, it may not be wrong to say that the constitution she inherited in 1947 was unitary but with strong federal features. Federalism, like democracy, is a matter of process and degree, and the last Act of the British Parliament laying down a pattern of government for India—the Act of 1935—pointed firmly in the direction of federalism. It was the penultimate chapter of a rather long story which began before the nineteenth century and included several themes besides the federal—in the later stages notably the movement towards self-government. Even the federal theme is at first uncertain and ambiguous, mixed with ideas about decentralisation. There is also a to-and-fro movement in the emergence of the federal theme. After all, before the Regulating Act of 1773 the three British settlements of Bombay, Calcutta and Madras, each grown into a Presidency, were independent of each other and separately related to the Directors of the East India Company in London. That Act established the superiority of Calcutta by making it the seat of the Governor-General and Council, but effective control over the other Presidencies and territories had to await the gradual improvement of internal communications and the tightening of provisions for central control as in the Acts of 1784 and, more conclusively, 1833. By the time the governing of India became in 1858 the responsibility of Crown and Parliament instead of company the system of rule was as centralized as it could be without being unworkable (and some have said it was more so). The units of British India are described as having been reduced, by the loss of legislative powers and by financial and administrative control, to the status

of agents of the centre. On the other hand, it has to be remembered
that other parts of the country—by no means inconsiderable in area
or population—were being deliberately left under the rule of Indian
princes who, while by no means independent sovereigns, nevertheless
enjoyed a great deal of authority within their states.

With some difficulty the tide moved after a while in the other
direction. Legislative powers were restored to the provinces in 1861,
but it may very well be that more important than this was the
increasingly careful and extensive consultation which went on
between centre and provinces on all important matters of policy. No
doubt it remained a centralized bureaucracy, but the men at the top
were not so stupid as to wish to ignore the variety of conditions in a
sub-continent, nor were they so arrogant as to do without the
opinions of their colleagues in the provinces. Yet consultation alone
was not enough and the voice of the decentralizers grew loud in the
land. At that stage it is clear that at least three themes were overlapping: administrative, constitutional and political. This was seen
in the difficulty experienced by the Commission on Decentralization
(1909) in restricting itself to the first. The solution to administrative
apoplexy involved a constitutional re-allocation of powers and this
was bound up at the same time with the need to associate developing Indian non-official opinion with the deliberative process—an
association which seemed more usefully and less harmfully effected
at levels lower than the central Council. The connection may be put
in another way: a weakening of provincial dependence on the centre
and an increase in the responsibility of provincial governments to the
people of the provinces could only be done well if done together;
for the latter without the former would be impossible while the
former without the latter would entail a multiplicity of local
autocracies.

These conclusions were less clearly manifested in the Morley–
Minto reforms of 1909 than in the Montagu–Chelmsford report and
the consequent Act of 1919. This Act attempted to carve out a range
of 'transferred' subjects suitable for entrusting to ministers accountable to elected provincial legislatures, a balance of 'reserved' subjects
being left in the hands of officials under the Governors. But this
scheme of 'dyarchy' required a preliminary relaxation of control by
the central government. This relaxation was not thought of as implying the introduction of federalism but at the same time it was
evidently more than could reasonably be conveyed by the term
decentralization; the favoured word was devolution. It entailed a
classification of subjects into those which were primarily the responsibility of provinces and those of which the centre continued

to be in charge. It also meant a separation of provincial and central sources of revenue (with provision for provincial contributions to the centre), independent provincial budgets and the removal of a host of administrative controls.

That the responsible ministers of the provinces should in time come to be entrusted with even the 'reserved' subjects and that some part of the work of even the central government should be handed over to Indian ministers may seem now to be developments in accordance with the natural course of events. They did indeed come about, but not without prodigious labours of investigation, agitation, negotiation and argument, whose record is to be found in such documents as the reports of the Simon Commission, Nehru Committee, Round Table Conferences and Joint Select Committee. Part of the difficulty lay in the failure of mutual misunderstanding and deepening distrust between the British government and India's political leaders. But another factor of importance was the considerable awkwardness, even with the co-operation of the best wills in the world, of discerning clearly the shape of the central government, in particular the way in which the logic driving towards a federation could work out in view of the presence of nearly six hundred princely states alongside the provinces of British India. Talk of a federation was common in the twenties but for the most part confidence and clarity could only be obtained by ignoring that half of the country. It is true that the scheme eventually envisaged in the Government of India Act of 1935 was odd, but it is unfair to present it as more odd than the situation with which it was intended to deal. There was to be a federation composed partly and in straightforward uniform fashion of the provinces, partly of such princely states as wished to enter, the latter joining by Instruments of Accession separately negotiated. The units of the federal state would thus have been most numerous, utterly diverse in constitution and varying considerably in their relations with the centre. The central government of this collection would itself have been constructed on dyarchy lines of a separation of ministers' subjects and officials' subjects. Neither those concerned nor students of institutions were able to see the creation completed and at work, for the stipulated prior condition that 50 per cent of the princes should join had not been fulfilled when the outbreak of war put a stop to all fundamental constitutional reform. Even so, the Act made three contributions to Indian political development. It established a full regime of responsible government in the provinces operated on an exceptionally elaborate division of powers vis-à-vis the centre. It established in the Federal Court a promise of the federation to come. Not least valuable, it provided in its 451 clauses a model for the Indian Constitution of 1950; for here, dyarchy with its hesitations and the princes with their Instruments notwithstanding, was a draft whose general vision and tendency to detail alike India was not able to throw aside. (It may be worth adding—without making it a specific contribution of the 1935 Act—that it proved, despite its complexity and detail, to be a remarkably adaptable constitution. Let us remember that it served, with ingenious modifications, as the basic framework for such different situations as British India during the varied period 1937–47, Pakistan from 1947 to 1956 and India from 1947 to 1949.)

The federal structure is thus an important part of the material legacy of government. But, as is evident, this was a later development of British rule. Like the parallel and related growth of responsible government, it was grafted on to a longer established system of rule by officials. Certain features of that system survived the pressures of nationalism and constitutional change so effectively that they too were handed over in 1947.

The paradoxical point about a centralized bureaucracy is that there are relatively few bureaucrats at the centre; the majority are dispersed over the country. Britain is not such a bureaucracy. Although it is no doubt geographically inexact to speak nowadays of the British civil servant as working in Whitehall, it remains true that he is a member of the staff of a central government department. In recent years regional and even local offices of central departments have increased in number, but it is still the case that an enormous part of the business of administering Britain is performed by a host of local authorities each with its own more or less independent bureaucracy. India's experience has been rather different. Much is heard in India these days about the indigenous tradition of local democratic self-government by village *panchayats*, but exactly how general and how effective were these councils of elders is a matter of doubt and dispute in the absence of adequate records. What is certain is that in the course of the last century British rule erected its own administrative system in which the focal unit was the district. All provinces were divided into districts. Their area and population might vary greatly as between one part of the country and another but a rough indication is given by the average figure of 4,400 square miles and perhaps one million inhabitants. In most provinces, districts were grouped to form divisions; in all provinces, each district would be split up into sub-divisions, these in turn being composed of smaller units called *Tehsils* or *Taluks* made up of a number of villages. This was the framework which, outside the larger towns with their own municipal governments, contained and covered the whole population. This framework was inherited by the new regime.

Three features of this order of administration are of special significance. In the first place it was a cardinal point of the system that in each unit there should be one official with overriding general responsibility: divisional commissioner; collector or district magistrate or deputy commissioner; sub-divisional officer; *tehsildar* or *mamlatdar*. Alongside the district officer there would be specialist officers such as district superintendent of police and chief engineer. They would be responsible so far as the specialist service itself was concerned to appropriate departments of the provincial government but in general district administration they would come under the district officer to whom they would look for leadership. Specialist functions of government were a later accretion; the substantial and senior tasks of government were the preservation of law and order, the settlement of disputes and the collection of the revenue necessary for the maintenance of the structure.

The second feature is closely related to the first: there should be no rigid separation in terms of personnel between administrative and judicial functions but, rather, there should be some measure of combination of the functions in the same person. In this there was nothing strange. Such had been the assumption not only of the Moghal predecessors of the British rulers of India but also of the British themselves; the separation of the judiciary from the rest of British government was first a matter of convenience and only subsequently a matter of principle. Moreover, it could become a matter of principle only when men began to think at least as much about their own rights against government as about their disputes with their neighbours. The British rulers of India with some exceptions (of periods and persons) saw no reason to assume that India had to follow that sophisticated line; government had better be simple and strong. This meant that the man entrusted with the peace and security of a district must also be responsible for the settlement of disputes; in adhering to the tradition of the land one would also be following reason, for if governments behaved themselves it could only be from disputes between subjects that order and internal peace would be threatened. The district officer was therefore collector, magistrate and administrator.

While the first and second features are original and fundamental, the third is subsidiary, unrelated and even incongruous. The conjunction of reforming impulses and public awakening brought about the introduction from the 1870s—and especially after Lord Ripon's resolution of 1882—of boards of non-officials (at first nominated, later elected) at the district and lower levels. The record of these local self-government bodies was not glorious. For one thing the role of adjunct to dominant district officer was not inspiring and could be tricky; yet the boards could not be given substantial responsibility without undermining in some measure the accustomed position of the key administrator. For another, almost by the time Western education in general and familiarity with public affairs in particular had become sufficiently widespread to furnish an adequate number of participants for these bodies, the nationalist movement was ready and able to persuade most likely members that this was an enterprise to be scorned. In the result, the boards contributed only a little to the satisfactory functioning of administration and the civic instruction of their members, while constituting not infrequently a source of tedium or irritation to the effectively responsible official. Nonetheless a mass of complex legislation regarding these bodies lay on the provincial statute books by 1947 and an inescapable part of the legacy of government was this somewhat inconclusive experience of arranging a marriage between local self-government and centralized bureaucracy. In the islands of metropolitan life, measures of munici-pal self-government had an earlier start, attracted more active participation and produced a more varied set of outcomes ranging from sober constructiveness to scandalous dissolution.

It will be clear that this administration was firmly hierarchical. From the provincial government (and, in the heyday of the system, from the Governor-General at the centre) the chain of command stretched steadily down through commissioner, collector and *tehsildar* to the village headmen. But this hierarchical character is only partly revealed if we look at the organizational structure; to complete the picture we must also see the personnel structure. This was *sui generis*, though in its historical evolution perfectly under-standable. The bureaucrats of India were not members of a single civil service; nor were there different services for manning the various levels of administration—central, provincial and district. Instead, the structure of services—each with its own largely self-contained schemes of recruitment, promotion and salary—cut unevenly across that of governmental organisation. Thus to the bureaucrat it was more important to know to which service one belonged than to remember what level of government one served. This has had certain important consequences. On the one hand, for instance, it had the advantage that officials were mainly disinclined to be narrowly loyal to a particular organizational unit; on the other hand, it produced a sense of service solidarity which made any general review of the service structure difficult.

The original, senior and most superior service was the Indian Civil Service. In a country where any kind of government employment carried appropriate prestige, membership of the highest service of all lifted a man into a social stratosphere. To belong to the ICS was not simply a guarantee of a good and interesting job, it was also a combination of a calling and an honour; no wonder one put the letters after one's name. More than that, it was practically the sole repository of power. For from its ranks were drawn not only the district officers and the senior officials of both provincial and central governments but also the Governors of most provinces, the members (until 1921 and in part until 1937) of provincial executive councils, most of the members of the Viceroy's executive council and even some of the members of the Secretary of State's India Council in London. The ICS was recruited by competitive examination, at first in England only and under the Civil Service Commissioners. Some Indians entered by this route, but not until the Lee Commission report (1924) planned a phased Indianization and recruitment examinations were organized in India did the number of Indian ICS men increase substantially. British and Indian alike were on entry assigned on a permanent basis to a particular province. They would start their careers in the districts with a period of attachment under the guidance of an experienced officer. In time they would themselves take charge of a district. They might serve for a period at the provincial secretariat. They might also be posted for a period on deputation at the central secretariat; if so, they nevertheless remained on the strength of their province of original allocation; to that province they would, in principle and often in practice, in due course return. The senior posts at the centre were reserved for the ICS, but the centre relied on these loans from the provinces for filling them. The term 'all-India service' therefore indicated a manner of recruitment and a coverage of all levels of government, but it did not imply transferability from one province to another. That was ruled out partly by the earlier tradition of independent presidency governments, partly by the importance attached to the civil servant's being familiar with the language, the needs and the ways of one region.

The ICS was the first all-India service but it did not remain the only one. Its members were general administrators and, at the higher levels, makers of policy. To assist them in dealing with a growing range of governmental activity there were established a number of all-India services of a specialist kind: the Indian Police, the Indian Agricultural Service, the Indian Educational Service, etc. Structured like the ICS whom they served, they enjoyed considerable status but still well below that of the senior service. Far more quickly

Indianized than the ICS (already the Islington Commission of 1912 accepted that), most of them also soon passed out of the control and protective eye of the Secretary of State as the subjects with which they were concerned became the responsibility of provincial governments. By 1947 only the ICS and the Indian Police remained as effective all-India services. The 'demoted' services, on ceasing to be all-India in structure, joined the second main group of services, the provincial. Recruited and employed within the provinces, these officers manned the less senior posts in the provincial secretariat and in the lower units of government.

Finally, a third group of services had developed which differed from the all-India and provincial services by being intended wholly for work at one level of government: the central services. One of these, the Imperial Secretariat Service, comprised the 'executive' and clerical grades in the New Delhi Secretariat. The others, such as the Customs and Audit Services, were engaged on the administration of central subjects. The most remarkable of this group was the Indian Political Service; mainly British, its members were employed in the two fascinating tasks of diplomatic supervision and guidance of the princely states and watchful (sometimes warlike) surveillance of the scarcely settled tribal areas of the north-west and north-east frontiers.

With the transfer of power in 1947, the British as rulers withdrew. Fresh British recruitment to the ICS had practically ceased some years earlier and the majority of Britishers still in the service retired, only a handful electing to continue in the employment of the new regime. But the great machine of government remained intact. Its build and shape, its manner of working, the relations of its parts—all these were firmly present, constituting an enormous fact of Indian politics. They were present not so much as descriptions in text-books and manuals of office procedure, not even as physical buildings, rooms, corridors and human bodies, but as established habits, prejudices, interests and expectations in both the great army of government servants and in the citizen body alike. It was scarcely possible for the new management to discard this legacy, to take the advice of a Lenin and 'smash the state machine'. Sardar Vallabhbhai Patel had to make the point in an impassioned defence of the all-India services in the Constituent Assembly in 1949: 'I have worked with them during this difficult period. . . . Remove them and I see nothing but a picture of chaos all over the country.' Only from Patel would some Congressmen take this; for many the ICS, even if wholly Indian, was a distrusted instrument from a resented past and they could not see what place it could have in a new order. Indeed, the problem was not simple: if wholesale destruction would be fatal, wholesale preservation might be absurd in the changed conditions. The humdrum and difficult task presented by the legacy was that of determining just which features of the existing machinery made sense only as parts of an imperial design, which were suited to more or less permanent demands of the Indian situation and which were fitted to meet new needs of government. This job was in some measure tackled by the makers of the Constitution, but there is more in a machinery of government than can be said in even the longest document and the work goes on today. Some aspects of the problem are discussed in Chapter 4.

Movement

If the new Indian rulers received a legacy of government from their predecessors, they assuredly carried over also a legacy from their own immediate past, from their experience of the nationalist movement. Indeed much of the character of modern Indian politics can be explained in terms of the interaction of these two legacies. Many of the 'lines of force' in Indian political life run between these opposite and strongly contrasted poles. But not all; as Chapter 2 seeks to show, certain other important lines run as between these two legacies taken together on the one hand and new factors of an even more sharply contrasted nature.

In fact it can be said at once that in one obvious respect the two basic ingredients of government and movement—the elemental data of Indian politics—were not contrasted but similar. In both the dominant emphasis was all-India, the final stress was on the note of the unity and integrity of the country. This must not be over-simplified, however; for this emphasis was not in either case attained without difficulty. We have already seen that in the sphere of government, concessions had to be made to decentralization, devolution and eventually provincial autonomy; that the provincial civil service grew considerably and to some extent at the expense of the all-India services; that even in the all-India services men belonged to provincial cadres—with all that could imply in terms of loyalty. For all that, the impact of the machinery of government was mainly unifying. Similar conflicts and a similar outcome can be found also in the national movement.

To give a brief account of this second legacy is difficult; a national movement has facets more numerous and less tangible than a governmental organization. We can do no more than select some of those which appear to be most striking and most significant in their influence on Indian politics today.

Probably the first point to be made is the very simple one that the Indian national movement had a relatively long history, reaching well back into the nineteenth century. Perhaps it would be more accurate to speak of an Indian political movement, for the explicit demand for national independence did not of course appear at the start. Nevertheless, it is important that the organization which was in a position to take over power at the end had been established very near the beginning. There had been several reform social movements earlier in the nineteenth century and even a few political bodies, such as the Bengal British Indian Society and the British Indian Association. But as their very titles in some cases indicate, they were mainly local in their appeal; they were in fact in the nature of select political clubs for a few Indian gentlemen of the presidency capitals. When the Indian National Congress was formed in 1885 it scarcely managed to be anything very different but at least it claimed an all-India basis. During the long period of its growth, its organization, mode of operation and goals naturally changed vastly. But it still counts for a great deal that in 1947 this body could look back on a life of sixty-two years; mere continuity of existence can be vital in encouraging in the members a sense of loyalty and devotion and a feeling of security and confidence. This has been a substantial asset (and only a slight handicap) for India's political leadership since independence. Reinforcing this is a related subsidiary point: it so happened that the generation of men who occupied the top positions at the moment of independence was that which had joined the movement in what was one of its most inspiring phases, the early twenties. But to explain this calls for some sketch of the strands and stages within the movement. Such an attempt is in any case useful, for the complex components of the movement throw light on much that is otherwise puzzling in post-independence political behaviour.

To speak at all of an Indian national movement is to simplify. Such a movement must be thought of less as expressing the aspirations and mobilising the energies of an already existing entity and more as a force, of ideas and organization, attempting to create that entity. It was a large task. Consider the ways in which man may be separated from his fellow men—by language, religion, class, caste and the rest—and discover which of these is not present in India, in its starkest forms and most ample variety, deposited and confirmed by long history. Almost it must seem as if Indian nationalism had only one strong ally—British rule, the consolidating common enemy.

It can therefore occasion no surprise to find that this movement was more often than not rather like a tailor's unfinished garment being tried on for size. It was incomplete, leaving whole limbs of the body uncovered, and even where it extended it was constantly in danger of coming apart at the loosely stitched seams. The particular question of regionalism has, as we shall see later, acquired growing importance in recent years as loyalities to Tamilnad or Bengal or Maharashtra produce regional parties, regional strains in all-India parties and regional pressures on the central government. Meanwhile historians have been uncovering considerable regionalism in the national movement right from the outset: the patterns of political life in Madras were quite different from those of Calcutta, the interests too differed as between Bombay politicians and those from Punjab. Moreover some of the ploys detected on the all-India stage had meaning only in relation to the persistent regional concerns of the actors. All this, however, can be overdone: it was still something to have created the all-India stage, for the stage then created its all-India audience and shaped its performers. The historians nevertheless have done well to remind us that regional strains are not exactly a recent development.

Before the twenties there had been two periods: the timid and restricted beginnings down to the turn of the century, and then a time of schism when cautious liberals concentrating on constitutional concessions had to face the challenge of younger men with greater ambitions and fewer inhibitions as to methods of work. These latter had come to the fore under the impulse of a wave of revulsion against Westernization and, in Bengal, in protest against the partition of that province in 1905. The rift between 'extremists' and 'moderates' was indeed wide, a gulf of generations and cultures. The older men had absorbed all the values of liberal England and sought only the gradual application of these to their own country; this was to be done by a process of rational argument and constitutional pressure on rulers who were worthy of every respect and whose intentions were honourable. On the other side were men who, even if they had received Western-style education—as most of them had—resisted bitterly its claims to superiority and rejected its values, seeking instead to revive memories of past Indian traditions. (It might be more accurate to say that while intending to reject all of the West, they in fact rejected only liberal values; their passionate nationalism was as Western as anything could be. One could add that even their rediscovery of India's past glories and spiritual and other greatness owed much to the research of Western scholars.) For these men the alien rulers were hateful and subjection to their regime an intolerable shame not to be endured by the true patriot. The influence of such ideas was geographically patchy, being largely confined to Bengal and parts of Maharashtra, but they did burn deeply into the minds of the youth of those areas during the decade before the First World War. Assassination became a rather noble calling and terrorism fired boys to feats of heroism and daring, but even in the most lively centres and at the most exhilarating times it could of course be only a small minority that found release in action. There indeed was the rub: a new high degree of interest in politics and desire for change could find no satisfaction in either of the two ways of doing political campaigning, for if one asked for too little the other called for too much. A third way was needed. It might in principle have been found in a mid-way position of a radical reform programme employing vigorous but lawful methods and backed by some eclectic compromise between wholesale acceptance and outright rejection of Westernization. In the event, the third way came rather differently. It manifested an element of creativeness; in a sense it achieved equidistance from the two poles but it did so by moving away in a fresh direction. When Gandhi emerged into prominence shortly after the end of the war he did so by an act of political invention which at once amply met the needs of a new and insistently Indian generation and was later to present itself as a universally valid challenge to 'orthodox' politics.

It does not matter that Gandhi's invention, like most inventions, was not wholly new, that one can locate sources and forerunners. Nor should we be reluctant to admit that his amazing appeal and his effectiveness owed a great deal to his own strange character and personality in which charm, simplicity and gentleness were combined with a capacity for ruthlessness, calculation and very great determination. It remains useful to see how his lines of thought and action had in them elements which could collect support from the most diverse sections and engender enthusiasm among very different persons. In the first place, he could appeal to many decent liberals of the old school—to Gokhale himself for instance, to Motilal Nehru. For Gandhi never seemed to reject liberal values; he only seemed to say that they were not enough. Moreover, as a trained lawyer he was not ill-at-ease or impatient in the discussing of constitutional niceties. Unlike the stormy terrorists, he was a quiet, reassuring man. Even if there was a touch of magic in his persuasiveness, there was also much reasoning and reasonableness. Indeed, the Gandhian way of non-violent civil disobedience was presented as an instrument of moral shock treatment designed to remove blind spots and thus enable the two sides to any dispute to see each other's point of view and come to a reasonable settlement. He appealed also to men of substance in Indian society. Though his own possessions were few, he was not without understanding of those with plenty. Here was no social revolutionary—at least not in the usual recognizable sense of a man set upon turning social arrangements upside-down.

On the other side—if that is not too gross a simplification—there was much here to attract also the more ardent spirits. There was that strong note of self-respect and pride, a detestation of weakness and the declaration that to follow his path called for the courage of a soldier and the willingness to sacrifice of dedicated souls. For men captivated but also disillusioned by terrorism, this message was irresistible. To be an Indian was not to be an imitation Britisher; it was something different, something worthy in its own right. It did not exclude absorption of some parts of the Western heritage, it did not require uncritical continuation of all traditional Indian customs; there was much good spiritual sense in the Bible and there was much that was wicked in the treatment of the 'untouchables'. Nevertheless one kept the *Gita* at one's bedside and one wore a *dhoti*. In terms of his concrete political demands, Gandhi struck many of his contemporary countrymen as awkwardly ambiguous, and to some seemed to be more concerned with slightly quirky social or personal issues— hand-spinning, chastity, dieting and prohibition—than with the central political problems. But no matter, from Gandhi such things could be tolerated. For one thing, even if his demands were not always clear, at least his tone of voice was different from that of the liberals; he did not beg or supplicate, he stated terms and bargained as an equal. For another, Gandhi had a reputation (from his South African campaign) for success. Perhaps most important of all, Gandhi promised to be able to make Congress keep pace with the times of mass politics, to work upon millions instead of thousands only.

It is worth pausing a moment on the last point. There can be no doubt as to the considerable extent of Gandhi's success in increasing the scale of Congress's appeal. On the other hand, some of the changes in Indian politics which have come about since independence and the introduction of adult franchise make it reasonable to ask whether the extent of the previous transformation has not been exaggerated. In the absence of any careful study of this subject, it is difficult to be certain, but it now seems possible that Congress under Gandhi only went part of the way towards introducing part of the masses to certain aspects of politics. This is not to belittle the pre-independence achievement; it is a long way from the top of Indian society to the bottom, and before Gandhi Congress was limited to a part of the top. If during the inter-war period Congress moved out from the presidency capitals and established a large and firm following among the middle and lower middle classes of the medium and smaller district towns, that was already a great deal. By 1921, Congress had a membership of some two million—which compares favourably with other nationalist movements. (The United National Party of Ceylon was perhaps at a '1918' stage of development when it obtained power; the wonder is not that it was practically swept away when politics then began to reach down to levels of the population previously untouched, but rather that it could so adapt as to achieve a come-back some years later.) But India, as Gandhi himself often said, lives in villages. Just how far they were touched is more difficult to say. The villages of some areas were more advanced than others; those of the princely states were mainly dormant. Here and there, of course, there were intensive, specifically peasant campaigns—such as that led by Patel in Bardoli, Gujarat, in 1928—and these no doubt made a profound and lasting impression. Again, Congressmen were active in the peasants' *Kisan Sabha* organizations, but these were patchily developed and often had about them, like trades unions in India, more the character of an organization for peasants than by them. Gandhian social workers went out into villages and Gandhi's name was widely known and respected, but probably as that of a new and impressive holy man with a devoted following. The strictly political appeal of Congress in rural India was probably limited to a very small rural élite—a few better-off peasants with sons going to college in the district town. The political public was no longer confined to an aristocracy of cultivated gentlemen but it was still quite sophisticated. One important consequence of this was that it could think in all-India terms and thus sustain an all-Indian leadership.

There was an ebb-and-flow movement within the rise of the Congress in the twenties—as Nehru's *Autobiography* indicates so vividly. But throughout that decade and into the thirties there was no serious rival on the political scene to the Gandhi-led Congress. To have a serious concern for the political advancement of India meant some kind of attachment to Congress. Only among Muslims was there some hesitation and holding back, indeed even a movement away if comparison is made with the period of Congress-Muslim League amity around the 'Lucknow pact' of 1916 and the Khilafat movement in the early twenties. It was in this period that most of those subsequently referred to as the 'Old Guard' of Congress determined to join the movement in a spirit of selfless dedication worthy of the cause and its leader. It was during this period that the image of Congress was fashioned—that image which as a standard of behaviour in public life still plays so large a part in modern Indian politics. Between images and reality one expects some gap and it is difficult to say how many moral supermen Congress created. A number from the middle classes gave up their professional careers and became full-time unpaid servants of the movement. This certainly meant something, but whether it meant as much as it sounds to Western ears is another matter. It is only just to bear in mind the employment position and the pattern of family life in India: in many cases, what was sacrificed was a dreary scramble for an uncertain pittance and what was secured was respect and excitement at no financial loss, for the other members of a large joint family were always accustomed to sustaining the odd younger brother or uncle who somehow never quite managed to earn. Even the periods in prison were not so appalling: long spells of separation are not unusual in India even for family men in normal times, the conditions were normally not punitive and the results were satisfying to honour. It is not suggested that this applied to all; obviously some real martyrs there were—men for whom perfect fulfilment lay in service to the party of Gandhi—but they were not as numerous as perhaps outsiders and, in retrospect, even Indians themselves imagine.

It could be said that in a sense the position of Congress and the supremacy of Gandhi's leadership remained—with the exception of the steady rise of the Muslim League after 1937—unchanged through the thirties and forties. Numerically the party increased and there were campaigns of great vigour and appeal—such as the early stages of the Quit India agitation in 1942. All the same, a change had taken place from about the middle thirties. Allegiance to Congress was substantially eroded not so much by any outside rivals—though the Communist Party was proving attractive to many young intellectuals by the late thirties and Dr Ambedkar had begun to organize the scheduled castes—but rather by dissatisfaction within. Criticism of Gandhi had never been absent; almost at the outset there had been the split between those (called the Swarajists) who wanted to contest the first elections under the 1919 Act and those with Gandhi who favoured boycott. Again, Nehru tells of the several occasions on which he and his father found Gandhi difficult to follow—though also, be it added, impossible to leave. These disputes, however, never touched devotion to the organization. The same could not quite be said of later challenges, coming above all from two sets of opinions. The first was represented by the Congress socialists who formed as a group in 1934 and pressed for an appeal to the workers and peasants on the basis of a policy programme wherein Congress would declare what it would do with power; their disagreement with the leadership was on both methods and goals for they considered only a mass movement could budge the British and only clear social goals could

B

rouse the masses. The second group is that most conveniently associated with the leadership of Subhas Chandra Bose. It was particularly strong in Bengal, perhaps deriving some force from local patriotism and memories of the terrorists. Their discontent was with the pace of the movement's advance and the excessive caution and decency displayed by Gandhi. It seemed to them as if the old man was holding back the potential fury of a subject people; leaders ought rather to stimulate and call forth popular anger. Sometimes these two strands of thought were viewed as 'left' and 'right' respectively and this was encouraged by Bose's disposition to be attracted by fascist ideas. But for the most part the distinction between the two was one of personalities rather than of ideology. ('Right' and 'left' have little meaning in colonial situations when a socialist often enough means no more than an ardent and impatient nationalist.) Nehru himself hovered with delicate uneasiness between both and Gandhi. In any event, the difference between these later discontents and the earlier disputes is that for the later rebels Congress was less an end in itself and more simply a vehicle to use so long as it was heading in the right direction.

Since the Indian National Congress was to become, as the Congress Party, the dominating political organization of independent India, it is worth asking further what its members can be supposed to have learnt in the way of political habits during the years of 'freedom struggle'. They learnt certainly to think of Congress as a body representing all the legitimate interests of the nation. Hence the profound and genuine wounding of Congressmen's feelings when they found that such groups as Muslims, scheduled castes and Sikhs were inclined to feel the need for separate organizations to protect their interests. To put themselves outside the Congress was to declare that they were in some degree un-Indian; that this should happen was a mark of failure on the part of Congress and error on theirs. This attitude of mind was one which it would clearly be necessary to abandon if Congress became a party among parties, yet it is very understandable that this would not be found easy. That Congress on the whole succeeded in shedding its former view of itself says much for its sense of political principle and of political realities. It may be true that it is less difficult to be tolerant of opposition groups when they are so weak as to constitute no threat. Against that it needs to be pointed out that this was also the situation in Pakistan in the first years of independence, yet even the most responsible Muslim League leaders continued to talk in terms of opposition being anti-national. One kind of organisation against which many Congressmen tend to take the view that it is not to be tolerated is any body which can be called 'communal' in character. Political allegiance to religious community, they recall, was one of the stumbling blocks on their road to comprehensive appeal; it affected not only Muslims and Sikhs but also those Hindus for whom Hinduism defined the nation; and even now they see communalism as a continuous impediment to national integration and a too frequent threat to social peace. Congress has also called Communists anti-national and has found warrant for this view in their equivocal attitude towards China's aggression on India's frontiers.

Congressmen were accustomed then to holding together in one organization many interests frequently thought of as requiring much reconciliation and mutual adjustment. Congress, that is to say, was used to performing in some degree the work of a national parliament where clashing viewpoints and concerns meet to determine a generally acceptable line of policy. Of course, in a situation of colonial rule most of the argument is about techniques of compaigning against the imperial government. But if the nationalist movement is permitted to enter legislative bodies—and Congressmen were present in fair number in central and state legislatures from 1921—and, even more, if the movement accepts some governmental responsibilities—as Congress did in eight provinces for the years 1937–9—then it is difficult to avoid adumbrating policies on a wide range of public issues. Congress had therefore to find ways of reconciling the views of its very different kinds of members. If there were a good analytical account of the internal working of Congress during the pre-independence period (or even afterwards for that matter), we should know just how this was done. As it is, two very general points must suffice.

The first relates to the roles of leadership and rank and file in the organization. In looking at this question we must of course take into account so far as possible both formal structure and customary practice. Where the former is concerned, the constitution of the Congress has undergone several changes during its life. It began merely as an organization of delegates elected 'by political associations and other bodies, and by public meetings'. By 1908 it had a hierarchy of elected committees from the All-India Congress Committee down through Provincial to District and even Taluka Congress Committees. After 1920 it changed both in scale and in methods: a membership basis was established and a strong Working Committee at the head was equipped to direct what was now seen as a political struggle. If the AICC was the elected Congress parliament, the Working Committee—whether chosen by the AICC or, following an amendment in 1934, by the Congress President—was its 'highest

executive authority'. It was responsible to the AICC and this gave
its members valuable experience in the business of argument and
management. All points of view found expression on the AICC and
at times a substantial cleavage of opinion was revealed. Sometimes
the Working Committee would represent a majority view and have
to hold the minority's loyalty; on other occasions (as in 1936 in
Nehru's presidency, when resignations were threatened by some of
his more conservative colleagues—including Rajendra Prasad, later
to become first President of the Republic) cleavage appeared on the
Working Committee itself. There was ample scope for Gandhi's
magic soothing effect but also for skilled leadership of a more
workaday variety. The urge was strong to confront the British with a
powerfully united movement, but it would be an oversimplification
to present the organization as autocratic. It is no doubt true that the
Working Committee exercised considerable directive power over
the hierarchy of elected bodies. It planned and managed the periodic
AICC conferences and full sessions of Congress, and had full
powers in the intervening periods. It was always familiarly referred
to as the 'High Command' and Gandhi often stressed how like an
army an effective political organization had to be. On the other hand,
of course, a party can lose its members by desertion more easily than
an army can lose soldiers. Just as the President, free to choose his
Working Committee as he pleased, would in fact be careful to secure
a team properly balanced in respect of opinions, regions or other
relevant factors, so the Working Committee, virtually free to issue
what directives it pleased, would naturally avoid giving leads which
would not readily be followed. There was nothing in the structure
of the party which made it impossible for the members to make their
views felt by the leaders, but exactly how much came up from below
is difficult to say. Caution is needed even in assessing the undoubtedly
exceptional position of Gandhi in the life of the movement. One side
of the truth is that on most but not all occasions what Gandhi
advised was done; the other side of the matter is that Gandhi was
most accessible and was engaged in a very great deal of correspondence and conversation with his followers. Before he announced the
decision that would become law for the party he had usually sounded
all substantial opinions. It may be fair to sum up this topic by saying
that Congress was an organization accustomed to carrying out
orders; that its structure permitted the formulation and communication of ideas and proposals; that its leaders were men with sensitive
ears; that nevertheless the policy-making process in the party was
one in which very few took any constructive part; that the resolution
of differences took place at or near the top and was effected as

discreetly as possible in order to preserve the unity and integrity of the movement. To say this is perhaps to say no more—but also no less—than that in these respects Congress was like most parties of a non-totalitarian kind.

A second aspect of the internal working of the party concerns the relations between the party organization and those of its members in positions of governmental responsibility. This matter has assumed great importance since independence, but it is worth noting that already in the short pre-war experience the problem had arisen. The existence of Congress governments in the majority of provinces between 1937 and 1939 had posed the question: to whom were these ministries primarily responsible—to the local electorate or to the national movement? The dilemma was real because the situation was unusual: Congress was engaged not in a parliamentary conflict but in a struggle against foreign rule. In any national organization a certain subordination of provincial leaders to the centre is to be expected; the Congress top leaders kept out of the ministerial jobs and sent second-level leaders to man the lesser parliamentary fronts. The Working Committee had given permission for Congress ministries to be formed and it subsequently called upon them to resign; as Nehru rightly said at the time, 'the ministries, being the creation of Congress, can be ended at any time by Congress'. The relation of party headquarters to the party's parliamentary groups tended therefore to be that of principal to agent. At the same time the manner in which control was to be exercised was not easily settled. The Working Committee (mainly through its Parliamentary Board) frequently rescued Congress ministries from 'embarrassing' attacks, often on points of administrative detail, launched by jealous rivals working through the party's provincial committees. The rescue operations saved something of the autonomy of the parliamentary wings but also served to underline the supremacy of the party centre. In the post-independence period the tussles between the organizational and legislature wings of the party take place in a much changed situation. Politics is no longer a battle for national freedom; Congress has been in charge of the central government as well as most of the states; before 1969 at least, almost all top men of the party were cabinet ministers in Delhi or state capitals; the state politician is increasingly a man of the local political soil, its product and its dependant. But although today's circumstances are different from those of 1937, the earlier experiences had their shaping influence and Congress is no exception to the rule that institutions are creatures of their past.

The legacy of the movement thus contains many features. It

accustomed its members to think in terms of the reconciliation of different interests and views within the one organization. At the same time it made them used to discipline inside the party. Although it covered the country rather unevenly, it thought fairly consistently in all-India terms and sustained an all-India leadership. It attracted in its vital middle period the devotion of a substantial number of able men from the middle layers of society and in doing so set forth a particular model of public life. If this were all, the contrast between this legacy and that of government would not be emphatic.

The contrast comes rather from the duration and the nature of its anti-government agitation. For the best part of a quarter of a century the country's principal acknowledged leaders were engaged in fundamental protest. Here is contrast indeed with the first legacy— the contrast that still today helps to account for a certain ambivalence of attitude towards government. Even after independence government is relied and leaned upon, and at the same time spat upon and abused. The same man who is 'looking to government' one moment may in the next take part in demonstrations involving violence and on a scale that threatens to make any government impossible. This unbalance owes much to the period of nationalist struggle when it could be the mark of the truly moral and noble soul to defy the law and suffer the consequences. For the purposes of Gandhi's civil disobedience campaigns, the British government of India was in a way perfectly suited: it was (at least until towards the end) strong enough to be able to control the situation, so that the demonstrators needed to have no anxiety about causing social chaos and collapse of order; at the same time, it was capable of being embarrassed. A government that was either weaker or more ruthless would have made a more awkward enemy. It is true that Gandhi frequently declared that it was not his intention to cause embarrassment to the government. Yet how this could be avoided and how morally obligatory organized protest could stop short of what Gandhi regarded as morally reprehensible mental coercion is difficult to see. It is to be acknowledged that Gandhi himself did on occasion call off or limit campaigns which promised to be damaging to order and it must also be said that one object of all his campaigning was to instil in his followers a capacity for discipline and self-sacrifice. Even so, the difficulty remains; its practical importance increases when with the death of the leader the weapons are left for other less qualified men to use. Despite Gandhi's warnings that civil disobedience would cease to be a normally appropriate technique once alien rule was replaced by responsible government with proper channels for the expression of grievances, it has become part of the Indian political scene. Gandhians claim that the weapons of non-violent protest could if more widely adopted resolve conflicts hitherto 'settled' by force. The Indian situation is that men are readily disposed to use these techniques in cases where settlement by discussion and compromise might have been hoped for. They will often prefer a pose of morally indignant protest to patient discussion and argument: they may not be wrong if they reckon they will get more that way; a premium is thus placed on impatience and intransigence. The range of methods is considerable: the dramatic fast to death is at one end, at the other the 'walk-out' by a parliamentary group; the attitude of mind is similar. Almost one could say that the weapon of last resort has in the Indian polity come into regular household use.

Mediating institutions

This heading is ambiguous and requires some explanation. Under it are to be considered those institutions which already in the British period stood as it were between the two contesting forces. For although the stage of imperial India was dominated for most of the twentieth century by the confrontation of government and movement, the dialogue between the two was modified by the presence of other actors. These forces which mediated between the two colossi prevented them from becoming wholly exclusive and self-contained worlds. They provided an area of overlap. In the transfer of power their integrity was not lost and they have been able to exert a continuing influence on Indian politics.

It might be legitimate to include under this head as a collective 'institution' the whole range of professions—teachers, doctors, lawyers, engineers and so on. In several senses they did stand between government and movement. They had become almost entirely Indian in personnel and would of course have been in general sympathy with the nationalist cause. From their ranks Congress drew its leading members. On the other hand a substantial number of their members were government employees—for instance, teachers in government colleges, doctors in the Indian Medical Service—and even others were connected indirectly with government or could be said to work under its aegis. Less concretely, the very subject matter of their professions associated them with the Western world of their rulers. In some cases the link was specifically with Britain—it was English law, English language, English history, in a word English values, which the professions served to transmit and develop. To abandon a career in one of the professions to devote oneself to the Congress was not only a matter of making oneself free in terms of time; it also signified a break of some kind in the connection with the government establishment.

There were, however, two specific mediating institutions of very great importance. First, there were the legislative councils and assemblies, the quasi-parliaments of imperial India. Here government and movement met on ground that belonged to neither. Here both had to abide by rules and conventions not quite of their own making. It is true that the legislative bodies of the nineteenth century began their lives as creatures of government, devised for its own convenience —in a position not unlike that of the first parliaments of Britain. It is no less true (and rather more important in the present context) that, as in Britain, the position changed. Membership of these bodies took both government and movement just a little outside themselves, forced each to speak to the other. Of course, success was limited; the separate worlds of the two main forces were far apart and proper conditions for a dialogue were scarcely ever present. In the councils set up under the Act of 1861 and then enlarged and made in some degree quasi-elected from 1892, the balance between the two sides was extremely uneven—almost all-powerful government and infant movement. By the time of the Act of 1909 conditions from this point of view are improved, but by that time also the extra-parliamentary and indeed extra-constitutional aspects of the movement are pre-dominating; within the movement, that is to say, there was taking place a shift in its centre of gravity. This point indicates the importance of the argument between Gandhi and the Swarajists in the early twenties. In fact one of the many 'ifs' of recent Indian history is the question as to how the nationalist struggle would have developed if the leaders had not consistently placed almost exclusive emphasis on the organizational wing and its campaigns of non-violent protest. A case can be made out for holding that a different bias, one in favour of accepting and exploiting every improved opportunity for entering and influencing the constitutional apparatus, would have provoked less resistance and repression, occasioned less distrust and misunderstanding and thus have made possible a less lengthy road to independence (and, therefore, most probably an undivided India). Obviously such a view requires a number of big assumptions. Here only three things need be said. First, such a concentration on operating through the quasi-parliaments might have kept the movement continuously split with an extremist wing wholly out of control. Second, a policy of parliamentary action alone might well have deprived the movement of much of that distinctive character which gave its members a sense of sharing in an Indian invention; to that extent many of the advantages of the legacy would

have been missing. Third, it is probable that a parliamentary movement would have made even less progress towards the lower social
levels; in that case, India would have arrived at independence with
leaders ill-equipped to survive the inescapable advent of popular
politics.

It may therefore be that if we had not to regret the distraction of
the movement's attention away from the parliamentary meeting-
place we should have even more to regret. In any case, as already
suggested, the assemblies and councils were far from being hollow
shams. Leaving aside the immediate effects of these bodies on both
parties—and these were not negligible—it is of inestimable value
that at least some of the leading men of the movement acquired a
skill and affection for parliamentary institutions. Mostly, of course,
the experience was that of being on the opposition benches. But in
the precious years 1937–9 there was also experience of government-
in-parliament at the provincial level. This went far towards avoiding
a groping in the dark when it came to constitution-making; they
knew what they were accustomed to and they found it good. It also
ensured that left to themselves they would in fact be able to work
such institutions and communicate the spirit of the rules to a
younger generation. Precisely what constitutes that spirit may be
variously formulated but it may be said to include at least the notion
of a dialogue or genuine discussion in which opinions and interests
to be found in the country find free expression and in which government, for all its power and prestige, has to give reasons for its
decisions and be willing to accept the responsibility and consequences
of failure. Even stated thus baldly, it can be seen that this world of
parliament is indeed a different world from that of government and
movement. Both, in so far as they took a real part in the proceedings,
were bound to be altered by the experience. That even the quasi-
parliaments of the pre-war period can claim to have done this is
remarkable. It could have been no easy road for formerly bureaucratic
governments. For Indian politicians of the nationalist movement it
must have been no less difficult; the impatient protest mentality
already noted was one obstacle and another was the probability
(discussed below) that in any case a real commitment to discussion
is not usually found in societies which are highly segmented and
also close to traditional ways.

The second great intermediate institution which was built up in
imperial India and became part of the legacy handed over in 1947 is
the system of law and the judiciary. This appears, and indeed is
intended, to cover a great deal: the introduction and adjustment of
the English common law; the Bentham-inspired codes of procedure;

the relationship of the legal profession to the judges; the training of lawyers in England; the structure of the courts and their relation to government. Of course, the manner in which law and justice served as an intermediary between government and movement is not as direct as in the case of parliament; here is not an institution in which the two meet but rather one which, while independent of both, attracted the respect of both and influenced their attitudes.

It is true that the independence of this institution in relation to government was incomplete. We have already noted how in district administration executive functions and criminal jurisdiction were combined in the same office of collector and magistrate. Above the magistrate's courts on the criminal side were the sessions courts. Here criminal and civil jurisdiction met, for the sessions judge and the judge of the (civil) district court were normally the same; the judges had no executive functions but they were mainly recruited from the ICS; however, the service had its special judicial branch and men's careers in the service did not usually entail movement between executive and judicial sides. At the higher levels, there may have been ambiguity and hesitation in some of the eighteenth-century developments (though the Calcutta Supreme Court very soon proved an awkward enemy of the administration); from the establishment of the High Courts following 1861, however, there was no doubt concerning the separation and independence of the judiciary, even though a certain number of the High Court judges were chosen not from the English or Indian bar but from the judicial services.

The influence of this institution on Indian life has been exerted effectively for a longer period than that of parliament. Moreover the values implied in its rules and procedures have been able to enjoy a prestige more immune from political attack. Though there was some opinion in the movement in favour of a boycott of the courts, it was never as strong as that opposed to participation in the assemblies. There have been Britishers who have doubted the suitability of English ideas on impartiality and evidence for Indian conditions, and it may well be that the results of the process of law were different from those anyone intended. But from the Indian side there seems to have been little criticism; indeed by attacking the mixing together of executive and judicial functions in the magistracy they implied a favourable view of the separate judicial ethos. Indeed, the political effects of the hundred years' growth of the legal profession in India have perhaps never been fully explored. Impact evidently occurred at the leadership level: almost notorious was the preponderance of lawyers among top politicians. This drew scorn and distrust from many British administrators who often regarded lawyers as unrepresentative of the Indian people as a whole and too prone to embrace criticism for its own sake. They overlooked the positive effect: the establishment of a political class habituated to a world of rules and resistant to arbitary autocracy. (Perhaps a Ghana would have shaped differently if its lawyers had been more numerous and stronger in political influence. Certainly significant has been the role of the bar associations as a centre of resistance to autocracy in Pakistan.) Impact would surely be discovered also at the lower levels of the small-town pleaders. It seems probable that these men performed a vital function of making a bridge between traditional and modern values. They operated professionally in the modern setting. of the courts but their clients were mostly embedded in an alien world of ancient custom. Who more effectively than the small lawyer kept rural India at least in faint touch with the cities where new political ideas were growing? Hired to manipulate the mysteries of a foreign legal system, would he not at the same time communicate something of the ethos of that system to his clients?

Here then was a set of standards embodied in and upheld by established independent institutions and an associated profession: that the parties to disputes stand equal in the eyes of the law and have equal access to the law; that an accused man is innocent until found guilty; that the evidence must be brought forward and sifted before an impartial judge; that the duty of the judge is to administer the law, having regard to principles of natural justice and with an indifference to the convenience of the politically or otherwise powerful. No less than the values carried by parliamentary institutions, these, while not native to the Indian soil, took firm root there. The movement may at times have welcomed the existence of any authority standing apart from government but this connection is unimportant; rather, these values had already conquered the minds of educated Indians and the movement drew some of its own leading members from the ranks of the legal profession. It is therefore little wonder that this legacy was taken over with respectful care. This is evidenced in the debates of the Constituent Assembly, in the Constitution's provisions concerning the judiciary and in the tone of that document as a whole. Even the inclusion of 'un-English' fundamental rights may be taken less as an imitation of some other constitutions than as a tribute to the judiciary in India and to the values it had preached for over a century.

Problems and promises

The subsequent chapters of this book can in part be viewed as an exploration designed to discover what changes have taken place in the legacies since they were taken over. But the scene is not fully set and the description of the starting line is incomplete without some sketch, however brief, of the problems which confronted the political system; for the legacy is composed of tasks as well as of equipment. Tasks and problems are to some extent independent of ourselves, but most of the tasks with which politics is concerned are of our own creation. Our needs are only in part given and inevitable, our hopes not at all. In looking for the tasks before the Indian political system, therefore, we need to see into the minds of the relevant men more than into the facts and figures.

This seems to be true even of a problem like that of the poverty of the Indian people. Doctors can tell us what intake of calories and vitamins is necessary to sustain a human life, economists can tell us the average income per head of the Indian peasant and demographers can give us information as to mortality rates from various categories of causes. But there are no tasks and no problems until someone wishes to change some of these facts. That the nationalist movement should have made this promise to itself can hardly be surprising to us now. As in other countries, however, preoccupation with poverty was by no means the first feature of national self-consciousness. The first generations of Westernized Indians seem to have focussed their attention—partly because their rulers did so too—on the reform of social and religious life. Only with works like that of Romesh Dutt (*The Economic History of India*, 1901) does the emphasis change. The early liberals of the nationalist movement (Ranade and Gokhale prominently) devoted considerable energy to exposing the ways in which imperial policies caused and did little to alleviate the poverty of the masses. Their hopes were that the government could be got to change its policies accordingly. In the later Congress period, under the influence of the socialists and of those, like Nehru, sympathetic to their views, the movement turns rather towards declarations of what it will do when it comes finally to power. The resolution passed by Congress in its Karachi session in 1931 expressed this most clearly. So much was this kind of promise in Nehru's own mind that one of his first pronouncements after independence made it a central point.

The leaders were thus committed to regarding this as a key task. (It is not to deny the primarily moral urge behind this to add that when the leaders speak of India's economic backwardness or under-development they indicate also a sense of shame at the implied international comparison and an awareness of a point of prestige.) This commitment itself then becomes a political fact of the greatest importance. It may be worth remarking that this does not yet establish the kind of rigid connection between economics and politics which is often postulated. People frequently speak as if they supposed that political stability in a country like India depended on the ability of the government to secure some particular, satisfactory rate of economic progress. (They also imply that this adequate rate of development is connected in a similar hard-and-fast manner with the achievement of a certain kind of popular-participation political system. On both these curious ideas, more is said in Chapters 3 and 7.) This is plausible only if politically relevant opinion itself makes the connection. If such opinion—and not a large body of persons is involved here—were persuaded that for some good reasons only a very low rate was attainable no matter what government might do, then that rate would be consistent with political stability. In a sense it is again the case that it is thinking makes it so.

This is not the place to consider the various economic policies which an Indian government could adopt. It is useful, however, to see that the movement had in a general way committed India's government not only to the goal of 'economic freedom' but also to certain ways of achieving this, in fact to two ways above all. The governments would have to see what each implied in terms of political forces and structure and how far they could be reconciled. The first was the use of some kind of governmental planning machinery. The notion had come from a wide variety of sources—socialist theory and Soviet experience, the American New Deal, universal wartime regulation and controls. A group of Indian industrialists had produced 'the Bombay plan' in 1944; Nehru had himself already presided over the investigations of the Congress-sponsored National Planning Committee during 1938–9; the imperial government had established a Planning Department in 1944 and had called on provinces to prepare schemes of economic advance. Apart from determining the kind of planning machinery required, the government would also have to decide on the relationship under any plan between private industry (with some of whose leaders Congress had close connections) and government enterprise. On the other hand, Gandhi and those who followed his economic preferences had insisted that the salvation, economic as otherwise, of the country must be effected at the very base. This seemed to mean the encouragement and protection of cottage and small-scale industries. The political corollary of such a policy might be an attempt to instil new life into bodies of a local self-government or co-operative kind. Related to this—though not in the sense that there was a clear Gandhian policy on these subjects—would be the questions of the pattern of agricultural economy and of land reform.

Another great range of problems would concern the formation to be given to the political structure itself. As already indicated, a system pointing towards federalism was inherited, but there were many quite unsolved difficulties as to the units of such a federation as well as of the relative powers of centre and units. The drastic partition of the country and the formation of Pakistan in a sense removed one problem but it left many others. What was to happen to the 562 princely states? The Congress had made no secret of its hostility to these regimes which tended to support the alien rulers; while restricting itself to British India, it had fostered and assisted the parallel organization of the States People's Congress. But how all these areas were to be ruled and integrated was not clear. Even so far as the provinces were concerned, the inherited pattern was not as settled as it seemed. Most of the provincial boundaries had been determined by the circumstances of conquest and acquisition. Some of them—Bengal for instance—corresponded fairly well to the areas of habitation of language groups; others like Bombay and Madras contained two or three such groups. These arrangements had given rise to no profound discontent but there was some sentiment in favour of linguistic (i.e. linguistically homogeneous) provinces. In two particular cases the imperial government had taken account of this: in 1936 new provinces of Sind and Orissa had been carved out on this principle. More important was the fact that Congress had in 1920 not only made a demand for a general revision of provinces but also revised its own constitution so that the Pradesh (provincial) Congress Committees operated with a few exceptions for linguistic areas and ignored the governmental units. Here then was an implied promise which would come up for redemption—though with what insistence few can have guessed.

Not only the political units of the state would have to be decided; a whole constitution would have to be prepared. That its general form would be a republican development of the federal parliamentary democracy towards which India had been steadily moving was fairly clear. There would still be important matters for decision—the distribution of powers between centre and units, the relations between heads of state (centre and units) and responsible ministries, and so on. But it was not the case that Congress had spent much time on framing model constitutions; after the Nehru All-Parties Conference of 1928 Congress had its hands full with the job of criticizing the proposals of others. On these matters therefore there would be room for argument, pressure and manœuvre. Only two structural questions might turn out to be difficult issues of principle. First, how much and what was to be done to incorporate the

Gandhian vision of a decentralized polity, in which decisions of vital importance would be taken near the base of the government pyramid and in which the higher levels would be actually constructed from lower organs? Second, while the demands of the largest religious minority had been met in the establishment of Pakistan, religious minorities would remain; so also would the religious majority, at least some of whom hoped for a state that would acknowledge if not 'establish' Hinduism. What constitutional recognition would be given to such fears and hopes?

Finally, just visible at the starting line, there would be the question of great importance, albeit indirectly, to political system: the future of the movement itself. Gandhi himself saw the matter clearly. For him as for all the other members, the main object of Congress was to gain independence from British rule, to achieve *swaraj*, literally self-government or self-rule. But in Gandhi's way of looking at things this was not a purely political task. Political independence would fall like a ripe fruit into the hands of any people who had achieved self-mastery. But the latter was a condition of moral regeneration and social reconstruction. For political independence it might be enough that a core of devoted workers had become ethically disciplined; in that case the work of spreading real *swaraj* would remain. This work was evidently not that for which a political party as normally understood would be suited. Congress had always been both more and less than a political party. With the achievement of independence it would be able to concentrate its attention on its moral and social role. It should, Gandhi suggested, cast off its political self and re-emerge as a *Lok Sevak Sangh*, an association for the service of the people. In that capacity it could continue with those tasks already begun: the breaking down of the backward isolation of the untouchables, the softening of the hard lines between other castes, the rectification of certain other undesirable features of social life that worked against the dignity of man. It would be as if India could go back and take up again that programme of social reforms which her first awakened leaders had taken up in the early nineteenth century but which had been put aside pending the political settlement. Now, not surprisingly, Congress did not choose to do as Gandhi suggested. It remained a political party—almost the only party ready in existence. This would pose problems of the relation between party organization and party members of government not unlike those of 1937–9 but on a vastly increased scale. Equally, the problem of social reform also remained in the minds of many of its members. They could be expected to pursue it; in doing so they would naturally explore how far politics could help—how far, that is to say, Congress control of the legislative and administrative organs of state could be useful in overcoming resistance to reforms, perhaps from the traditionally minded. But that, as the next chapter will show, is only one of several connections that politics and society would establish once the alien rulers left power behind.

2

POLITICS AND SOCIETY

A problem

Reference was made at the start of the first chapter to political systems in their relations to social structure. It is a fact that many accounts of the politics of modern states have given scant attention to this relation. This may have been in part a consequence of specialization in social studies. The student of politics found sufficient to command his attention in the forms and working of political institutions ever growing in number, complexity and importance; he may sometimes have been anxious to demonstrate the self-contained nature of the material examined by his particular discipline. The close connection which often existed between political studies and law may have encouraged this attention to institutions. Even the links between philosophy and politics did little to discourage the tendency; indeed, the effect here was often to produce over-rationalistic accounts of institutions, describing them as if they were nothing more than attempts, more or less successful, to embody purposes and values existing in a realm of ideas.

A strong reaction against this somewhat blinkered view of politics has become especially evident in the last two decades. In some forms this is referred to as the behavioural approach. The implications of this term may not everywhere have been the same but it has usually included several elements: a distrust of formal descriptions and a desire to uncover an 'inside story' of actual operations; a preference for particular and limited-scale studies of a strictly empirical character; an aspiration towards precision and objectivity seen as contrasted with unscientific and impressionistic studies. If this approach implied some closing of the doors leading to law and philosophy, it opened others. The use of surveys, a preference for quantitative data, the attraction of sister-subjects engaged in close and exact studies of other kinds of actual behaviour—all these draw politics as a subject towards the company of social statistics, anthropology and sociology. This led to a new or revived interest in the impact of social factors in political life. In the study of electoral behaviour—one of the great fields for the display of the new approach—attention came to be given to the influence on voters of class, family relations, local social habits and so on. But this was not the only consequence; it naturally happened too that certain guiding background terms and concepts derived from sociological and anthropological theory entered into political analysis. A political system came to be seen less in terms of its own institutions—parties, legislatures, bureaucracies—and more in terms of interests, functions, élites and roles. At best, both consequences were all gain, in that new aspects and fresh insights were obtained. At worst, however, there was some loss of grasp of the internal coherence and independent influence of political institutions. Exploration of the activities of pressure groups, for instance, tended to concentrate on showing how they upset the accepted orthodox accounts of legislatures—sometimes at the cost of failing to see how the pressure groups themselves were shaped in a measure by the political institutions on and through which they sought to operate.

It is not an accident that behavioural studies, although originally developed (and still more advanced) in relation to political systems such as the United States and Britain, have been flourishing at a time when increasing interest is being shown in the politics of 'new states' or 'developing areas'. One reason is no doubt that, confronted with the challenge of incorporating such areas within the framework of 'comparative politics', it seemed more hopeful to turn away from an institutional treatment involving such categories as 'legislatures'—which often do not even exist in new states—and look for more effective, more universal categories of analysis. But there is another reason: the relationship between politics and society in the new states is often of a kind which for Western students of politics is novel and arresting. If political studies of Western countries did until lately tend to ignore the social structure with which the polity is inevitably impregnated, it was surely not out of a mere desire to carve out a separate subject of politics. It was also that the social patterns had come to be largely taken for granted—and this for the reason that society and polity had grown up together, continuously influencing each other through the country's history. The neglect of sociological studies of British politics, for instance, may have been unwise and unfortunate but it was prevented from being absurd or disastrous by the fact that a fund of historical background relating social and political factors could be taken as read. The crucial fact about new states like India is that this trick no longer works at all. For under alien rule society and polity do not grow together in the same way.

The consequences of Westernization are many and complex. The central feature that concerns us here is that so long as alien rule prevails the impact of Westernization on the political system is well-nigh complete whereas the impact on society is partial and uneven. This at any rate is the Indian experience. The incoherence of polity and society is fully disclosed only with the start of an independent polity. Moreover, in such a polity the incoherence is unstable and from both sides forces move in to establish consistency. This is the process which gives rise to so many of the fascinating features of Indian politics today. It also provides a strong and special reason for believing that without attention to social forces the study of such politics is peculiarly partial and even misleading.

This position can be expressed in several ways. It was put very curtly by someone who remarked that 'there has not yet been written an honest book on Indian politics'; the suggestion is not that authors have been lying but that to the full truth there is a difficulty of access. While the political life of every state has its 'inside story' and every 'honest' book must try to bring it out, is there not a special difficulty in the case of Indian politics arising out of its inside story being very concealed and very different from outward appearance? The observer of political life in India can indeed quickly form the impression that the main thing he has to learn is that nothing is ever quite what it seems or what it presents itself as being. At first he may put this down to his own faulty vision, to his unavoidable tendency to try to fit new things into categories which he has brought with him. But later he realizes that the matter is not so simple; there are different categories operative within the Indian context itself. This should not be surprising. Indeed, it would be odd it if were otherwise. Everyone knows that in India's economic life and in her social life, too, whole European centuries coexist within the present moment. The bus-ride from the airport to city centre announces this enormous fact even to the passing traveller. Why then should we expect her politics to belong to any single simple style?

Yet it is worth emphasizing that for most students of politics this phenomenon is unusual and for that reason at first baffling to the understanding. Of course the idiom in which political activity is conducted certainly varies from country to country. The Britisher who seeks to understand American politics knows that he must master a new idiom—one which is dictated by the size of the country, the peculiar character of the nation-building process which has taken place there, the separation of powers, and so on. But at least it is, by and large, just one idiom. The general variations are related to the main theme. The conversation of American politics may be 'tapped' at any level and any place and the language will remain the same.

It may be argued that the matter is one of degree only—but then the range is very wide. We may concede at one end that even in this socially tight island politics looks rather different according as to to whether it is seen in Whitehall or in a miners' lodge. But the differences are, as it were, of tone and volume, not of basic language. For all participants have shares in a common culture. In some other countries of Western Europe, such as Belgium and France perhaps, the variety of political styles may be more marked; it may be a long way from Clochemerle to Paris. Further along this scale would come a country like Italy where culture contrasts between the south and the north are pronounced. But even there—with the exception perhaps of Sicily's Mafia—politics could be said to be in one language with several dialects.

The case of communist regimes seems different in an emphatic way; if we are to speak of differences only of degree, then at least we must say that here is a sizable jump along the scale. For in communist countries it seems that an idiom of politics derived from Marxism is found along with a primarily national idiom; the two may not mix in such a thorough way as to form a coherent new language. The observer of the political life of such a state may easily get the impression that things are not what they seem. The incoherence is in the situation itself and can express itself in different ways. Men may act in one political fashion but give an account of their acts in another set of terms. Or some men may act more or less fully in one political manner while others of their countrymen, within the same political institutions, act more or less thoroughly in another manner. Or it could be that the same men act in different styles according to occasion and context.

Languages of politics

This way of putting things may or may not be helpful in understanding communist political life but it certainly proves an aid to probing the nature of Indian politics. Tentatively three main languages in which political life in India is conducted can be distinguished. The least inappropriate of a poor set of labels for them would be 'modern', 'traditional' and 'saintly'. (It will have been already noticed that I speak of these as 'languages' and 'idioms' while also referring to 'manners', 'styles', 'fashions'. Perhaps all these terms indicate a particular view of politics. Perhaps they all seem ambiguous and unclear. Some of the ambiguity attaching in particular to the word 'language' is, however, quite fitting. As already suggested, I wish to talk both about behaviour and accounts of behaviour and I intend to use the same term to extend over both. I am content to do this partly because there is a similarity between learning or acquiring a language and adopting a way of behaviour, partly because it may be useful to emphasize the close interacting relation between practical behaviour and descriptions of behaviour.)

The contrast between modern and traditional languages in particular is, of course, a contrast between the political institutions of a nation state and the structure of an ancient society and, as already suggested, the key to Indian politics today is the meeting of these two as strangers. Political system and social structure, so far from having grown up together, have only just been introduced to each other. Before independence, limited franchise and alien rule kept them apart. Even the great national movement, for all its long history and wide appeal, seems in retrospect to have skated quite lightly over the surface of Indian social relations, cutting it up, as it were, only in one or two patches, such as Gandhi's untouchable campaigns. With the disappearance of the white outcastes and the introduction of adult suffrage, polity and society come to meet. However, to speak of languages of politics still seems valuable. It serves to stress that no social relations—however ancient and no matter how far bound up with religious ritual—are devoid of political content. Traditional India is not non-political, only it contains a different kind of politics from that of the 'modern' state. This way of putting the matter also makes it easier to bring out the peculiar third language of saintly politics.

The language of modern politics is undoubtedly important in India—more so than perhaps in most other parts of Asia. This is less on account of the long period of British rule in itself than because of one of its consequences—the existence for nearly a hundred years of an Indian élite steeped in its grammar and masters of its accents. Members of this élite were not only the agents of much of the administrative and economic development of the country; they also provided the leadership of some of the more important movements of social reform and of the nationalist movement itself. It is true that an important change came over the nationalist movement with the impact of Gandhi's leadership after 1917, but it would be a mistake to imagine that Gandhi did not employ the modern idiom; he combined it with another, but by no means abandoned it or prevented its continuous development.

This language is so widespread in India that it has seemed possible to give comprehensive accounts of Indian political life without moving outside its terms. This modern language of politics is the language of the Indian Constitution and the courts; of parliamentary debate; of the higher administration; of the upper levels of all the main political parties; of the entire English Press and much of the Indian language Press. It is a language which speaks of policies and interests, programmes and plans. It expresses itself in arguments and representations, discussions and demonstrations, deliberations and decisions.

Within this idiom are conducted several momentous conflicts of principle and tussles of interests. These are so wide-ranging that observers could be forgiven for greeting this Indian politics as a well-recognized familiar friend and, assuming that this is the whole of Indian politics, the complete story. One kind of 'debate', for instance, is that which is carried on—partly within the Congress Party, partly between it and the Swarantra Party on the 'right' and the Socialist and Communist Parties on the 'left'—about the size of the public sector of the economy, the degree and forms of governmental controls and the direction and pace of land reforms. This looks very like some of our own doctrine-and-interest conflicts. Another 'argument'—still conducted within the modern idiom—relates to the 'federal' theme, and will also sound familiar to Western ears. Here men will discuss the relative roles of centre and state governments, the impact of the Planning Commission on the federal structure, the Supreme Court's influence on the federal balance through its interpretation of the Constitution, and so on. (The whole range of disputes between India's linguistic units concerning the division and boundaries of territories—the splitting of Madras and Bombay, the demands of the Sikhs, the violent hostility between Bengalis and Assamese—can up to a point be regarded as falling within this category; but, as we shall see, only up to a point; to get the full meaning we have to move into a different language, for the reason that those involved are operating in a different language. The same is the case with the strictly linguistic tussles between Hindi and the regional languages and between both and English.) A third example of 'debate' within the modern idiom would be most discussion about forms of political organization and relations between organizations. Here one would place conflicts between party organs and party groups in legislatures; relations between ministers and back-benchers and between minister and civil servants; the composition and powers of the Planning Commission; relations between governments and opposition parties.

Most evidently, then, this is an important language of politics, covering most of what is to be expected as politics. A good index to a book written in these terms on Indian political life would bear comparison with a standard work on Britain or the United States. This is not to say that there would be no items peculiar to India; nor that many of the apparently familiar items would on closer examination prove so readily recognizable. It is only to say that if this modern language comprehended the whole of Indian politics, then as a subject it would for all its distinctiveness be susceptible to analysis by the same methods as French or Dutch politics. But this is not the case. The observer of Indian politics will not look at his subject for long before he gets the feeling that he is missing something. This feeling can perhaps be described only be metaphors. The actors on a stage do not know why the audience should laugh just then, because they have not seen the cat which is playing with the stage curtains. Or, again, the audience may detect an awkward pause but they do not know that the actors are preoccupied because the hero's make-up is coming apart. Such a feeling with regard to Indian politics is perfectly justified; what the observer has so far not taken into account is a play within the play.

That India is even after partition an extremely heterogeneous society is too well known to require emphasis. If the British had not already made it clear, India's leaders have amply done so in recent years. So frequently did Nehru in particular inveigh against communalism, linguism, casteism and the like that the composers of newspaper headlines must be hard pressed to make the theme arresting. But there is a big difference between the periods before and after the transfer of power. In British times the division of political importance was communal—that is, as between religious communities—a phenomenon primarily of urban and middle class origins which was nevertheless capable of seizing hold of popular emotions at certain times and places. What is significant in the present period is the series of divisions that rise out of the caste foundations of rural Hindu society. (Minority religious communities may still be important even here—in so far as they often behave and are treated as if they were component parts of that system.)

What is caste? Until quite recently, the answer would have been given in terms that have become familiar: Hindu society is traditionally divided into five great strata, ranked in terms of social and ritual status, marked and left separate by endogamy and by the possession of distinctive attributes and *mores* appropriate to occupation. These strata consist of the four castes (*varna*) of *Brahmin* (priests), *Kshatriyas* (warriors), *Vaisyas* (traders), *Sudras* (labourers), together with the outcastes or untouchables (associated with a variety of 'unclean' occupations). Students of caste worked mainly on religious texts and similar literary sources and were interested primarily in its origins as a system and in its ritual aspects. The smaller caste-like strata (whose existence in contemporary India had been emphasized by the very different investigations done by British administrators acting as amateur sociologists) were presented as sub-castes derived by some process of division from the basic strata. But soon after independence the study of caste became remarkably transformed and the new work, embodied in an already considerable literature, has presented caste rather differently. Social anthropologists whose previous attentions in India had been devoted to primitive tribal groups began to approach caste from the opposite end to that of the indologists; they concentrated their studies on small units, usually single villages. Their main interests were not religious but social; sometimes there was a practical purpose in view —such as the discovery of factors relevant to the progress of the government's community development programme. The consequence has been to give prominence to caste not as *varna* but as *jati*, that is, as the relatively small and relatively local strata formerly dismissed vaguely as sub-castes. Here is the basic unit of social stratification in traditional rural India, the effective social grouping. That is, social realities are not well revealed by analysis in terms of *varna*; for this purpose the sense of caste which is most relevant is *jati*. The sub-division becomes the division and the fact that each *jati* can be allocated to one of the large *varna* groups is of reduced significance. (It seems not even to be historically the case that there were first *varna* which became sub-divided into *jati*; *jati* were real groups before *varna* categories were applied to them.) For purposes of social analysis as distinct from ritual ranking, it is more important to know in Andhra about the differences, and battles, between *Kammas* and *Reddis* than to know that both are usually regarded as *Sudras* now though perhaps at one time as *Kshatriyas*. In a Gujarat village the dominant caste may be the *Patidars*, in Mysore it is the *Okkaligas* and in Madhya Pradesh it is the *Rajputs*; these are real groups, while the fact that the first two are *Sudras* and the third *Kshatriya* is of less interest.

Seen thus, castes are not five but innumerable; in each small locality—varying in area in different parts of the country but always to be thought of as a cluster of villages rather than a region—there is a distinctive constellation of castes. Each caste is an exclusive endogomous group and no person is outside the system. Each caste is associated with a particular occupation or a limited range of occupations, the interdependence of castes and the exchange of services making for an organic unity in each village. Although each local constellation of castes is distinctive, some castes (even in the *jati* sense) may be common to several. Castes indeed vary interestingly in geographical spread, some being local, others regional. (Brahmins are a somewhat special case. Their spread is nearly complete—but then it is not the spread of a *jati*. The *Chitpavan* and *Namboodri* Brahmins might be *jati*, but then they do belong to particular regions). Each caste in every constellation will have its own customs, ritual functions, distinct features; it will often or perhaps normally occupy a separate group of dwellings even in the smallest village. There is virtually no mobility for individual persons between one caste and another; a man stays in the caste into which he is born. But it appears that a certain amount of group mobility has been present—even before today's social changes. Changing economic conditions could bring about a decline or an improvement in the fortunes of a caste group; the demand for its services might be reduced but it might move into some new 'unallocated' occupation. It had been noticed that castes moving in this way up the economic ladder and thus acquiring strength normally ask for ritual and other recognition of the change; they make claims usually in terms of the *varna* model, pretending to *Kshatriya* ancestry or adopting strict rules of diet associated with 'purity', and in time such recognition comes to be accorded. The existence of a hierarchy of ranks is therefore compatible with group mobility but this is more true at the middle levels where there is ambiguity and room for adjustment than at either the top or the bottom. It has also been observed that although Brahmins are at the top of the *varna* hierarchy, this is not completely so in the case of *jati*. A Brahmin in any village will always have the highest ritual rank but this does not prevent non-Brahmin castes from being normally the politically and economically 'dominant' caste of an area. Brahmins are in fact to be found dominating only when they are also possessors of the key to rural power: land.

This is only the barest sketch of a model. But it may suffice to indicate some of the characteristics of the language of traditional politics. First, and most evidently, it is the language of a host of tiny worlds. *Varna* has all-India meaning, but in the little worlds of *jati*, *varna* is only a reference scale relevant in a limited range of relations. The arena within which *jati* and village interact is a microscopic box, in principle sealed away from the other boxes. It has—again, in principle—no direct experience or sense of the other boxes or of being part of a larger whole; India, even say Andhra, is merely the vague outside. Second, it is a world in which men have their stations and from these stations in the little society they derive exclusively their rights and duties, their whole code of behaviour, even their outlook on things. Here opinions and interests alike belong not to persons but to groups. As there can be group mobility, so there can be shifts in opinions and interests, but these will be shifts by groups. Third, it is not a world in which influence and power are absent, but they are present only as attaching to the *jati* groups. For one thing, leadership is fragmented, each caste having its own leaders. For another, in so far as there is any leadership common to the village as a whole, it will come from the ranks of the locally dominant caste who will regard themselves and be regarded as the natural hereditary repositories of such political status. Indeed, the furnishing of political services will be a recognized duty to be performed by that *jati* in the same way as it will be that of another *jati* to cut hair, of another to wash clothes. The location of political authority is no question of choice, will or election; it is given—by station in the social structure. Finally, the nature of political operations is clear. The work of the caste leaders is to ensure the conformity of members to the caste code, to maintain the position of the group in the village community, to achieve appropriate readjustments in that position if the relative strength of the caste should for some reason increase. The job of the village leaders is twofold: to produce a 'consensus'—that is, to resolve and settle inter-caste disputes in such a way as if possible to maintain the *status quo* or if necessary to secure a smooth readjustment of positions; at the same time to represent the village as a whole in relation to the outside, protecting it from interference and securing favours from whoever happens to be *Raj*. This too, then, is a comprehensive language of politics—for its own scale. But it may be noted that this language is more important as behaviour than description; it is by comparison with modern politics inarticulate, acted upon rather than spoken about. This is for the simple reason that on questions outside the little worlds it has nothing to say, whereas within those worlds it is so familiar that there is no need for it to explain itself.

But the studies which have provided us with a model of the *jati* system have been undertaken at a time when the system is itself undergoing great changes. What is happening to the system of castes understood as *jati*? In particular, is it the case that caste is becoming more important or less? The generally held view has been that with the growth of industrialization, the improvement of communications, the development of urbanization and the spread of education, the power of caste as a focus of loyalty and a determinant of social life has been declining. It might also be added that social reform movements within Hinduism have been engaged with some success in modifying ritual exclusiveness. Moreover, the national movement itself had impacts in the same direction: it provided a point of attraction independent of caste, and by virtue of Gandhi's own social gospel brought many people to feel a sense of shame at such aspects of the caste system as untouchability. There is some truth in all this. But these forces, though operative over more than half a century, have been doubly limited in their influence: quantitatively in that so much of Indian society was left little touched, qualitatively in that it has been mainly the ritual, especially 'pollution', aspects of caste that have been weakened. Moreover, in certain most important respects these very factors making for some weakening of caste have in other ways provided caste with fresh power. For example, social reform has often been anti-Brahmin in tone and purpose and its effect has often been actually to increase consciousness of caste on both sides. More significantly, the improvement of communications and even the growth of cities has made possible for the first time a wider, more effective, positive organization of caste. *Jati*, an essentially local group, has been able to throw out links to its 'opposite numbers' in neighbouring localities; caste begins, that is to say, to manifest itself as regional rather than local, increasingly independent and competitive in relation to other castes rather than interdependent and co-operative, and as an organized association rather than a natural social group.

The third language of saintly politics is to be found 'at the margin' of Indian politics. By this is meant the fact that it is in some quantitative sense relatively unimportant, spoken only by a few and occupying a definitely subsidiary place on the political page. But 'margin' may also be allowed here to have something of the importance given to it in economics: there may be few or none actually at the margin, but the location of the point has an effect on all operators as a kind of reference mark. In other words, saintly politics is important as a language of comment rather than of description or practical behaviour. The outstanding figure of nation-wide importance in this idiom is Vinoba Bhave, the 'Saint on the March' who tours India on foot preaching the path of self-sacrifice and love and 'polity without power'. His effective active followers may not be many but his own activities and pronouncements are reported week by week, almost day by day, in the Press. The direct impact of Bhave is a matter of some uncertainty and dispute. The startling initial success of his call

for donations of land for distribution to the landless prompted all
political parties to pay tribute to him and accord him respectful
recognition. Subsequently, doubts about the motives of land donors
and a certain ineffectiveness in the distribution programme have
lowered the temperature of enthusiasm. Some time ago, there
occurred the experiment of taking Bhave's help in dealing with the
dacoit menace in the region south of Delhi; police action was called
off while Bhave went in to talk to the brigand gang leaders; the
present impression is that the dacoits were keen to benefit more
from the withdrawal of police attention than from the message of
Bhave.

But the direct effects of Bhave are less important than the indirect.
This language has a widespread appeal to all sections in India. For
many people it is identified with the political style of Gandhi. This
is a bad over-simplification: for one thing this was only one of
Gandhi's styles; for another, this idiom was already present in
Indian society before Gandhi undertook its systematic and organized
development. For it is in no way far-fetched to relate this language to
the ideals to be found expressed in classical Hindu religious literature;
the doctrine of the four *asramas* or life-stages with the emphasis on
renunciation and transcendence of self in the two later stages seems
always to have exercised a powerful fascination for the Hindu mind.
Be that as it may, the influence of 'saintly' politics in India cannot be
ignored. Admittedly it affects men's actual behaviour very little;
remarkably few men engaged in political activity within the other
two idioms are striving to be saintly. Its influence is rather on the
standards habitually used by the people at large for judging the
performance of politicians. In men's minds there is an ideal of
disinterested selflessness by contrast with which almost all normal
conduct can seem very shabby. Such a standard is not of course
applied continuously or to the exclusion of other standards. However, it does contribute powerfully to several very prevalent attitudes
to be found in Indian political life: to a certain withholding of
full approval from even the most popular leaders; to a stronger
feeling of distrust of and disgust with persons and institutions of
authority; finally, to profoundly violent and desperate moods of
cynicism and frustration. This is not to make 'saintly' politics a sole
cause of these sentiments; only to say that it can add, as it were, a
certain bitterness and 'edge' to them. It may also be suggested,
though more tentatively, that the existence of this standard may if
anything affect actual behaviour in a morally adverse manner: if the
only really good life is one which seems to belong to a world beyond
reach then a man might as well not strain too hard in that direction

and indeed might as well be hung for a whole big black market sheep as for a little irregular lamb.

That saintly politics is worth listing as a third idiom does not imply that it is wholly unrelated to the other two. In curious ways it takes in much from both; indeed in this lies much of its power. A Bhave talking of the corruption of party politics appeals at once to the modern notions of public spirit and civic conscience and the traditional ideas of non-competitive accepted authority working through a general 'consensus'. Similarly, and even more conspicuously, a man like J. P. Narayan (see also below, especially pp. 258–9), speaking of public 'participation' in a 'communitarian' democracy, stirs the imagination of the advanced radical and the conservative traditionalist alike.

Corruption and distrust

The tale of three idioms may help us to understand certain both general and particular aspects of Indian political life. Consider, for instance, this matter of the gap between profession and practice, the difference between the way things really get done and the way in which they are presented as being done. Of course, this kind of contrast happens everywhere: in England, for example, different sorts of 'old boy networks' are to be found smoothing the course of politics in city council, parliament and Whitehall alike. There is a cement of informality that holds together the formal bricks. But this is not the same as the mixing of entire political styles that happens in India. It is not simply that those people whom a foreigner is likely to question will reply in the 'Western' idiom for his benefit—though this certainly happens. It is also that such people will in any case habitually use that idiom when explaining things to each other. That is to say, Indian political life becomes explicit and self-conscious only through the 'Western' idiom; that is practically the only language in which the activity of description, giving an account of matters, will normally take place. But this does not prevent actual behaviour from following a different path. This situation is of course to be found in many spheres besides the strictly 'political'. 'Applications for scholarships will be considered by the Committee on the basis of recommendations submitted by the Head of the Department', but the natural tendency will be for the aspirant to tackle this problem in terms of 'favours' and 'influences'. Likewise with such matters political as the casting of votes, the selection of candidates and distribution of portfolios, and with such matters of administration as the siting of a new school or the granting of an industrial licence. One must be careful not to exaggerate and careful not to imply that in

English local government or in American party organization everything is as in the text-books. Still there is a substantial difference.

The gap between supposed and real patterns of behaviour is a
much wider matter than corruption but the two are closely related.
Corruption—the fact itself but, even more important, the talk about
it—occupies a great place in Indian politics. It is of two kinds. Much
of what is called corruption is no more than behaviour conducted in
terms of one idiom being looked at in terms of another. Anyone
holding any kind of position of power may be inclined to regard that
position in both modern and traditional terms. Even if he is himself
peculiarly free from the grip of traditional categories and loyalties, he
will be subjected to steady pressures framed in those terms—and it
will be very difficult not to give in. Of course, the proportions in
which modern and traditional are mixed will vary greatly: there may
be 100 per cent modernism in the Planning Commission and 90 per
cent traditionalism in a Mandal (local) Congress Committee in
Madhya Pradesh. But at most levels two mainly antagonistic sets of
standards will be in competition for the power to control a man's
conduct. Equally important, these two sets will also be employed—
frequently by the same persons—for judging his conduct. The
behaviour which the traditional language holds to be irresponsible is
for the modern idiom responsible and that which the modern
regards as improper is for the other the very opposite.

This type of contrast can be greatly sharpened when the third
idiom is present which happens more often than one might imagine.
This is not simply because of the personal influence of Bhave
or the traditional appeal of those ideas or even because of memories of the saintly aspect of Gandhi. It is also on account of the
actual experience of many people in the nationalist movement. That
movement did bring out of ordinary men and women a remarkable
standard of behaviour. From a sense of dedication or merely from
sheer excitement and exhilaration men forgot about themselves and
thought only of the cause. Even if there is a tendency today to
exaggerate this in retrospective glances at the golden age of comrade-
ship and unity, it still contains a big element of truth. There is a
natural unwillingness to accept that period as exceptional and
therefore a strong inclination to be severely critical about the decline
in standards.

The second kind of corruption is in a way the opposite of the first.
The first is a demonstration of the power of the traditional idiom; the
second is a sign of its weakness. When a man 'fixes' applications and
licences in disregard of merit but in accordance with group loyalties
he is obeying a law of social conduct more ancient than that of the

upstart state. But when a man puts into his own pocket moneys intended for some organization, when he relentlessly exploits every situation for perfectly private gain, this is not obedience to the rule of any traditional society. No doubt in every society some men have been very selfish when opportunity was provided. But within a compact and tightly knit social unit of India's traditional kind the checks on anti-social selfishness would be very strong indeed, the sanctions against it awesome. There can be little doubt that much present corruption in India is the work of men not long released from one set of firm social bonds, not yet submissive to a new set. Both corruptions can flourish side by side, for two social processes are contemporaneous: the intrusion of caste into the new fields (mainly of regional and even national politics) and the erosion of caste as a feature of social life as a whole. Corruption is at once what one political language calls the other and what happens when one is displacing the other.

Related to this is a further striking general feature of Indian political life—and again it is a feature rather of social life which politics shares: a certain caution and distrust in relations between people. In the courts a man in India is innocent until he is proved guilty, but in social and political life the position tends to be reversed. One has noticed the wariness with which people encounter each other and the relative difficulty of establishing friendships except within 'community' groups. If we understand the character of caste, this is hardly surprising, for its little worlds are worlds of mental attitudes and styles of behaviour. To have dealings of any intimacy with a man of a different world from one's own is an adventure into a dark unknown and best avoided; personal relations, in the strict sense, are not contemplated in the scheme of Indian traditional life. In politics this has its counterpart in features such as the extra-ordinary extent to which the other man's motives are suspect and the enormous difficulties attending any attempt at concerted action. One particular manifestation of this character is the resistance to unification which is often found in political groups with almost identical policies and the great readiness of many groups to split and break away into factions. Myron Weiner in his *Party Politics in India* offered the explanation that in many cases party had become a substitute for *jati* and that what members demanded above all from their political group was the snug and reassuring coherence of a unit in which there are no strangers or outsiders. A more general, though not incompatible, explanation would be that even in the sophisticated world of urban party politics men have not so far left behind the atmosphere of traditional politics that individuals can be taken as persons; on the contrary, frankness is killed by suspicion and every disagreement becomes a situation of intolerable distrust. Edward Shils, in his study of the Indian intellectuals, found them exceptionally conscious of being 'cut off' from the people. But he commented that this awareness went beyond the actual situation; the reality is not any special 'alienation' of intellectuals from society but rather the 'alienation of most Indians from Indian society', the awful way in which caste consciousness (at least in its present-day forms) 'cuts off most human beings from each other', giving rise to a kind of 'social blindness'. The intellectual's exceptional awareness of this does at the same time give him a special longing for unity and an acute nostalgia for past moments of fellowship.

Thus man as man, man as clerk in an office, employee in a factory, even student in a college, is placed at a distance from his fellows; indeed, it is not easy to recognize the other as fellow. But this is not all. Present-day India strikes many observers as a ruthless and unkind society—and this by the way of contrast with the recent past. This may seem strange in view of the well-known efforts of the present regime to establish a welfare state and raise the living standards of the impoverished masses. Yet the impression has some basis. As the status society slowly crumbles, personal ambitions are released and new men press hard on the traditional holders of authority. Perhaps it is to be expected that men escaping from a world of set status may for a while swing violently to the opposite extreme of competitive struggle for all kinds of power. To caution and distrust of the other man there comes to be added disregard. This tendency, already present before independence, was somewhat held in check by the spirit of fellowship in the freedom movement; it has now been let loose.

The role of politics

It is, then, the presence, the confrontation and, indeed, the mixing of political idioms which dominates the Indian political scene and gives it distinctive tone. For although the 'pure' expressions of each language occupy certain areas, these are less significant than the areas of co-habitation. But what is happening in this great encounter? Does one language gain over the others?

Our understanding of much that is happening in Indian political life today is due to the social anthropologists. For they have to follow caste as a social institution wherever it may lead them, and it has led them firmly into politics. The central discovery is that politics is more important to castes and castes are more important in politics than ever before. The regionalization of *jati* was in some areas a well-established tendency even before independence. The anti-Brahmin movement in Madras during the inter-war period was perhaps an exceptionally advanced manifestation of this development. (It has been usual to regard this movement—in the shape of the Justice Party—as a provincial expression of an all-India anti-Brahminism and to add that it attained political status in Madras because anti-Brahmin sentiment was peculiarly strong there. But it is equally important to see it as a coming together, on the relatively wide basis of a linguistic region, of a number of local non-Brahmin *jati*.) The process has been greatly quickened since independence. India's modern-idiom rulers are no longer protected from the influence of traditional politics by the three bulwarks of British administrators outside the caste system, the national movement and a restricted franchise. All three safeguards have gone and the little worlds of caste have been drawn upwards into the big arenas. The top leaders may proclaim the goal of a casteless society, but the newly enfranchised rural masses know only the language of traditional politics which so largely turns about caste. Nor does caste keep outside the city limits. Although the long-run effects of urban and industrial life may be to weaken caste loyalty, the immediate effects are the opposite. Since immigrants from rural areas keep very close economic and social ties with their villages of origin and since also they often tend to settle in distinct caste 'colonies' within the city, the consequence is greatly improved facilities for organizing. Moreover, cities teach men to forget caste as a co-operative element making for interdependence; caste becomes instead the unit in which men associate for competition against others.

The result is not merely, not even mainly, the rise of particular caste parties. It is rather that in any kind of politics away from the highest levels, caste becomes a category to be reckoned with. So, in the middle and lower reaches of all parties—and in the administration too—realistic men learn what language they have to talk if they are to be understood and effective. What sounds fine in the Delhi Parliament or for the newspaper-reading public makes little sense at the grass roots. Therefore, behind the formal electoral returns, knowledgeable observers discern the intermediaries who join together the ballots of a caste group to the candidate with a party label. Behind the formal lists of party candidates nominated for the contests, there is probably an inside story of careful calculation in terms of caste appeal. Or again, the wrangles of Mysore politics, which the sociologically innocent might describe in terms of relations between parties and between parliamentary and organizational wings of the Congress, come to be seen as a new stage on which is being played an age-old drama of inter-caste rivalry.

C

But in the mixing of idioms the effects are by no means all in one direction. For the modern idiom is moving out of its base in the élite just as surely as the traditional idiom is emerging from its hitherto hidden habitat. Therefore the attempt to show how modern political institutions are open to manipulation and exploitation by traditional social forces has to be accompanied by equivalent attention to the way in which such institutions by their existence constitute modern social forces. Detailed, careful empirical studies of the working of 'inside' politics in India began to appear only in the late sixties and there is still much to be done. It was then that we were given, notably by Paul Brass and Myron Weiner, the first close-ups of that institution, in many ways the most central on the Indian political scene, the Congress Party. This organisation has clearly been, in the terms of our analysis, a crucial meeting ground of the three languages of politics. Within the party are to be found many men who speak the modern idiom—most of them with skill and polish, some of them even with love. Most of the internal party debates would seem to be conducted in this language; for instance, the arguments between the 'right-wingers' (supposedly, for example, Desai, Pant) and the left (Menon and members of the one or two 'ginger groups') on the size of the public sector, the seriousness with which land reforms are to be tackled, the tone of voice to be adopted when speaking to China and the US. When commentators noted the wide range of opinion held together by Nehru, it was a range within this one language which they had in mind. (The same range is to be found, though more obscurely, in the top administration.) The 'federal' tussles within the party are also for the most part in the modern idiom—the location of new steel mills and the choice of ports for development.

At the other end of the machine, so to speak, there is to be found a very different kind of person engaged in a very different kind of operation: the Mandal and District party leaders. Now admittedly local party secretaries in England and ward bosses in the US are concerned with rather different issues from those which preoccupy the parliamentary and senate leaders. The difference in India is, however, a profounder one of the very manner and style of behaviour; the difference in social setting imposes quite different techniques and is associated with quite different values and standards. But who is the present-day Congress worker? Most observers would agree that some change has taken place since independence in the character of the men who do Congress politics at the lower levels. Older party workers will often explain with regret and scorn how new men of the wrong kind have got into the organization. The voice of saintly politics is often heard in this strain. But the point has some validity.

Of course, the motives which impelled a man to join and work for Congress in pre-independence days were more numerous and varied than the old-timers would have us believe, and 'national sentiment' no doubt covered a multitude of different characters. But the new men are indeed different.

Some investigators seem to have found two kinds of new men inside the Congress machine. First, there are the leaders of the new village establishment. Until the introduction of adult franchise, the politically active sections of rural India were generally men of higher castes than the peasants and for this reason even a mass party like Congress was manned by Brahmins and other high caste men out of proportion to their numbers in the community. The politics of adult franchise has in many regions raised the influence of the non-Brahmin middle peasants who are at once numerous and—as compared with the hardly less numerous untouchables—economically substantial. Men from these groups seem to be more prominent in Congress than before. The opponents of the party cry out that Congress is courting and capturing the influential leaders of rural life. Of course it is. But it is equally true that such leaders have in their own ways been courting and capturing Congress. Village India, playing its own game of politics in relation to outside *Raj*, has been adjusting itself to Congress power. The men who for economic and electoral reasons count in any area naturally regard it as one of their functions to get to positions from which they can do what is expected of them by their clients and dependants.

Secondly, however, there may have arisen an even newer kind of local Congressman—the man who relies not on his local social status as a member of a dominant caste but solely on his political skill in the new politics. Whereas the first type would operate in the traditional idiom as a matter of course, this second brand of newcomer is really a modern who is simply able to exploit that idiom. (In addition to both these, there naturally continue to be many party workers who belong to those sections who, while numerically and even economically weak, provided social and intellectual leadership in the past.)

Thus Congress is one of the great meeting-places of the three languages of politics. That the party has in some measure gone traditional under the impact of mass electorate politics seems clear. But it must not be forgotten that a political party *as such*—its very organization, as well as the character of Congress national leadership and the fact of its governmental responsibilities—is a modernizing influence. So which language wins? The question is not yet answered and in a sense cannot be final, for the mixing is thorough and continuously changing. Research subjects abound: the procedures by which Congress's internal elections take place; the negotiations leading to the choice of parliamentary and, even more important, State Legislature candidates; the relations between Pradesh Congress committees and Congress State ministries; the character of the agitations and campaigns on linguistic and communal (e.g. reservation of posts for scheduled castes) issues; the extent and character of party pressures on State Congress governments in relation to land legislation. On each topic there would be at least two main features to examine. First, the extent to which community and caste considerations were present and influential; second, the extent to which the exercise and reception of authority was conducted in modern terms of the institutions and offices or in traditional terms of social status and customary respect. Lest it be thought that all this is in some derogatory sense academic, let it be said that the battles being conducted within the modern idiom as between 'right' and 'left', 'centralist' and 'statist' will be most significantly influenced by the outcome of the underlying conflict between the two languages. The traditional way tends to point to the right and certainly points away from the centre.

Consider also India's representative institutions. In this world, too, as in the world of party, the two idioms meet (with the third idiom again keeping up, as it were, an influential running commentary on the proceedings). There is general agreement that the central Parliament in New Delhi is a powerful instrument of political education for members and public alike. The education it conveys is almost entirely in the modern idiom; this is certainly true of the debates on the floor of the House, in all the parliamentary committees and in some party committees; it is less certainly so in the case of certain other party committees and in regard to general lobby conversation. The members are powerfully influenced by its atmosphere and they are under that influence for by far the greater part of the year. The public that reads papers is also accustomed to watch it closely—so large is the space devoted by the Press to its proceedings. The talk is all of issues and problems and programmes and the scale is emphatically all-India. As Asoka Mehta strikingly said, parliament is the great unifier of the nation. This is true; it has taken over that role in large measure from the freedom movement. (The parallel with the Tudor parliaments is close and instructive: Nehru was 'King in Parliament'; in no other place did he 'stand so high in his estate royal'; with him parliament learnt how it could, in time without him, keep the country powers subdued and in order.)

Much less clear is the character of the State Legislative Assemblies. Students have already pointed out that the members of these bodies are drawn from layers much closer to those of traditional politics. Also they are in the Assemblies for quite a short part of the year; the rest of the time they will be in their home districts which are, increasingly, their constituencies. No one can visit the lobbies of a State Assembly without realizing quite vividly that the Member of a (State) Legislative Assembly (MLA) is 'in touch with' his constituents; the corridors are full of them, some still bearing the dust of the village tracks if not the earth of the fields themselves. The MLA is thus another critical point in the drama of Indian politics: which language of politics does he speak? He is himself undergoing 'modern' education from his seniors on the front benches, but the 'courses' are shorter and of a fairly 'elementary' nature. Still he learns to think of his state (even if not yet of India) and to talk of power projects (even if the big decisions are taken in Delhi). At the other end there are the pressures from home and in the corridors—to remember that he comes from the Vidarbha part of Maharashtra, or that he is a Mahar or that he must please those who count in his district party. So evidently he becomes 'bilingual'. But we would still like to know in which language he does his thinking and his dreaming. Anyone anxious to secure the victory of the modern language over the traditional would do well to concentrate on the MLA and should presumably try to strengthen the links that join him to circles where the modern idiom is spoken. The MLA is one of the great 'gap-closers' in Indian politics but we do not yet know whether he is achieving this in ways favourable to the modern or to the traditional style. Even state ministers have to operate in the two languages. Indeed, one might say that the successful chief ministers are those who are equally skilled in both idioms. Chavan of Bombay was a good example of this kind. When Kamaraj was Chief Minister of Madras, it seemed that his role was, by his unfamiliarity with English, confined to the informal politics of the state, while a colleague handled policy talk with Delhi. But Kamaraj has since shown impressive 'bilingualism' without English.

Recently students of social change in India have developed certain of these points further. For instance, the suggestion just made that behaviour in political parties is in some ways an extension of behaviour learnt in a world of caste groups has recently been neatly expressed by Harold Gould. For him much of Indian politics manifests a largely unconscious *jati* model; in other words, even where caste as such is not a unit for political action, the groups which are real units—notably factions in parties or in bureaucracies—are modelled on 'the principles of solidarity, reciprocity, exclusiveness and ethnicity' which characterize caste. If caste is seen retreating in the face of new institutions it must also be seen as having in some measure already shaped its replacements. In the terms used in this chapter, one might say that the language of even the modern sector has taken its grammar from the language of tradition while adding a new vocabulary.

Such a view of the process may attach too much weight to traditional styles but it underlines our emphasis on the great mixing of political idioms which is going on. When we spoke of antagonistic sets of standards and asked which 'language' was winning, it was by no means intended to endorse a notion that the only possibilities are outright victories for one or the other with defeat implying destruction. On the contrary, by 'political bilingualism' was implied the emergence of a new political idiom formed from the blending of the three analytically separate languages, the manner and proportions of the blend requiring investigation. The work of Lloyd and Susanne Rudolph has in this connection been most helpful, stressing as it does that mode of change which consists in the persistence of traditional elements but their modification and adaptation to new roles—in their words, 'the modernity of tradition'.

The combination, the containment in peaceful interpenetration, of these diverse and in principle competitive languages of politics is the great achievement of political life in independent India. Vast social and economic changes are being accomplished steadily and without obvious drama and are being accommodated and digested by and within a political structure which is successfully flexible, 'politically multi-lingual'. The instruments of this achievement are, first, the two great legacies which India inherited from the days before 1947: the Government and the Movement, a stable administrative structure and a capacious political organization, both equipped with able leadership. To these must be added India's parliamentary and local government institutions—in many respects a development of post-independence politics, yet owing much of their present success to earlier beginnings.

Fig. 1. India: political divisions 1946

3

EVENTS AND ISSUES SINCE 1947

While the purpose of the first two chapters has been to set the scene of Indian politics and indicate some of its distinctive features, that of the present chapter is to give a short narrative account of the main developments in the political system since 1947. In order to avoid excessive overlap with the later, more analytical chapters, the survey is deliberately bare and sketchy; it is intended only to provide a certain perspective of time. Even so, no strictly chronological order is observed and the events are grouped rather according to character. It does seem useful, however, to divide the period into three parts. The first, from 1947 to 1952, can be represented as a period of construction: not only is the constitution itself considered and adopted; in every part of the system there is, after the shock of partition, a kind of self-discovery and mutual assessment. Individuals, institutions, groups are finding their way about in the new world, taking stock of themselves in relation to others—parliament in relation to the cabinet, Congress in relation to other political groups and the strands inside Congress to each other, civil servants in relation to politicians, politicians in relation to voters. The task is to hold things together, to ensure survival, to get accustomed to the feel of being on the water, to see to it that the vessels keep afloat. Although said in the context of a discussion on the reorganization of states, a remark of Nehru's in 1947 had a general validity: 'First things must come first and the first thing is the security and stability of India.' But it is not a negative task. For it involves also exploring the legacies—their relation to each other and to the needs of the new state as the new government begins to discern them—and sifting them. The period from 1952 to about 1964 is one in which a system which has achieved recognizable form and stability undertakes its operational voyage. It is a period not without substantial difficulties and these make necessary significant readjustments and amendments in the system. It is also a period in which the more profound and long-term disparities and discontinuities of Indian society come more clearly into view. But on the whole there is an achievement of containment—in which the forces which demand recognition also begin to undergo a process of taming and domesticization under institutions now more firmly established.

The third period appears initially to be a reversal of the earlier two, a period of destruction and deadlock. In this light indeed is it often seen by some Indians and many foreign observers who sense that several things have been falling apart and that the relative order and coherence of the fifties have given way to processes of disintegration and a condition of fragmented instability. Even the less alarmist view which is taken here must concede that the period has to be characterized as one of political flux and uncertainty. We should still speak of an operational voyage but we must then allow that during the fifties the course stayed within sheltered waters whereas subsequently the open seas, with not a few storms, have been encountered. The 'open seas' are the rich complexities of Indian social structure manifested in a population of massive and increasing dimensions that is both backward and on the move as never before. It is change, not stagnation, which brings problems, change which as ever comes unevenly and hence with pain. One might quite properly say that only in the third period has the full impact begun to be felt of that decision to introduce adult franchise which was taken in the first period. The formal delineation of a comprehensive citizen body is in process of becoming a political reality. The political universe is not, as in established polities, constant but rather constantly expanding. The 'disparities and discontinuities' mentioned as having come clearly into view during the Nehru period, those regional and social cleavages and rivalries whose clamour outside the walls was heard with such distaste, horror and anxiety by the rulers within—these are now the very stuff of political life, in occupation of the central durbar hall itself. The sight is not a pretty one and there is much untidiness; the money-changers are in the temple and there is a noisy boom in political futures. In this situation it is remarkable that the main elements in the political system have been able to survive, not unchanged but through changing. And it is still correct to speak of an achievement of containing and domesticating the forces that threaten disintegration. It is a period of challenge.

Period of construction

An important preliminary point to be made concerning the first period is that it was one of tragedy and peril as well as of construction —so much so in fact that it is a matter for some wonder that any deliberate construction could take place at all. Independence opens with partition slaughter moving down from divided Punjab into the streets of the capital city itself. In the other divided province of Bengal, earlier killings were not repeated, thanks mainly to the almost miraculous fast by Gandhi who acted, as Mountbatten put it, as a 'one-man boundary force'. Before 1947 was out most of the bitter fruit of partition had been gathered, the final estimated totals being half a million killed and a further twelve million refugee survivors of whom perhaps seven million came into India. What this horror deposited in the minds of the newly responsible ministers was a vivid sense of the power of community-feeling to burst through the ties of neighbourhood, citizenship and humanity. The smouldering resentment which it left in other minds made itself manifest in the almost unbelievable event of January 1948 which so shook the country: the assassination by a Hindu fanatic of Gandhi, 'the father of the nation'.

Not only from emotional frenzy was internal security in danger; men of calmer passions were also working to provide other storms. The Communist Party of India, formed as early as 1924, had little opportunity for growth before the war—so unchallengeable was the Congress in the only campaign that mattered and so effective were the legal and administrative disabilities imposed for most of the time by the government. But in 1942 the ban on the party had been removed on its expressing its willingness to be associated in what had become, since Russia's involvement, a people's war. Their policy alienated them gravely from nationalist sympathy, but freedom for activity at a time when Congress was in suspense enabled them at least to do much to build up a firm organizational structure and develop the training of cadres. This proved useful for it put the party in a position after independence to establish strong points in certain areas around particular grievances. One such area was Telengana, the Telegu-speaking portion of the princely state of Hyderabad. Here the discontent of an impoverished peasantry and hostility to the somewhat harsh and unsympathetic regime of the Nizam had already become manifest during the latter months of 1947. Local communist leaders on their own initiative were quick to lend their organizing assistance and at times certain districts were out of effective government control. A change in the party's national

leadership and a sharp 'left' switch of policy early in 1948 transformed Telengana's status in communist thinking from a slightly
puzzling eccentricity to a glorious guerilla warfare centre which
could be the starting point for the revolutionary conquest of power.
The peasant war was supported by vitriolic exposures of Nehru's
right-wing policies and by dedicated efforts to stimulate and exploit
all forms of urban and industrial unrest.

The fact that the communists' attempted rising took place in a
princely state was not wholly accidental. As already mentioned,
Congress activity in those units had always been on a reduced scale
and its relative advantage over other parties therefore less marked.
In some states the winds of political change seemed scarcely to have
touched either the rulers or ruled. In 1947 the Nizam of Hyderabad
certainly failed to understand the world into which he had survived.
Hereditary ruler of by far the largest princely kingdom, he saw no
impermissible incongruity either in his position as old-style autocrat
or in being Muslim ruler of a mainly Hindu population; if British
India was moving to independence through the passions of communalism and democracy, Hyderabad could move to her own independence by other and older ways. Through the middle months of
1947 envoys from His Exalted Highness's court, together with
intermediaries like Sir Walter Monckton, went silently to and from
Delhi carrying terms and proposals, feelers, and conditions. By
November no more than a standstill agreement had been secured
from the Nizam and in the following months stubborn negotiations
continued, to the accompaniment of free-lance arms-running from
outside and a crumbling of order from within. To the threat from
communist-led peasants of Telengana was now added ugly peril from
a violent and fanatical group of Muslim militants, the Razakars,
aiming at the maintenance of an Islamic bastion in the Deccan,
certainly making the most of the last days of this remnant of the
Moghul empire. By September 1948 the Indian government, with
fewer other worries and with no prospect of absorption by negotiation, ordered its army to move. The 'police action' took four days;
outside Pakistan, foreign protest was negligible despite the efforts of
escaped Hyderabad notables. The Nizam himself made a surprisingly
speedy adjustment to circumstances and became the nominal head of
state.

Along with Hyderabad, Kashmir was another problem left
behind unsolved at the time of the transfer of power. The Hindu
ruler of this Muslim-majority state adjacent both to Pakistan and
India had not at that time decided to which of the new states his
kingdom would accede. An incursion of tribesmen from Pakistan in

October 1947 quickly threatened his capital of Srinagar and in
desperation he asked India for military aid. This was given only on
the ruler's agreeing that Kashmir should accede to India. For the
government of India it was announced by Lord Mountbatten as
Governor-General that 'as soon as law and order have been restored
in Kashmir and her soil cleared of the invader, the question of the
accession should be settled by a reference to the people'. The
condition remained unfulfilled and the undertaking unimplemented;
instead, Indian and Pakistan forces were soon engaged in hostilities
which came to an end only with the cease-fire agreement of 1
January 1949. As the Kashmir dispute pursued its subsequent sad
course through UN debates and commissions and unsuccessful
bilateral talks, the cease-fire line has become a *de facto* frontier,
each part of Kashmir being incorporated in practice in the territories
of India and Pakistan.

Hyderabad and Kashmir were the two salient points of physical
force along the line of the problem of the princely states. But the
whole line was intimidating in its complexity and potential for chaos.
Here it was a case of being bound to construct, and construct
quickly, if worse peril was to be avoided. The British had been
adamant in their view that their relations with the princes, expressed
in the term paramountcy, could not be transferred to the successor
states but must simply lapse. The most they felt able to do was
through the last Viceroy, Lord Mountbatten, to discourage separatist
aspirations by emphasizing the compulsions of geography. But the
interim government set up already from 1946 with Nehru as its leader
had already taken the matter in hand: by August 1947, all the 552
states (with the exception only of Hyderabad, Kashmir and Junagadh)
had been persuaded to sign Instruments of Accession and Standstill
Agreements which had the effect of surrendering their powers in the
three fields of foreign relations, defence and communications and
maintaining unchanged all arrangements in other matters. The
energy and determination of Sardar Patel who was in charge of the
specially created portfolio had much to do with this preliminary
success; these qualities were also needed to see the process through.
No fewer than 216 smaller states were fairly quickly abolished as
separate units and merged into the provinces. In certain parts of the
country princely states covered large contiguous and mainly homogeneous areas; these, numbering 275 in all and including some
substantial units, were integrated to form five new unions, one ruler
from each being chosen as the head of state (or equivalent of
provincial governor) and called *Rajpramukh*. With a third group of
sixty-one states neither of these solutions seemed appropriate; for

Fig. 2. India: political divisions 1954

(*By kind permission of the Government of India, Ministry of Information and Broadcasting. The cease-fire line between West Pakistan and India, in Jammu and Kashmir, is based on the unofficial map of the United Nations, No. 1609 (b), August 1965. This shows the approximate location of the line.*)

strategic or other reasons they were instead brought under direct central government administration, either as separate units or in consolidated blocks. Hyderabad, Mysore and Kashmir were left unaffected by these changes. This massive tidying-up operation called for a great deal of negotiation. Even when completed it called for much patient administrative readjustment: the extension of provincial administration into the merged areas; the approximate assimilation of the position of the new unions to that of the provinces in their relations, financial and administrative, with the centre, and also in their internal system of government; the establishment of almost new regimes for the centrally administered units.

This work settled some immediate problems; it also dictated certain features of the new Constitution which was under discussion during the same period. In particular it meant that the units of federation would not be of the same kind but that these would be nine 'Part A' states (former provinces), eight 'Part B' states (the five unions of states plus Hyderabad, Kashmir and Mysore) and ten 'Part C' states (under central administration). To this work of constructing a constitution we may now at once turn our attention. (A decade or so ago no special justification would have been required for giving a certain priority to the constitutional aspect of a political system. The behaviourists in political studies have, however, made any marked attention to legal and institutional forms seem such *vieux jeux* that reasons had better be given: first, the constitution happens to play at times an important part in Indian politics; second, the process of its manufacture provides an instructive introduction to many central problems; finally, the Indian leaders themselves considered it worth while devoting a not inconsiderable part of their energies to the constitution-making task.) The Constituent Assembly, formally the maker of the document, was a body of varying size. Originally elected (indirectly by communal groups of provincial legislators) in 1946 on an all-India basis it in fact transacted little business before the transfer of power; it met without the presence of the boycotting Muslim League members and contented itself in the uncertain circumstances with a very general Objectives Resolution. After partition, the representatives of the Pakistan areas went to compose the separate Constituent Assembly at Karachi, while the Muslim League representatives remaining in India now felt able to attend. Its composition also changed as representatives (mostly nominated) from the former princely state areas were added. A body of some 300 members, simultaneously acting as legislature for the new state, required to have its task carefully organized if it was to be successful. This was done in three main ways. First, committees were set up to report on the main issues of principle, and in these national leaders like Nehru and Patel played a big part. Second, the Assembly's Constitutional Adviser brought together a great deal of data on foreign constitutions and prepared, on the basis of the committee reports, a rough draft. Third, a Drafting Committee under the very able chairmanship of Dr Ambedkar prepared the detailed Draft Constitution. Ample debate took place on the committee reports and above all on the Draft—165 days in all, spread over a period of more than two years.

Reference will be made in appropriate places to particular parts of the Constitution. The central pillars of the construction are three, and to each of these special attention was given by the Assembly's committees: (a) a system of government by ministers responsible to legislatures chosen by adult franchise is established at the centre and in the units (Committees on Union and Provincial Constitutions); (b) a federal relationship between centre and units is worked out in detail (Committees on Union Powers and Financial Relations); (c) the relations among citizens and between citizens and the state are set in a framework provided by the sections on fundamental rights, directive principles, minority privileges and the independent judiciary (Committee on Fundamental Rights and Minorities).

On the principle of cabinet government there was no deep cleavage of opinion but there were sufficient presidential enthusiasts at least to force an adequate statement of reasons to be given by the leaders. The most powerful argument of the critics was that only by making the executive independent of the legislature could its strength and stability be secured. This was countered partly by the view that English experience showed that weak, unstable governments were not a necessary feature of the cabinet system, and partly by the point that the stable president was likely to be in frequent conflict with the legislature and this state of disharmony was a source of certain weakness. There was also the further point peculiar to India: if presidential government at the centre implied the same system in the units, how could the *Rajpramukhs* be fitted in except by the retrograde step of making them the real state rulers? But most telling of all was the simple argument of experience: the British model had been before them for a hundred years and they had been operating it in a qualified form in the provinces and now in its completeness at the centre itself: 'After this experience,' said K. M. Munshi, 'why should we go back upon the tradition . . . and try a novel experiment?' That decided, there remained the determination of the relation between the President as head of state and his ministers. The executive, legislative and emergency powers of the President as listed in various parts of the Constitution are most formidable. On the other hand, the Council of Ministers with the Prime Minister at the head is 'to aid and advise the President in the exercise of his functions', and it was repeatedly stated that this formula was intended to convey that the President would act as constitutional head only. That this is what has in fact so far happened is fairly clear—though President Rajendra Prasad did express his own views both publicly, in speeches and in one significant message to Parliament (on the Hindu Code Bill), as well as in private discussion and correspondence with the Prime Minister. That this may not be the case in every conceivable future situation is equally obvious. It was Prasad himself in the debates who seemed anxious on the score that no provision was being included that would explicitly bind the future President of the Republic to act only and always on ministerial advice. In deciding against this course, the constitution-makers may be assumed to have reckoned that the flexibility that is desirable for the unforeseeable crisis cannot be secured without giving a margin of discretion which might be abused. In a situation where even the impeachment procedure which has been included will not save the Constitution, the probability is that nothing else would either.

This cabinet system is reproduced in the units, but with some differences. That the position of the Governor of a state does not correspond to that of the President is indicated by the different modes of selection. The President is chosen by an electoral college composed of all central and state legislature members with voting powers weighted so as to give the state legislators power equal to that of the central members, and also to give each state legislator power proportional to the population represented. The Governors are appointed by the President and may be dismissed by him. This was a fairly late (1949) reversal of the original plan (1947) to have elected Governors. The change reflected the leaders' experience of the early period of independence: India could not be held together without care and effort: 'It is very important', said Nehru, 'for us not to take any step which might lead towards loosening the fabric of India.' The risks of conflict between head of state and head of executive which were accepted at the centre would be intolerable if reproduced in every unit. Moreover, clearly structural unity would be assisted if Governors were in one aspect agents in the states of the central government. The Governors are in normal times constitutional heads, but already since the Constitution was inaugurated a variety of abnormal situations has arisen in the states and the important discretionary role of the Governors has been evident. Some instances are mentioned later.

The position of Governors in relation to the President is only one of the special features of the federal aspect of the Constitution. The whole question of centre-state relations was one of big issues in the Constituent Assembly debates. The Objectives Resolution of 1946 was passed before partition was certain and when there was something to be said in favour of a promise of autonomy for the units which might yet avert the division of the country. By 1949 the leaders had enough experience of trouble in the states and enough imagination to see more ahead. They were sure that only a central government at least potentially all-powerful would suffice. Many politicians, especially those with strong links with particular regions and their governments, did not share this fright and, moreover, attached great importance to a wide area of state jurisdiction. At several points, therefore, long debates were required; many members remained dissatisfied and indeed the argument continues.

The Constitution lists elaborately the subjects of government. A central emphasis is to be found in the size and importance of the Union List; in the possession by the Union of residuary powers; in the supremacy of Union over state legislation in regard to the concurrent list (except if Presidential assent is secured for a state law); in the provisions for central invasion of the state list in special and limited circumstances. In a similar way the Constitution lays down a comprehensive division of sources of revenue: union sources; state sources; revenue levied and collected by the union but assigned to the states; revenue levied by the union but collected and appropriated by the states; revenue levied and collected by the union and distributed to the states. This last category includes income tax and may include excise, and the division of proceeds in these cases is made in the recommendations of the independent Finance Commission appointed at regular intervals by the President. Other financial matters may also be referred by the President to the Commission but its second specific duty is to make recommendations as to the principles which should govern grants-in-aid from the centre to the states. More remarkable still are the explicit statements in the Constitution concerning administrative relations between union and state governments. Not only must the executive power in every state be exercised so as to 'ensure compliance with the laws made by Parliament', but the union government is empowered to give 'such directions to a state' as may seem to it necessary for this purpose. Further, the centre is able to give directions to secure no impediment to its own functions in the states. States can be entrusted with central functions and vice versa and the union Parliament can impose duties in the central field on state governments. Nor should it be forgotten that the union Parliament requires no more than a simple majority to dismember existing states or create new ones.

To those in the Assembly who tended to form a 'states' rights' school of thought, the most scandalous proposals of all, utterly destructive of federation, were those contained in the emergency provisions. Indeed, many other Congressmen found these difficult to swallow, so closely did they seem to resemble those of the pre-independence period against which they had campaigned so ardently. Even the leaders protested their distaste for these provisions and their sincere hope that they would not be required in practice. As to the necessity of their inclusion even brief experience had left them in no doubt. Three types of emergency are envisaged: a threat to security by external aggression or internal disturbance; a breakdown of constitution in a state; financial crisis. In each case, the emergency is announced by Presidential proclamation which requires parliamentary approval within two months; in the second case, it is made on the basis of a report from the state governor. A significant consequence of the first two kinds of emergency is that the fundamental rights guaranteed by the constitution may be suspended and steps to secure court action prevented. The security emergency frankly entails the suspension of federalism; financial and legislative autonomy goes and the states become centrally administered. The financial emergency permits such directions from the centre as it thinks necessary. While financial emergency has not yet arisen, a security emergency was proclaimed in October 1962 at the time of Chinese advances across the frontier in the north-east, and was still in force, though with limited practical effect, several years after the Chinese withdrew to the cease-fire lines. Constitutional emergency proclamations, on the other hand, were made on nine occasions in the twenty years up to 1967 and on ten occasions in just three years since January 1967. A failure to carry on the government of a state 'in accordance with the provisions of the Constitution' might arise for several reasons; in practice it has come to mean a situation of chronic instability, though (as will be seen below) this can arise in more than one way. Government by ministers is replaceable either by Presidential or Governor's rule; legislation on behalf of the state is undertaken either by the central Parliament or by Presidential ordinance. The normal duration of a constitutional emergency is limited to six months but this can be and has been extended.

On the desirability of including in the Constitution some body of fundamental rights there was no disagreement in the Assembly. The notion had for many years had great appeal not only as representing advanced democratic thought but more particularly as a convenient way of setting at rest the fears of minorities. Some difficulty was, however, experienced in achieving a satisfactory formulation of the rights. Many leaders were anxious to avoid what they took to be a somewhat unfortunate American experience; they sought some means of safeguarding majority-determined policy from frustration through an over-enjoyment of rights by particular persons and groups. A solution was found in the careful and explicit inclusion in the Constitution of a number of qualifications to which the rights must be regarded as subject. This by no means leaves the judiciary with no interpretative role in regard to these rights, but it does mean that the constitution-makers wanted to make the necessarily limited nature of rights perfectly clear to the courts. Thus, a group of 'rights to freedom' is listed in Article 19 (1), and the list is followed by six clauses, all of which take the form 'Nothing in clause (1) shall affect the operation of any existing law in so far as it imposes, or prevent the State from making any law imposing, reasonable restrictions on the exercise of the right in the interests of'—public order, decency or morality, friendly relations with foreign states, and so on. 'The freedoms guaranteed by this Article,' said a critic in the debates, 'become so elusive that one would find it necessary to have a microscope to discover where these freedoms are whenever it suits the State . . . to deny them.' In fact the framers went further: chased by the nightmare of a government hamstrung and enfeebled by constitutional provisions, unable to act firmly in a crisis, they laid down that in declared emergency the whole procedure for the enforcement of rights may be suspended. If the government of India should ever fail to control the country it will not be for the reason that the constitution denied it the necessary power.

A related problem was what to leave out and what to include as rights. The American and French draftsmen of rights in the eighteenth century had an easier task. For one thing, theirs were in the nature of brave declarations, scarcely envisaging minute judicial interpretation. For another, they antedated the practice of democracy and the later notions of the welfare provisions demanded by social justice. What was India to do about matters like social discrimination and economic exploitation? Some 'leftish' pressure to make fundamental rights all-inclusive was resisted on the common-sense ground that it was pointless to give men guaranteed rights to things that no one would have the capacity, for at least some time, to provide. The Irish Constitution came to the rescue: under the heading of 'directive principles of state policy', the status of a place in the Constitution was secured for rights to work and free education, the desirability of decent standards of living, village self-government, international peace and other similar objectives; at the same time these were expressly declared not to be enforceable by any court. Despite the use of this convenient device, the fundamental rights chapters of the Constitution still contain some remarkable provisions. These include: rights of minorities to cultural and educational privileges; prohibitions against forced labour, certain forms of child labour and several forms of social as well as administrative discrimination; and the perhaps incongruously declamatory 'abolition' of untouchability.

The Constitution's fundamental rights are thus doubly limited: first, in the measure that they are qualified so as to permit certain forms of state action which might infringe such rights of some people; second, in that the category of justiciable rights has been drawn up in such a way as to exclude the merely desirable aspirations. To these limits may be joined two further considerations. It is not open to the courts to create rights; the Indian Constitution, unlike the American, does not suppose that there may be fundamental rights which it has not stated. Secondly, the fundamental rights are in no way especially 'entrenched'. On the contrary, they are not even among those ('federal') parts of the Constitution whose amendments requires ratification by half the state legislatures; like the rest of the Constitution they can be changed by vote in Parliament, provided only that the majority is two-thirds of those present and voting and also an absolute majority of the total membership. When in a surprising ruling in 1967 the Supreme Court held that fundamental rights were beyond the reach of Parliament to alter or abolish, government and legislature opinion reacted strongly but showed no hurry to seek a confrontation with the Court.

These limitations were not designed (though it could be held that it is their effect) to weaken the guaranteed character of such rights as are at any time stated in the Constitution, but only to give Parliament the continuing last word in the stating of the rights. Short of that last word the guarantee is indeed firmly present. The Constitution not only expressly states that any law which takes away or abridges any right shall be void but it also includes in the rights the right to move the Supreme Court for their enforcement. Moreover, the Constitution devotes considerable care and attention to the judiciary; appropriately so, for it is the judges who swear by their oaths of office to uphold that constitution. Every effort is made to make substantial the scope of their jurisdiction and the independence of their position. The authority bestowed by the Constitution on various parts of the state machine is open to review not only for the protection of fundamental rights but also for guarding the established federal balance; the Supreme Court has jurisdiction in any dispute between the centre and states or as between two or more states. The judicial system is made strong also by being integrated. Unlike some federal judicial arrangements, those of India ensure a single system of courts from the subordinate courts through the High Courts in the states to the Supreme Court which has supervisory powers and appellate jurisdiction. The judges' independence is aimed at in several ways. The mode of appointment is by the President but only after consultation with senior judges. Tenure is fixed (sixty-five for the Supreme Court, sixty for High Courts) and removal is only possible by resolution of both houses of Parliament on grounds of proved misbehaviour or incapacity. Qualifications, salaries (the actual sums of money, charged on the Consolidated Fund and therefore not subject to a legislature vote), allowances, privileges and immunities are all set out in the Constitution and schedules.

Political construction could not wait on the making of the Constitution nor would it be confined to matters of which a constitution could take cognizance. A large part of government and politics alike began to take shape before 26 January 1950, when the new republican Constitution finally came into force, and the work went on afterwards. With states to be integrated, refugees to be rehabilitated, a constitution to be drafted, communists to be controlled and mouths to be fed, it is not that India's leaders were free to contemplate in calm leisure the structure of government. Nevertheless, several lasting changes in the machinery of government forced themselves even on desperately busy men. Indeed, many of the changes were needed just because there was so much to be done. This, in part at least, explains the adjustments in the ministerial structure. The cabinet of independent India which was sworn in as successor to the Executive Council of the Viceroy was a body of fourteen ministers. In the following five years several junior ministers came to be added. Gradually—and helped by the recommendations for orderliness made in the report of Gopalaswami Ayyangar, himself then Minister of Transport—a hierarchy of four ranks emerged: cabinet ministers; ministers of state (also referred to, for prestige rather than clarity, as ministers of cabinet rank) who may have independent lesser portfolios or be in charge of a department within a ministry under a cabinet minister; deputy ministers; parliamentary secretaries. By now, the ministry as a whole numbers over fifty while the cabinet has shown a tendency to increase slightly to between sixteen and nineteen. (In recent years shaky governments in certain states have prolonged their existence by grotesque expansion of ministerial numbers.) The parliamentary secretary rank is disappearing.

The changing composition of the ministry had also political

significance. The chosen fortress-holders of 1947 included many with little or no connection with Congress. It was a coalition government in two senses. First and foremost, it contained a strikingly careful selection of representatives of communities and regions—far more so than any later governments. Secondly, it was a policy coalition also, though not by virtue of containing a balance of opinions: on the contrary, the non-Congress opinion represented was all (with the possible exception of Ambedkar) in some sense markedly conservative. By 1952, much had altered and the directions of future change were also clear. Of the men who disappeared from the government, it can be said that they were usually strong either as representatives of established groups or as personalities, or both. Some were removed by death: most important, Vallabhbhai Patel; later, Kidwai and Ayyangar; most recently, Azad and Pant. Others went by resignation on grounds of policy differences: Mukherjee, Neogy, Mathai, Ambedkar and Baldev Singh before mid-1952; subsequently, Deshmukh and Krishnamachari. Others again have left to take appointments as state Governors—perhaps one of India's equivalents of a seat in the Lords: Munshi, Prakasa, Gadgil, Giri and Katju. There has also been some to-and-fro movement between the central government and chief ministerships in states: Rajagopalachari and Mahtab moving outwards, Pant, Desai and Chavan coming in. This indeed was during much of the Nehru period a main fresh source of strength for the centre, many of the other cabinet members being quiet and rather colourless men of uncertain ability and distinction whose merit has been to avoid giving or taking offence. (Mr Krishna Menon belonged to neither category.)

A government is not simply a group of ministers. It heads an administrative body. It is true that in India the (in some ways) opposite origins of ministers and bureaucrats might have made a joining difficult. But what circumstances demanded in the name of survival and stability a powerful realist like Patel was able to achieve. It is no doubt true that just as nothing short of access to private conversations would reveal the whole story of ministerial movements, only inspection of confidential files would disclose some of the 'adjustments' which were called for and effected in the higher bureaucracy. Of general tendencies made evident during the period of construction, three may be mentioned here. First, the basic civil services structure was preserved in its non-unified character: state services, central services and all-India services. While several new central services have been established, the key all-India services remain the Indian Administrative Service and the Indian Police Service. The former is the successor service to the ICS and had already been established in anticipation of the transfer of power. But the shortage of top bureaucrats was acute; a committee of civil servants which investigated the position in November 1947 (and recommended the speedy recruitment of an emergency cadre of the IAS) estimated the need at 250 men, and this was no more than a minimum replacement that took little account of expansion. Yet such expansion was precisely what was soon required and this gave rise to other tendencies. There was a good deal of change in departmental structures—personal factors, uncertainty and genuine experimentation all playing a part in such vicissitudes as were endured for some years by the departments of industry, commerce, supply, works, production and power. There were also the beginnings—envisaged already in the Industrial Policy Statement of 1948—of a fresh movement of the state into industrial and financial enterprise—and here too variety (under the sometimes legitimate designation of undogmatic experimentalism) was marked. In addition to direct departmental management, which was already present in ordnance factories, railways, telephone manufacture, etc., trial was given to the public corporation form (e.g. Damodar Valley Corporation, 1948) and to the government-owned company (e.g. Sindri Fertilizers and Chemicals Ltd, 1951). In any case, the top management of the enterprises was another job for the civil servants and it became usual for boards of directors to be appointed from 'parent' ministries, with the permanent secretary of the ministry often as chairman of the board. Finally, just two months after the Constitution was brought into force, there came into existence, by simple resolution in Parliament and comparatively little public discussion, the Planning Commission. The idea of planning was not new; rather, as already indicated, this was a commitment inherited from the past. But the new body came suddenly upon the scene—unannounced by the Industrial Policy Resolution of 1948 and only hurriedly preceded by an appropriate statement from the Working Committee of the Congress Party—and it seems likely that few foresaw the part it would play or the controversy that would soon surround it. However, it could be reasonably guessed that with Nehru as its founding father and its chairman it would enjoy great influence of some kind. It would provide another illustration of the rule that in any fluid political situation battles are half won if there can be established an organization or institution around which habitual procedures and loyalties can grow. In this case the battle was not merely or mainly one of policy in the cause of planned economy; it was one of constitutional structure in the cause of strong central direction of governmental economic programmes.

If political construction must be understood to comprehend administrative structures, it must also be taken to include party organizations. In this part of the tale Congress deserves most of the space to itself, for at the coming of independence who else was present? The creation of Pakistan had left the Muslim League for the most part looking unseemly and feeling futile. The Hindu Mahasabha had little coherent and effective support except in patches, and the RSS (Rashtriya Swayamsevak Sangh), which moved in its shadows, was exclusively dedicated to the militant training of Hindu fanatics and therefore only potentially a party in politics. The Communist Party had been far from idle in its brief season of legality, but its support of the Soviet–Allied war, and then its readiness to see the Muslim League demands as legitimate and even progressive, had crippled its capacity to appeal; its only listeners were to be found among the ultra-sophisticated who might be willing to go beyond nationalism and those whose horizons had not yet taken in the nation.

Yet if at independence it was only Congress that mattered, it is also true that independence posed for Congress the question of whether it should be a party. It was posed not for the first time, nor for the last. Gandhi had created and fostered an organization which was insistently different from a 'mere' political party, not simply by virtue of its 'total' claims to speak for a national interest but also by that side of its activities which was designated 'constructive work'. This was an aspect of *swaraj* itself, understood not as 'mere' political independence but as real self-rule through self-reliance; it covered the non-political part of the campaign for *swadeshi*—the use of home-made goods—through encouragement to hand-spinning and the wearing of *khadi*; it extended to social reform with movements for prohibition and the uplift of the untouchables; and it included voluntary social welfare activity on health, hygiene and education. 'Constructive work' served many purposes in the nationalist struggle. Not only did it attract and occupy and supply a mission for some of the members all of the time; it also proved convenient as a sector of retreat and withdrawal for most of the members some of the time —whenever, in fact, a pause was for some reason indicated on the political front.

Now, in 1948 on the eve of his assassination, Gandhi in a solemn document proposed that this part should become the whole and that politics should be left to others. It must have seemed to him that there was little in common between party politics and 'movement' politics; or, using other words, that overall national service and not political management was the main meaning of Congress and that therefore the organization should properly move into a field where that meaning could be preserved. In this view, he showed insight: there was at least truth in the implied confession that his own distinctive contributions to Congress—'constructive work' and the techniques of *satyagraha* or non-violent civil disobedience—were not the stuff of which workaday politics is made. But he was mistaken if he imagined that his own contributions were limited to those parts which were distinctive; his inventions were extra-political but his practice included much politics. He was even more mistaken if he thought the other leaders would be willing to preside over the dismantling of what could become a powerful political machine. The reply of the leaders to Gandhi's plea had in effect been given in anticipation of the event: Shankarrao Deo, as General Secretary of Congress, had explained in a party circular in August 1947 that India's need for unity and stable government in the coming period of trial and peril could only be supplied by 'one big political party' and that there should accordingly be no break in the continuity of the life of Congress. He added—and Nehru subsequently stressed this on many occasions—that the unfulfilled pledges of Congress in economic and social matters pointed to the same conclusion. The Gandhi document was laid gently on one side, but the issue has never been wholly stilled. Like the sayings of Bhave, the Gandhian vision of a *Lok Sevak Sangh* hangs as a reference point in the sky above politics, and in certain kinds of awkward times—as when party membership qualifications are under discussion or when party devotees seem not to be as well appreciated as party parliamentarians —men will be found lifting their eyes in that inspiring direction.

To decide that Congress would be a party was not to dispose of problems but only to settle the range from which they could arise. (Even the decision itself, which at least in principle implied a degree of competition with other parties, could get overlooked in moments of special emotion: in 1953 Nehru said: 'The Congress is the country and the country is the Congress.') A key question was: who could no longer be accommodated within the organization? In 1948 the socialists had their minds made up for them by a decision banning parties within the party. The Congress socialists became the separate Socialist Party. But parties within the party were one thing; another related question was whether members of Congress could at the same time be members of another political organization. There had been a long-standing rule making membership of Congress committees incompatible with membership of committees of communal organizations which the Working Committee found anti-national. In 1948 this was doubly extended—mainly with communists in view: it now covered membership of 'any political party, communal or other, [having] a separate membership, constitution and programme', and it also applied not only to committee men but to all 'qualified' members. (In 1951 this was further extended to cover even 'primary' members.) But the 'right'-ward approaches needed guarding almost as much as the 'left'. Naturally those Congressmen who were most zealous in ridding the party of its radicals were less assiduous in attending to the other side. Even so, it was remarkable that the Working Committee should have permitted itself in 1949 to take advantage of a period when Nehru was absent abroad to agree that men associated with the RSS could be members of Congress—and this within only a few months of the lifting of the ban on that body which had been imposed at the time of Gandhi's death. That Nehru saw to it that the decision was reversed is less surprising than that it could ever have been taken.

Any political party expects that with luck it will one day enjoy or at least share in the responsibilities of government. In the case of Congress it was inconceivable that it should require any help from fortune in this. But this at once revived the problem of the thirties: the proper relation between party and party-as-government. 'At once' is correct: already within two months of independence Acharya Kripalani resigned from his position as President of Congress, explaining that there was no harmony between government and party and that his own position was impossible since he did not enjoy the confidence of those members of the party who were ministers. Prasad's election in his place brought a period of calm at the centre, but it quickly appeared that there were as many similar difficulties as there were states with Congress in power. In most states, indeed, Congress governments seemed to have more troubles with their own party organs than with other parties; in the Pradesh Congress Committees were collected a fair proportion of disappointed men, envious of those in office and occupied by no tasks of sufficient interest to distract them from resentful criticism. From the central office issued a steady stream of excellent general advice, encouraging mutual consultation between party and government leaders and urging the former not to try to control the activities of the latter. Such exhortations proved none too effective and by mid-1949 the Working Committee had to direct party committees to refrain from passing—as in Rajasthan they had just done—no-confidence resolutions against Congress governments; complaints, they added—with an attempt at tightening the centre's control—should be lodged with the Working Committee.

The lopping-off of certain radical branches and the check on the entry of some 'right' communalists had not secured perfect harmony of viewpoints among the leaders. Nehru and Patel, the tallest of the tall leaders, had for long been regarded as standing for different things and had on more than one occasion been ranged on opposite sides in the movement's internal debates. Now they constituted the 'duumvirate' as it has been called—the 'strange alliance' of contrasted opinions and temperaments which saw India through to safety. But although each recognized the indispensability of the other and both exercised admirable tact and discretion, tension was present. It found clear institutional expression in the elections for the Congress presidency in August 1950—an event which introduced a critical period of thirteen months in the party's history.

This was a closely fought contest. The electorate consisted of delegates to the annual session of the Congress, and the fact that they had been chosen in turn on the basis of membership rolls of doubtful validity made it difficult to know whether the vote reflected accurately the state of opinion in the party; there were those who said it reflected which side had control of the party's own electoral machine. Purshottamdas Tandon, accepted as Patel's candidate, conservative and orthodox Hindu to the point of communalist, won with 1,306 votes. Kripalani, a radical Gandhian, and taken, despite the large differences, as Nehru's candidate, obtained 1,092, while Shankarrao Deo, a middle-way Gandhian, had 202. The necessary absolute majority was secured by twelve votes and the party dived towards schism.

Whether things would have been easier if Patel had not died before the end of the year is difficult to say: as it was, they were bad enough. Kripalani set out at once to counter Tandon by organizing what he no doubt hoped would be regarded as something less than a party within the party, the Congress Democratic Front. It aroused considerable hostility, and although Kripalani for some months evaded and resisted gentler forms of Working Committee pressure on him to dissolve it, he had to surrender to a firm directive of April 1951. This prepared the way for Kripalani's departure from Congress at the end of that year to form the Kisan Mazdoor Praja Party (KMPP). While the 'rightist' leaders were happy to use discipline on radicals, Nehru took advantage of the situation to turn the same weapons against those who, perhaps with some encouragement from the right, were snapping at the government's heels and even trying to dictate policy. In one of his periodic bursts of anger, Nehru hit out at 'undue interference' from party organs and got the Working Committee directive to cover such activities also. But restive elements were to be found on all ideological sides and some of the state politicians who had to be disciplined—Prakasam of Madras, for instance—became recruits for the KMP.

In this ugly year Nehru emerged more clearly than before as a determined political fighter. His taste for intellectual arguments and his habit of delicate and hesitant self-examination in public had perhaps made people all along prone to underestimate his capacity for skill and determination in tough situations. Now, more on his own than ever before, he moved steadily towards a major show-down. It seems likely that one of the decisive considerations with him was the need to control so far as possible the nomination of Congress candidates for the coming first general elections—nominations which could greatly influence the character of legislatures and ministries in both states and centre. Certainly the first action he took after his victory was the despatch of a strongly worded circular which not merely reiterated the ban on groups inside the party but went further in prohibiting any association of members with communal organiza-tions, and requiring men of 'progressive social outlook' to be chosen as the party's candidates.

Tandon was ousted from the presidency of the party by forcing the party to choose between him and Nehru. Nehru's claims were total: control over the leadership of Congress. Either Tandon would have to permit a 'reconstitution' of his Working Committee or Nehru would resign from that body. For nearly two months the other members tried to reconcile the contestants, but Nehru saw that the party's need for him was so great that he could win all, and finally Tandon saw this too. On Tandon's resigning in September Nehru himself was chosen as President of Congress. Not only was the duumvirate at an end both within the government and within the party; it was also out of the question in Nehru's lifetime that party and government at the centre could be other than in complete harmony, each having the same master. This did not mean that Nehru would thenceforward rule as he pleased; the political system was free, Congress contained a variety of opinions and Nehru's was a sensitive ear. It meant that his was the final word; to influence policy entailed persuading him.

Period of operation

The crisis in Congress and its resolution have such importance as would without further help warrant our saying that 1951 ended a period. But if Nehru's victory in the party is one piece of the gateway out of the stage of construction, the other is the general elections of the winter of 1951–2. Before the elections took place there was a certain tentativeness about political life despite the inauguration of the new Constitution of the Republic in January 1950. Indeed, until the elections were held, the Constitution was not fully in force; this, appropriately enough, was the period not only of the 'temporary and transitional' provisions but also of the 'Provisional Parliament'. In a sense, the people had not yet come on to the stage; or, up to now it was but a rehearsal. 'Provisional Parliament' was only a new name; the body was still the Constituent Assembly, put together under British rule five very long years earlier and now freed of its constitution-making function. How different would be the new Indian Parliament chosen by adult franchise?

It is worth remembering, twenty years later and after three further elections, how bold a step this seemed at the time—as bold as it was inescapable: 'a leap in the dark' and 'an act of faith', said the leaders. The 176 million voters of 1951–2 represented nearly a five-fold increase on those exercising the franchise in 1946. What would these silent, illiterate, untapped levels of the people now say? Even if Congress politicians might claim some familiarity with the people of the former provinces of British India, who could say what would happen in the former princely states? The shocks were, in the event, not severe. First, the administration survived. Nearly a million government servants for varying periods manned the vast electoral machine under the directions of the independent Election Commissioner who had earlier been responsible for preparing the rolls and delimiting 3,772 constituencies. To avoid the voter's having to mark his ballot paper in any way, he was required only to place it in the box displaying the symbol of the candidate of his choice; this meant over two and a half million ballot boxes had to be made, distributed and collected from the 200,000 polling booths. Just over 50 per cent of the voters went to the polls. Not all of them understood the nature of this new ritual and some were no doubt victims of others who understood it wrongly and too well. Invalid votes totalled over one and a half million and election tribunals were at work for over a year deciding on a mass of petitions filed by unsuccessful candidates. But the accounts of observers left little doubt that large numbers of people became aware that they were important enough to be courted and that a smaller but still not insignificant number realized that some kind of choice was open to them. To say this is not at all to underestimate the importance of group voting and its corollary, so vital for the politician, that success demands an understanding of how groups are led.

Seen from above, the campaign was dominated by Congress and especially by its leader, who strove with fantastic energy to rouse the party from its year of agony. From below, too, Nehru counted for a great deal. But near the ground other considerations could also be felt: some candidates were successful because they stood for Nehru's and Gandhi's Congress, but others were given the Congress label because they were going to be successful. Men of great local influence were not easily to fail at this examination. Even those whose allegiance was not secured before the elections—and the number of independents was very large—often attached themselves to Congress afterwards. In the Lok Sabha, the lower house of Parliament Congress's majority was massive: 364 out of 489, and the next, largest group, the communists, had only twenty-three. In every state, Congress emerged the largest party. Against this, however, its share of the vote was only 45 per cent and in four states it failed to secure an overall majority of seats. Thus, it was firmly in power, yet with the knowledge that a majority of those voting preferred others. Only the mixed character of these 'others', scattered on all sides of the giant, saved it. On the other hand, only such a wide scatter of candidates could have gathered in so many non-Congress votes; independents alone accounted for 521 candidatures and 15 per cent of the votes. (For details see Tables at pp. 184–90.)

Nehru had campaigned mainly against the conservative communalists—partly from personal preference and conviction, partly from his recent experience within Congress, partly perhaps from a sense of where the longer-term threat lay. But certainly the results seemed to point in a different direction. The three main Hindu parties—Jan Sangh (very new but vigorously led by Shyama Prasad Mukerjee), Hindu Mahasabha and Ram Rajya Parishad—mustered only six million votes and ten seats in the Lok Sabha between them; the communists alone had nearly as many votes and twenty-three seats, while the socialists, together with Kripalani's KMP, gathered over seventeen million votes though only twenty-one seats. Such totals of votes may, however, be misleading. As between socialists and communists, for instance, they do not reveal the number of constituences over which the votes were secured. In fact, the socialists and KMP together spread their optimistic effort and put 391 candidates in the field, while the communists chose to concentrate on seventy constituencies. (Unfortunately, it is impossible to estimate what would have happened if different policies had been followed. Both parties did in fact reverse their policies in 1957, but that was five years later and provides no more than a possible answer.) Even looked at from the viewpoint of votes per candidate the performance of the communalists was the poorest of all.

Perhaps more significant was the fact that more than half the seats (and not much less than half the votes) that did not go to Congress did not go to the main known rivals either, but went into the categories of 'other parties and independents'. The 'other parties' were almost entirely those with a purely regional appeal and basis; leading examples were the Akali (Punjab Sikhs), Jharkhand (Bihar tribals), Dravidian parties (Madras) and Ganatantra Parishad (Orissa). The independents (1952 is referred to here; the tale changes somewhat later) were more local than even regional, representing no eccentric ideologies but rather position, status and influence of greater value than any party label. The success of these groups and individuals can be regarded as having posed at the outset of the period of operation of the new Indian polity a literally basic question: could adult franchise sustain a genuinely all-India polity? The full dimensions of the problem were, however, not fully disclosed merely by this evidence. Rather, the critical aspect lay as yet mainly hidden in the internal affairs of the major party itself. How far the surviving all-India leadership could communicate downwards its integrating influence was to become a decisive consideration in the years to come. Such influence would be exercised of course not through Congress and other all-India parties alone but also through institutions such as parliament and the administrative machinery of government.

It is not an excessive oversimplification to say that the period of operation has been dominated by two great issues: national integration and economic development. These issues are not resolved within the decade; they are at least formulated in some of their key aspects.

National integration

'National integration' appeared in so many words at the end of the fifties but was of course present as a problem from the start. Its territorial aspect was manifested in two phases with only a brief interlude between them: the work of integrating the princely states was barely completed before the reorganization of states on linguistic lines was on the active agenda. Thus an important job of construction was held over into what we have called the period of operation. Yet the anomaly is not too awkward, for this particular task of construction was one which at the same time entered very fully into the operations of Indian politics—to the point where it became perhaps the chief concern of very many politicians in the fifties.

The proposal to redraw the boundaries of the units to coincide with the language areas of the country had met with some British approval and had been so emphatically endorsed by Congress for thirty years (see p. 46 above) as to have about it the quality of a promise. The matter was raised early in the Constituent Assembly and received the first of its three major studies in the report prepared for that body in 1948 by a Commission presided over by Justice S. K. Dar. The verdict was firm and hostile. Linguistic states could not be established without a loss of administrative efficiency, the creation of unhappy linguistic minorities on the wrong side of any possible borders and, above all, a substantial and unnecessary threat to national unity at a time when every effort was required to preserve it. To concede the demands, the report indicated, would be irresponsibly unpatriotic. But so many aspirations—political and economic as well as cultural—had developed in association with the regional languages over half a century that they were not to be easily stilled. They might bide their time a little, but soon they would try to demonstrate that to ignore them would damage unity more than to recognize them. Especially insistent were the voices from the south: Telegu-speakers were in parts of three states (Madras, Hyderabad and Mysore) and demanded an Andhra state of their own; Kannada-speakers were dominant in Mysore but also present as minorities in neighbouring states; Maharashtrians looked to a state of their own in place of a Bombay shared with Gujaratis: similar dissatisfactions and hopes were felt among the Malayalees and Tamils.

The frustrations were sufficient to cause anxiety inside Congress, and the party, late in 1948, appointed Jawaharlal Nehru, Vallabhbhai Patel and Pattabhi Sitaramayya as the ('JVP') Committee to look again at the question, presumably from a more purely political standpoint. Their report also advised against linguistic states, but did so with certain reservations. It was evident to good politicians that indeed a point might be reached when unity would be not helped but harmed by continued resistance. Unfortunately for the *status quo* they in almost so many words said so. In particular, they rather singled out the instance of Andhra (Sitaramayya's home area) as one where a strong case could be made and on which at least an open mind had better be retained. This was an irresistible invitation to the Telegus to bend their energies to closing the minds of the leaders in the right direction. (This is not to say that concealment of the political assessment could have postponed indefinitely the day of reckoning with linguistic movements; to arrest the general movement would have probably required increasing repression.) A mounting sentiment for Andhra soon led to growing support for the communists, schism and disaffection among Madras Congressmen and a state increasingly difficult to govern. It required only a Gandhi-styled exercise in moral pressure to produce violence: when at the end of 1952 Potti Sriramula went through to death with his fasting in the cause of Andhra, indignation burst the bounds of order and the government gave in.

Fig. 3. India: political divisions in 1970

(By kind permission of the Government of India, Ministry of Information and Broadcasting. The cease-fire line between West Pakistan and India, in Jammu and Kashmir, is based on the unofficial map of the United Nations, No. 1609(b), August 1965. This shows the approximate location of the line.)

The new state was conceded almost at once and came into existence within the year.

But the case of Andhra was not unique; if, to be convincing, what the other areas lacked was fervour, this could be put right. Partly to head off other agitations, the third and largest investigation of the problem was undertaken. The States Reorganization Commission (SRC) was composed of men of independent standing and reputation: Fazl Ali, Panikkar and Kunzru. Their terms of reference told them to bear in mind national security and the need to preserve and enhance national unity, the viability of the units and the welfare of the people including linguistic minorities. Still, 'reorganization' was in their title as well as in everyone's mind, and it did look as though much would depend on the amount of feeling and support which could be mobilized. Over wide areas of the country, politicians' energies were devoted in this direction throughout the Commission's two years of work. Congressmen were affected as much as anyone; the party directive of 1954, requiring that members, while allowed to submit their views to the SRC, should not conduct agitations or associate with other groups for such purpose, was flagrantly disobeyed. But the agitation and campaigning directed at influencing the SRC was mainly sedate and constitutional; it entailed much ink and no blood. This is more than could be said of the activities that followed the publication of the report and which were directed at coercing the government.

The SRC report recommended substantial changes to meet the wishes of Malayalees and Kannada-speakers but baulked at the splitting of Bombay. Instead, they recommended forming a state of Vidarbha out of parts of Bombay and Madhya Pradesh. This no doubt gave some Marathi-speakers a state of their own but it left the main body in a weaker position vis-à-vis the Gujaratis in undivided Bombay state. This compromise sold badly and eighty people were killed in Bombay city rioting in January 1956. With this, the problem landed firmly on the table of the Congress Working Committee. (How far it came before the cabinet is difficult to judge since the two members of the cabinet who have expressed their views seem to contradict each other flatly. C. D. Deshmukh, Finance Minister from 1950, resigned on precisely this question. He alleged that neither the cabinet nor any cabinet committee had discussed the matter and that he had not even been individually consulted. The Prime Minister insisted that there had been consultations with every colleague and decisions taken with the full consent of the cabinet.) The problem was by no means easy and although much wobbling was done—and, worse, was seen to be done—'firm decision' might have worked no better. One attempted solution was to split the state in two but give Bombay city to neither, making it ito a separate centrally administered area. In the end the States Reorganization Act of 1956 provided for a Bombay state undivided and enlarged by the inclusion of additional Marathi-speaking areas. This pleased neither the Maharashtrians, who still wanted their own state, including Bombay city, nor the Gujaratis, now become an even smaller minority in the undivided state. Moreover, both sides were by now thoroughly well organized. Almost, the political parties had been effectively replaced by two language-front organizations, composed initially of leftist parties but soon attracting support from many even non-political people: Samyukta Maharashtra Samiti and Mahagujarat Janata Parishad. The drawing together of diverse sections—rural leaders, students, artists, business men and civil servants—in a common enthusiastic sentiment and sense of unity paralleled, on its regional scale, the best days of the nationalist movement. A shaken Congress organization was reduced in the 1957 elections from a position of near-monopoly in the Bombay legislature to one of a slender majority (though it managed even then to hold on to the bulk of its voting strength). Further agitation and violence finally secured in 1960 the splitting into Gujarat and Maharashtra.

In 1961 the government, in a slightly desperate attempt to put an end to a troublesome war with the Naga tribal people of the north-east frontier, agreed not merely to release them from subordination to the government of Assam but to allow them to form a separate state of the Union. Effected in 1963, that brought the total of states to sixteen: Assam (Assamese language but with significant Bengali and tribal minorities); Andhra Pradesh (Telegu); Bihar (Hindi mainly); Gujarat (Gujarati); Jammu and Kashmir (Kashmiri mainly); Kerala (Malayalam); Madhya Pradesh (Hindi mainly); Madras (Tamil); Maharashtra (Marathi); Mysore (Kannada); Nagaland; Orissa (Oriya, with tribals); Punjab (Punjabi and some Hindi); Rajasthan (Rajasthani and some Hindi); Uttar Pradesh (Hindi); West Bengal (Bengali). (It should be added that Kashmir consists only of those parts of the former princely state on the Indian side of the 1949 cease-fire line and that even these areas are disputed by Pakistan.)

The states as reconstituted seemed in the main to be stable entities, though further minor boundary adjustments were not to be ruled out. The only really awkward case appeared to be Punjab—and a decade later there was ample evidence that appearances were not deceptive. Here the issue was not a simple one of language; Punjabi as a spoken language is closely akin to Hindi. Rather, Punjabi is the language of the Sikh community whose sacred book is written in the distinctive Gurmukhi script. Moreover the Sikhs, former rulers of the Punjab and even in British days prominent in the life of the state, were now fearful of losing influence and even identity; with the disappearance of both the British and the Muslims they had moved from an exploitable quartet situation to one of direct confrontation with the Hindus. The Sikhs had for many years their own political organization, the Akali Dal, and talk of a Sikhistan was heard by the British (1946) Cabinet Mission. Disappointment on securing no special recognition added a bitterness to the community's migration sufferings and retaliations. Separatist political claims for Punjabi Suba were put forward again in the early fifties, but made little impact on either the SRC or the government. The leadership of Master Tara Singh seemed, as so often in the past, to be at once fiery and uncertain—reflecting perhaps the community's own divisions and its inability to agree on whether intransigence or conciliation would secure most. The main leaders agreed in the 1957 elections to back Congress—though Tara Singh attempted a last-minute reversal —and a compromise formula on language policy in the state was adopted. But dissatisfaction and distrust manifested themselves very soon; the new agitation, involving mass arrests, culminated in Tara Singh's allowing himself to be pressed by ardent supporters into a fast to death for the cause of Punjabi Suba. The government remained firm and Tara Singh lost much face by abandoning the fast in return merely for a promise to have a commission to enquire into Sikh grievances; the newspaper photos showed him engaged in the menial task of shoe cleaning as a penance for his unwillingness to die.

States reorganization is best regarded as clearing the ground for national integration. It seems at least likely that refusal to grant political recognition to the cultural areas would have focussed and held all political attention on this one spot. The newly fashioned units, it is true, have a self-conscious coherence and pride, but they are willing, thus equipped, to do business with the centre, to work as parts of a whole that is India. This would not be true of those who support Dravidisthan movements in Madras, but these movements contain other elements: caste feelings and further aspects of the language problem. (But see below.)

The political importance of language was indeed not exhausted by the reorganization of states. In the first place, the new states' governments were bound to advance the local language by every means—including the educational system. The reorganization Act had expected such linguistic patriotism and had provided for two institutional checks. There were to be five Zonal Councils (see also below, pp. 155-6); these advisory bodies under the chairmanship of the Union Home Minister and consisting of Chief Ministers and two other ministers from each state in a zone were to draw neighbouring states together for the settlement of disputes and the organization of joint activities. Most of the councils have achieved little but the Southern Zonal Council has done useful work as a meeting-place for neighbouring governments and, through its committees, of officials. Among the more important subjects handled are irrigation waters, police reserves and linguistic minorities. The last of these was also the subject of a second provision of the Act: the establishment of a Commissioner for Linguistic Minorities. The two measures together have gone some way towards meeting the dangers of unfair treatment of minorities in the new states; in particular, provision has usually been made for appropriate educational facilities. (This is not to say that minority problems have disappeared everywhere: for instance, the mutual distrust of the Assamese and Bengalis in Assam remains and in 1960 reached tragically violent proportions.)

In the second place the new enthusiasm and scope for the dominant regional languages impinged not only on liguistic minorities but also on the position of Hindi as the all-India language. The Constitution had distinguished between 'languages of India' (of which there were fourteen listed) and the 'official language' for all-India governmental purposes. For the latter Hindi was chosen but English was to continue to be used as such until 1965. This outcome of one of the Assembly's most bitter debates was a useful compromise for 1948, but to those concerned fifteen years soon ceased to seem a long time. The Hindi enthusiasts realized that a real change-over from English could be achieved in 1965 only if the process were started without delay. Their opponents saw that the best way to keep off the evil day was to postpone all preparations. With the best wills the problem is extremely difficult. A country can have two or even three official languages, but hardly fourteen. Moreover, the claims of Hindi and English are different: the former is the language of the largest number, though not quite of the majority (42 per cent); the latter is the language of all parts but only of the 'educated classes' (1 per cent). The drawback to Hindi is that it places the non-Hindi areas (and especially South India whose four languages belong to the distinct Dravidian group) at a disadvantage in relation to the rest; yet to select English as official language would be to accept a barrier between government and people inimical to democracy. The opposition to Hindi came robustly from South India, less so from Bengal, only to a limited extent from the educated classes of other parts. With the Report of the Official Language Commission (set up in 1955 in accordance with a constitutional provision), the question came to a head—at the very time when states reorganization was giving certain regional languages ground for pride and joy. The protagonists of the newly powerful regional languages were by no means pro-English but they were sometimes anti-Hindi; certainly the Hindi enthusiasts for their part did not find it easy to look on while all the other languages received encouragement. The Commission undertook a massive examination of the subject and the majority concluded in effect that the Constitution's formula could not be improved. English had all manners of virtue and Hindi might have several shortcomings, but the Union's official language would have to be Hindi. Strong dissent came from two of the twenty members, one Bengali and one from Madras; they expressed alarm and despondency at the damage that would be done to the unity of India, to her educational system and public life, and to the people of the non-Hindi areas who would be placed at a serious disadvantage in all competitive fields. In the south the cry of 'Hindi imperialism' came to be sounded loudly. The balance of forces was delicate: on one hand, the south made up for lack of numbers by impressive ardour and unity on this point; on the other, Hindi enthusiasm had gone so far as to frighten much neutral or uncommitted opinion. When by 1958 the Commission's report was reviewed by a special committee of Parliament (a further procedure imposed by the Constitution), the issue had become one of first political importance. The Committee, while very firmly endorsing the Commission's views, expressed anxiety about a too hurried switch to Hindi. In this situation the Prime Minister gave an effective casting vote on the side of a go-slow policy. In an important statement in 1959 he sought to avert a collision between Hindi and English. He was opposed to any 'imposition' of Hindi on non-Hindi areas and he thought English could remain for an indefinite period as an additional or associate official language. The retreat from a rigid 1965 switch-over was made official in a Presidential Order in 1960, and two years later legislation was promised which would establish this 'associate' status for English for an indefinite period. The Chinese war, and perhaps some Hindi pressure, secured a delay in 1962 but the south was evidently not to be bullied; in 1963 the Official Languages Act was finally passed. However, anti-Hindi jubilation was guardedly muted and Hindi resentment unconcealed; a battle was over but the war would go on.

Thirdly, these questions intimately affect education policy at several points. The medium of instruction at the primary level is everywhere the regional language—which for over a third of the country's children will be Hindi. (There are of course exceptions; fee-paying sons of the well-to-do or very ambitious will be taught in English in the private schools which are appropriately called public in imitation of their UK models.) The interminable haggling among educationists and politicians has focussed on the secondary and higher stages. Formula has clashed with formula and even when one has seemed to gain victory the struggle has merely shifted to differences in the implementation. The government inched its way slowly towards the 'three-language formula', which should have meant that in addition to the regional medium Hindi would be introduced at some secondary stage in the non-Hindi areas and some other Indian language in the Hindi areas; English or some other foreign language would complete the trio at a later grade in secondary schools. At first it was parts of North India who defaulted by choosing Sanskrit rather than, say, Tamil, but when the aggressively anti-Hindi Dravida Munnetra Kazhagam (DMK) came to power in Madras in 1967 Hindi as second language was the first casualty. There is not much doubt that although educational expansion has brought larger numbers of children into some contact with English, general standards in that language have declined; some halting of the process may be expected from the attention being given to the novel techniques for the teaching of English as a foreign language. This affects the problem at college and university levels. Here the pressure, educational as well as political, has been to switch to regional languages; resistance, which is strongest outside the Hindi areas, has been effective mainly in checking unprepared switches and encouraging gradualism. The nation-wide pattern is therefore utterly varied though master's level work is in most places still in English. The problem is that oral instruction in English has in many places broken down and teachers find themselves able to make themselves understood only through the regional language. At the same time the literature to be read by the student is still scarcely available in these languages. Students with capacity for advanced studies are therefore frequently handicapped by incompetence in English. The situation may in time be improved from both ends: translations may increase in volume and improve in quality; greater attention may be paid to the teaching of English at least to those selected for advanced studies. The placing of university education into regional compartments would certainly have great disadvantages even if standards did not fall; the all-India community of scholars would be in danger of disintegration and student migration, already limited, would cease.

These questions of regionalism and language have been so much in the forefront of Indian politics and are so readily related to events in India's recent political history that it is sometimes difficult to realize that they do not constitute the whole of the problem of national integration. Social divisions are as troubling as the territorial. Since an attempt was made in Chapter 2 to give an interpretative presentation of the bearing of social cleavages on political life, only a little more needs to be said here. At what points has India's social heterogeneity, ever active in the body of her politics, made its appearance on the face of events?

Although the divisions of religious community have been less obtrusive since independence than before, they have not been wholly absent. The real mood of the substantial body of Indian Muslims is perhaps one of the mysteries of Indian life. Dazed and subdued by partition and the disappearance of their main leaders, the community seemed to accept as inevitable a loss of political identity. Separate electoral rolls were dropped and the leading political party of the community, the Muslim League, died a natural death except in the south. While no doubt some integration of a political kind has taken place through Congress and other parties, it is far too soon to say that this part of the communal problem is finished. On the contrary, communal violence at the end of the 1960s touched levels never reached in the previous decade, one of the most frightful riots taking place within sight of Gandhi's *ashram* in Ahmedabad during the centenary year of the man who tried to bridge the communal gulf and failed. Riots apart, the agitation in and around Aligarh Muslim University, the Muslim Convention of 1961, the role of the Muslim League in Kerala and reactions to it—all these testify to a situation of continuing communal consciousness in which the Hindus' distrust and discrimination and the Muslims' sullen and despairing isolation feed eagerly upon each other. The Indian Christian community, previously irrelevant in politics, has become prominent in Kerala affairs through its substantial identification with the Kerala Congress. The political aspirations and frustrations of the Sikhs in the Punjab have already been mentioned.

As stressed in Chapter 2, social cleavages within the Hindu community have been of greater political importance than those between the communities. But these have for the most part worked their way into political life through existing institutions, above all through Congress itself. Only a small part of this massive iceberg makes a distinct appearance in political events. A few examples must suffice. In the legislative field, the tussle over the Hindu Code Bill—originally a single comprehensive measure of social reform, subsequently processed piecemeal through years of legislative discussion

—illustrated the stresses within the community when confronted with reform imposed by a secular state. The political position of the scheduled castes or untouchables is that they have mainly exchanged a separate political party (the Scheduled Castes Federation, led by Dr Ambedkar) for a status of legal and constitutional equality and the nominal freedom to compete for political power through any party; if this has been checked and in some areas negated by the hostility of socially powerful castes, it is supported and made substantial in others by their own strength of numbers and growing sense of power. The 'backward classes' (a more loosely defined category far wider than the scheduled castes and including significant *sudra* groups) have been able to secure such privileges as to place some of them in some states in positions of supremacy over the higher castes; A Supreme Court decision in 1962 found that the Mysore government, in reserving 68 per cent of places in certain institutions of higher education for backward classes, had gone so far beyond the fundamental rights provision (which permits special assistance to such classes) as to have perpetrated 'a fraud on the Constitution'. Finally, it can be said that while caste loyalty is almost everywhere present as a factor in political relations, in a state like Madras the rapid rise of the non-Brahmins has not merely dominated the whole shape of Madras politics but has in particular made a significant contribution to the movement for Tamil consciousness expressed by the DMK which for a period in the early 1960s backed separatist demands.

Disintegrative factors and tendencies have thus been at work, often as causes of major events in the nation's recent history. The forces of integration—and this category includes every all-India institution almost by virtue of its mere existence, whether a political party or an administrative organ—tend to work less obtrusively. Their silent ways have been in many eyes their great defect and leaders have searched for means of increasing this force by providing more explicit institutional forms. Most extraordinary was the campaign culminating in the setting up of the National Integration Council in 1961. Although Nehru had almost from the moment of independence regularly and unceasingly inveighed against all kinds of particularisms, it was not until 1958 that the phrase 'national integration' (coupled with 'social cohesion') achieved prominence when it appeared in a Congress Working Committee resolution. It seemed to come to the fore mainly as an expression of concern at the possible consequences of the new linguistic states. But it soon acquired further point. Communal feeling following the violence in 1960 at Jabalpore gave rise to the demand even among Congressmen that communal organizations should be made wholly illegal. Perhaps in an effort to calm and placate Hindu opinion, perhaps in the hope also of reassuring fearful Muslims, an all-India Muslim Convention was called together in Delhi in 1961. Muslim MPs and even former ministers attended and Nehru sent a message. While on the one hand the voice of submerged Muslim protest was clearly heard—the demand for proper recognition of the Urdu language and a cry that Muslim 'life, honour and property' were still unsafe in India—on the other hand communal organization was disavowed and Muslim adherence to 'national integration' emphasized. Only two months later, in August 1961, a States Chief Ministers' Conference on National Integration was held, at which attention was given to communalism and language problems; three firm decisions were made in favour of a common script for all Indian languages, the establishment of new all-India civil services and the prohibition of any secessionist demands (such as the DMK had begun to put forward in Madras—and which were later made unconstitutional by the 16th Amendment). The National Integration Council, set up as a permanent body and composed of Prime Minister, Home Minister, chief ministers, party parliamentary leaders, educationists and others, set to work in 1962 and soon stimulated a campaign at several levels—from the elaboration of a press code and the creation of new all-India civil services to the organization of a National Integration Week and the taking of a national integration pledge by schoolchildren and citizens. Before sceptical minds had much time to cast doubt on the value of some of these measures, the Chinese invasions (October 1962) of the northern frontiers took over from the campaign organizers and achieved, at least for a time, an almost unprecedented integration of the nation.

Economic development

The place of national integration as an issue in political life is both important and clear; that of economic development seems at once much less certain and probably less important. Let it be said quickly that this is not how the matter is normally viewed in India itself. There it is widely believed that simple strong links join economic developments to politics. Each tends to be thought of as an efficient means for the solution of the other's problems. Economic development, if fast enough, will cure political troubles; if too slow it will prove fatal to the present political system. Then again, from the other side, economic development can only be secured by a kind of mass political awakening, a mobilization at least substantially political in character. These views imply a relation between politics and economics which is too simple to be true. They underestimate the autonomy of these two aspects of a society. Rapid economic development may cure some political troubles, leave some untouched and aggravate others. Whether or not a poor rate of economic growth is damaging to the political system will depend on many factors—above all, perhaps, on the extent to which it is accepted as the best possible by those who lead in the formation of opinion. On the other hand, a political awakening of itself may hamper almost as easily as it may help economic development. Equally, its absence, far from being fatal to economic development, might be of little importance or even beneficial. Investigation, not dogmatic assertion, is called for.

In the meantime and in this place it will be enough to indicate a few of the political implications of economic development which became evident during this middle period. They can be grouped under two heads: first, problems of policy and the effect of these on political life; second, problems of organization and administration and their effects on the structure of government.

There is a general impression that economic policy has scarcely been a lively issue in Indian politics, that here is a land where all are 'socialists' now. This is not wholly true but it has some foundation. For one thing, Indian politicians schooled in the nationalist movement were not exactly accustomed to looking for issues in the realm of constructive economic policies. It took a few years for these to take sufficient shape to be grasped; the first general elections which somewhat helped this process came only four and a half years after independence. Moreover, there was indeed little disagreement anywhere in India at least on what the economic problem was: to increase production in order to remove abject poverty. Agreement would even prevail over the spelling out of this prescription to mean attention to investment, industrialization, land reforms and the creation of employment opportunities. More than this, no one could imagine that these tasks would not require in the Indian situation a large increase in governmental initiative and activity. Beyond these two factors of lack of practice in economic policy argument and the existence of much fundamental agreement lay a third factor: Congress's advantage in occupying a large and central position and its skill in exploiting it. But in examining this we shall see that development policy has after all influenced the shape of political alignments.

This third factor became prominent in the period between the first and second general elections (1952–7). By this time public debate on problems of development had begun to get established and some of the latent disagreements on policy were emerging into clearer light. It became apparent that while most people could agree on certain general goals, their policy interpretations could differ: what kind of land reforms, what sort of industrialization (cottage and small-scale or steel mills?) and whose investment (public or private?)? At this period the main policy criticism came from left of Congress. The economic and social conservatives were comparatively quiet by virtue of their location: those outside Congress were in political parties (Hindu Mahasabha, Jan Sangh, Ram Rajya Parishad) whose main platforms are religious and communal and whose economic programmes are imperfectly worked out; the larger number inside Congress worked mainly behind the scenes, urging caution and effecting inaction. Nevertheless, the challenge to Congress was not powerful. The non-communist left (Socialist Party and KMP) emerged sobered from the 1952 elections in which they fared disappointingly; indeed, they quickly effected a merger to create the new PSP (Praja Socialist Party). Nehru's own electoral campaign had also impaired their self-confidence; by directing his main attacks against the rightist groups (and minor ones against the communists) he had seemed to imply that socialists were either insufficiently strong or insufficiently different from Congress to worry about. Moreover, the Congress government had moved in two important directions, each of which was pleasing to different socialist sections. The more modernist-minded were satisfied that the establishment of the Planning Commission and the shape of the first plan meant a decided step towards a planned economy with large-scale industry and a growing public sector. The more Gandhian elements were able to approve the inauguration of the Community Development projects (and related National Extension schemes) as a start to a programme of 'constructive work' on rural reconstruction.

At the same time, Congress had emerged from the elections in pensive mood; it was difficult to be wholly jubilant about the massive majorities of seats when these were so often based on a minority of votes. It seemed to Nehru—then Congress President as well as Prime Minister—that party and government advantage coincided with common sense: since the socialists and Congress were in fundamental agreement on the key matter of economic development, they 'should not fritter away their energies in mutual opposition'. Out of the need of each for allies could be constructed the benefit of a co-operative effort by men of goodwill dedicated to building the nation; only the communists on one side and the communalists on the other would be excluded. On Nehru's initiative, talks with socialist leaders took place in March 1953. Nothing came of these despite the discovery of wide areas of agreement; the socialists brought with them a fourteen-point programme but Nehru felt unable to enter into such a commitment. Both sides' leaders wanted co-operation but found the others' price too high—if not for themselves at least for their followers. But whereas Nehru drew back from any course which would have threatened Congress unity, the socialists found their unity imperilled even though the talks had failed. Some of them, led by Dr Lohia, greeted the failure with relief because it meant that their insistence on the 'equidistance' of socialists from conservatives (Congress) and communists alike could be maintained. Others, represented notably by Asoka Mehta, were not convinced about the theoretical validity of 'equidistance' and were certain that it would doom the party to a long period of practical ineffectiveness just when a great national regeneration was in prospect.

The Mehta view made virtue of necessity. The socialists alone could not create an effective opposition, but then was this what India required? Might not the usual idea of opposition be inappropriate to an underdeveloped economy where what seemed to be both called for and attainable was a united front or coalition in a war against poverty? Mehta certainly argued thus: 'The economic backwardness of India exerts inescapable compulsions on our policies', and this was held to require in particular that socialists search conscientiously for areas of agreement and co-operation with Congress. J. P. Narayan, formerly top socialist leader, meanwhile had concluded not only that oppositionist politics was misplaced but that all conventional politics was inadequate and improper for India; his socialism became Gandhian *sarvodaya* (roughly, social regeneration by voluntary service instead of state action) and his road the one of Bhave's *bhoodan*. It was not surprising that in these circumstances Dr Lohia should find support for resistance against both these counsels of apparent despair; many militant socialists gathered round his banner of ideological purity. For over two years the Praja Socialist Party groaned with internal divisions.

Congress made matters no easier for the socialists by stealing their words for pinning to the Congress banner. Already within a few months of the failure of the PSP–Nehru talks, Congress had put into its 'social and economic programme' some of the left's fourteen points. More important perhaps than general phrases about equitable distribution, socialized economy, welfare state and full employment was the translation of vague 'land reforms' into a mention of 'the fixation of ceilings on land holdings'. None of these developments, however, attracted as much attention as the quickly famous declaration of the Avadi Congress session of January 1955:

'planning should take place with a view to the establishment of a socialistic pattern of society'. This has received almost as much commentary and explanation as a Biblical text and no clear meaning has yet emerged. It made some business circles anxious and it increased the distance between the Mehta and Lohia segments of the PSP; it was swallowed with quiet grace by conservative Congressmen. If subsequent decisions can be regarded as implementing the declaration, it may be safe to say that it has come to entail several policies: the most rapid practicable expansion of the public sector of the economy, not by the reduction of private enterprise but by its exclusion from some of the main sectors of growth; moves towards a more equitable distribution of wealth by such means as appropriate tax policies: general removal of privilege and increasing equality of opportunities for all classes by aid to backward sections, general expansion of education and social services and attacks on some social bases of inequality such as landlordism. These policies found expression in budgets, in the second Plan and in legislation in the late 1950s.

A centre party can hardly avoid conducting a war on two fronts. The Avadi operation was successful in that it seemed to scatter the left and enthuse much of Congress itself without unduly alarming the conservatives inside or beyond the party. But in leading the party towards a 'socialistic' society, Nehru was certainly following his own inclinations and not merely a line of tactics. Those inclinations took him a further step four years later, to a resolution at the Nagpur Congress of 1959: 'The future agrarian pattern should be that of co-operative joint farming in which the land shall be pooled for joint cultivation, the farmers continuing to retain their property rights and getting a share from the common produce in proportion to their land. . . . As a first step . . . service co-operatives should be completed within a period of three years.' This seems to have proved more alarming to more people than the socialistic pattern or even the talk of 'ceilings'. Conservative elements evidently considered that a general aim of socialism could be dealt with more satisfactorily as and when it emerged in specific measures, while the move to impose ceilings on land holdings could be (and indeed has been at least in some measure and in some areas) undermined by quiet pressure at the state legislature level designed to ensure sufficient legal loopholes. But farm co-operatives appeared as a different matter, at once concrete and difficult to circumvent. This may not have been a correct calculation—would the substantial peasants have found it too difficult to capture and 'fix' local co-operatives?—but it contributed to an important political development: the formation later in the same year of the Swatantra Party, the first primarily 'ideological' and policy-based party of the right. While it is thus clear that some events in political life have been closely related to policy questions arising out of economic development, it would be misleading to pretend that this is the whole story. On the contrary, it remains the case that many policy questions have occasioned surprisingly little political debate and that many important decisions in the field of economic policy have been taken on mainly expert advice and with little subsequent political repercussion. This could be said of most of the decisions embodied in the plans. Political party opinion has not found it easy—outside the more sophisticated sections of the PSP and, later, Swatantra—to form on such policy matters. However, this is not to say that economic development has not given politicians much to do. They have been very active on the 'spoils' side. This has entailed at least three directions of energy. First, politicians have worked to secure for their regions (or, less often, for their community groups) the benefits of government enterprises—in terms of employment in a state factory, for instance. Politicians have taken great interest in 'location of industry' problems. Second, they have found themselves useful as intermediaries who may be able to influence the operation of governmental controls (e.g. licences for export–import business) on behalf of 'clients' and 'allies', actual or potential. Third, with the growth of rural development expenditure increasingly in the hands of new elected local bodies, politicians have found much to do in cultivating faction leaders who may be able to offer useful votes in return for suitable pressures applied from above on local officials and petty bureaucrats. When government activity expands, so, in these ways, does the job of the politician. His need and desire to make friends and influence people find new means of expression.

Problems of economic policy in relation to the need for development have affected governmental administration as much as they have influenced political alignments and the activities of politicians. It is by now very well understood that economic development depends on much more than economic factors. It depends on cultural values, on social structure and social forces, and on political climate. (The relations are extraordinarily complex and it is doubtful if their full character has yet been mapped. Those who argue that traditional Hindu values, extremes of social inequality and political frustration are obviously and in every respect obstacles to economic growth in India are by no means having things all their own way.) It depends in some, though perhaps limited, degree on the system of government administation. Since development rests so largely on government initiative, control and even management, the administrative machinery is called to new tasks. Sometimes wholly new organs are required, sometimes existing instruments have to learn new uses. In both cases adjustments of attitudes and acquisitions of skills are at the heart of the matter. Some examination of these changes is given in Chapter 4, where the present governmental administration is described. Here it is necessary only to indicate some of the main events and the general manner in which economic development policies have evoked administrative adjustments.

At the level of the union government, the most important change, the establishment of the Planning Commission in 1950, posed problems of three main kinds for the machinery of government. First, there were problems arising out of the composition of the Commission and its staff, chiefly centring on relations between responsible ministers, civil servants and non-official experts. Second came problems concerning the relations of the Commission to other parts of the central machinery, notably the ministries and in particular the Finance Ministry. Finally, the central planning machinery has had its impact on union–state relations. All three areas of adjustment have been subject to the influence of the National Development Council. Established in 1954, this body, composed of members of the Planning Commission together with chief ministers of the states, has become a significant manifestation of co-operative federalism, an all-India cabinet standing above both union and state governments. To be sure, this is not spelt out in its terms of reference, but its membership along with the indefinite ramifications of planning policy have made it into a key institution of the governmental system.

Another development, mainly out of the central government, has been the setting up of a large number of state enterprises. Here, too, different sets of problems have emerged. One group concerns the form and personnel of these organizations. Should they be run as departmental branches of central ministries (e.g. railways and their locomotive works), or as public corporations (e.g. Air India), or as limited companies in which the government is principal shareholder? Should they be staffed by civil servants expected to turn to these tasks as general administrators or should a special managerial corps be recruited from the world of business? The answers to these questions (discussed further in Chapter 4) were on the whole given unobtrusively and with little public attention. More rousing have been the questions concerning the relation of these bodies to Parliament—the extent to which parliamentary scrutiny of their affairs is desirable and the manner in which it is practicable. Most explosive of all has been the problem of ministerial responsibility for these enterprises; the case of the Life Insurance Corporation (otherwise known as the Mundhra affair), culminating in the resignation of the Finance Minister, ensured for this issue the widest publicity.

Apart from these developments, which were new in kind, the central government has changed much in degree, in the extent of its activities of control, supervision, initiative and sponsorship. These changes have given rise to problems of departmental structure, of personnel qualifications and of bureaucratic morale: suitability and adaptability of organizations, capacity and integrity of people.

Equally clear have been the administrative changes at the opposite end of the line of government, at the local levels. These have come in two main phases. The first consisted in the setting up, at first on a limited and 'pilot'-character scale, of Community Development projects. Experiments in rural development had been undertaken before the war by Gandhians and also by dedicated British officials. Further experiments with American foundations' guidance and support had been initiated in the post-war period and had by 1951 led to fifteen pilot projects. Within a year enthusiasm from the Indian government and the offer of funds from the US government had brought into existence a Community Development (CD) Programme. All aspects of rural life were to be within its province—from agricultural methods and communications to education and the uplift of backward sections. It was to be distinct from other government agencies in its method: the use of government to initiate schemes which would rouse the villagers to new efforts on their own behalf. It had still at the outset a pilot character: fifty-five 'development block' areas were designated in all parts of India. The 'block' idea has justified itself and is now the key unit for development administration. The average population of a block is 60,000–70,000, covering an area of perhaps 150 square miles and comprising about 100 villages. At the centre, a Community Projects Administration was created, independent of any ministry but responsible to a special committee under the Prime Minister and including all members of the Planning Commission. By 1956, when the number of blocks had been increased to 1,200, covering over a quarter of the rural population, the Community Projects Administration gave way to a full-fledged Ministry of Community Development. The network of blocks was extended to most parts by the mid-1960s.

The erection of this new apparatus has entailed the recruitment, training and despatch into rural India of an army of new-style government men—by the end of 1963, about 6,000 Block Development Officers (BDOs) and nearly a hundred times as many Village Level Workers (VLWs). This army is to awaken village India—by

encouragement, by demonstration, by offers of material help to those
who will stir to help themselves. Finding this army, ensuring that it
is properly equipped for its task and giving it continuous direction
in the field is only one of the new political and administrative
problems thrown up by this campaign. The others concern the
relations between this army and other elements already in the field at
district level and below. Three sets of relations have turned out to be
important: those with the ordinary government administration—
district officers in particular; with local political leaders; and with
the various sections and groups in village life.

These last problems have been in some measure transformed by
the second phase of local adjustment to the rural development drive.
When the CD programme was well advanced, its progress was
examined by a special study group under the chairmanship of
Balwantrai Mehta, a leading Congressman. The report (1957) of this
body recommended in effect the integration of the whole CD
structure into a new system of democratic local government.
Substantial powers and resources for development purposes were to
be placed in the hands of popular representatives, chosen by direct
and indirect elections; the new bureaucrats would be their servants.
State legislation to implement these proposals was put into force in
Rajasthan in October 1959, in Andhra soon afterwards and subsequently in most other states. The rule of elected bodies (the terms
democratic decentralization and Panchayati Raj are used indifferently
in India but the latter, more evocative, term is now the commoner)
has changed much; exactly how they have become related to the CD
officials, to the general government administration in the districts, to
the politicians and to the group bases of village politics will require
analysis below.

The impact of the issue of economic development in terms of
administrative events is thus fairly clear at the levels of central and
local government. That much has also happened at the level of state
government and is no doubt true. But the facts are less well known,
less accessible and less susceptible of sure generalization. It seems,
however, that most states have officers (together with committees of
ministers and officials) designated as responsible for the co-ordination of planning and developmental activity. They look upwards to
the Planning Commission in Delhi on the one hand and down towards the local apparatus of development on the other.

Period of challenge

Let us admit it is not easy to settle on the right label for the period
since 1964. Reference was made above to its being a time of 'flux

and uncertainty'; that is true but inadequate to convey its full nature. 'Disintegration', while valid in certain respects, implies a view as to the outcome which is not that taken here and for which there is insufficient evidence. Some have favoured 'transition' which is safe in the sense that all periods can be seen as transitional but which at the same time tends to minimize the very real possibility that many of the key features of this period are here to stay, that India has reached her normality. Challenge can at least be imagined as continuing; it conveys too a sense of excitement which the period certainly contained; above all, it expresses the notion of a testing time, in which a system has to deal with difficulties. In that respect there is more in common between the first and third periods than between either and the second.

As to the dating of the period, here too there can be argument. The earliest date for which a case could be made is 1962, the latest 1967. The effects of the Chinese invasion in the former year were threefold. India came face to face for the first time with external insecurity and was compelled to redistribute its resources sharply in favour of defence needs. Secondly, the events were a profound shock to Nehru himself; perhaps by themselves they were not crippling and ten years earlier he could have taken them; as it was, though he had resilience enough to resume an outward poise he never recovered capacity for sustained initiative. (Two things must be remembered, however: first, we must not exaggerate the forcefulness of Nehru's leadership even before 1962—he was politician enough to like to see how others were feeling before he gave a lead; second, we have to admit that, in the important matter of the 1963 'Kamaraj Plan'—the scheme put forward by the Madras Chief Minister whereby Congress ministers would resign office to take up party organization work—he showed that he was still capable of exploiting skilfully the initiative of others.) Most important of all, the invasion destroyed a hitherto settled assumption at the back of the public mind, an assumption not indeed of governmental infallibility but of a certain impregnability of the rulers. Although the blow was external effects were felt internally; these were strikingly made manifest in the loss by the governing party in the following year of three prestige by-elections. The case for choosing 1967 is even simpler: the general elections of that year witnessed a drastic shrinking of the Congress overall majority in the Lok Sabha from a luxurious 228 to a poor 48, accompanied by the loss of any overall majority in no fewer than eight of the sixteen state assemblies. The arguments against either of these dates is equally clear: 1967 only registered openly a change that had already occurred, while 1962 only initiated a process

which required a little time to mature, a process moreover that could
not be fully released as long as Nehru was physically present. On
balance it does make sense to make 'the end of the Nehru era' come
with the end of Nehru.

This is not to make charisma a sole determinant of political
stability; it is only to say that in a situation that was poised for
change the death of an outstanding leader could supply the push. So
long as Nehru continued to preside, the undercurrents of change were
concealed and disguised which later were exposed. If Lal Bahadur
Shastri had lived to rule for longer than the seventeen months
between May 1964 and January 1966 it is conceivable that the
tremors would have been much subdued and the sense of upheaval
absent. After all, the delicate operation of arranging the succession
had been smoothly managed, there was about Shastri a quiet
maturity and sturdy poise which were displayed over a number of
awkward issues, while his restrained but decisive and successful
leadership during the Indo-Pakistan war of 1965 built him up into
almost heroic proportions quite out of keeping with his appearance
and style. His death at Tashkent without political heir made the
question one of the 'ifs' of history. (There is an appropriateness
about the documents associated with the last days of these Indian
leaders: Gandhi, the blueprint for a social service movement;
Nehru, the aspirations embodied in the 'Democracy and Socialism'
resolution put to the last Congress session he attended; Shastri, the
business-like terms of peace negotiated to end a war.)

What then were the undercurrents of change? The picture is in its
details highly complicated but the key has been mentioned already:
the ending of the myth of the rulers' impregnability. The consequences subdivide along two broad channels: an upward leap in the
level of disenchantment with government and a proliferation and new
intensity in political rivalry and competition.

No visitor to India in the fifties would have got the impression
of contentment. The more articulate sections, engaged as usual in
an enthusiastic love-hate relation with government, were highly
critical and even abusive towards those in power; satisfaction with
affairs might have been more easily found where there was least
basis for it, at the bottom of the social heap. But on the whole even
the cynics were polite, there was little anger in the air and the private
view of many a public critic would be that things were being managed
reasonably well: the five-year plans were getting bigger, rural back-
waters were being stirred by community development, reorganization of the units of the country into linguistic states was being
achieved, the institutions of the political system were in fair working

order and India enjoyed a certain status in the world community. At what points then did disenchantment begin to gnaw into political life? Mention has already been made of the Sino-Indian border war but this was by no means the sole factor.

The generation gap deserves some notice. In any country that undergoes a regime change, as from colonial to independent status, this assumes special significance. By the mid-sixties no one under the age of about 35 could have had any meaningful direct experience of the phenomenon of 'the freedom struggle'. The basing of the legitimacy of rulers on their contribution to that struggle could make lively sense for many of the middle-aged and elderly but for a whole new generation of young people it had at best little and vanishing appeal and at worst was already an irritant. Nehru was the last one from whom an appeal in such terms might have been tolerated—but he used it little anyway. So those in power had to justify their positions in terms of results rather than records.

The past might in that sense be discarded as irrelevant, but in another sense it lived on. Out of the national movement had come high standards of public morality (pp. 59–62) which still persisted not as guides to one's own behaviour so much as criteria for the judging of others'. For some years after independence 'the old guard', never spotless but nevertheless somewhat shaped by these standards, had occupied most of the key positions of power. By the mid-1960s their places were largely taken by men who had made their political careers in the post-Gandhian period. They had come to power the hard way, up the tricky, greasy ladders of 'machine' or 'boss' politics; the self-restraint of the aristocrat was not for them and they threw their newly acquired weight around with some satisfaction. Such curbs on personal greed as they would understand would be those imposed by the obligations to reward friends and provide for relatives. Although they were in this respect more earthily Indian than their predecessors, their Indian public judged them harshly and when in doubt regularly assumed the worst. To meet this consequence of the widening recruitment area for the political élite would have required more than a weary Nehru could achieve. There had been popularly exciting corruption scandals in the fifties but as the Nehru era drew to a close the issue became politically significant: Home Minister Nanda put himself at the head of an organized crusade dramatically pledged to root out corruption within two years and a full-scale investigation (by the Santhanam Commission) of corrupt practices was launched, while at the same time angry campaigns were mounted against some hitherto powerful state chief ministers. (Shastri did much to restore the standing of government by securing the speedy resignations of two such men, Kairon of Punjab and Mitra of Orissa, following independent enquiries.)

It has been insisted above that there is no simple and automatic relationship between economic failure and political crisis. If there had not been other factors making for disenchantment with government the economic difficulties of the mid-sixties might not have translated so readily into grievances and discontent. It was India's bad fortune that at a time when her planned development was already running into difficulties and when she was being forced to divert more resources towards defence, she should be afflicted by a couple of monstrously inadequate monsoons which resulted in poor harvests, food shortages, famine in certain areas, a set-back to industrial growth and steep price rises throughout the system. Nor were the political effects of these disasters confined to the traditionally articulate sections of urban areas. Community development programmes did not effect the production increases that were hoped for but they did bring about a heightened political awareness in rural areas. This awareness mainly focussed on local situations and expressed itself in caste or factional rivalries but it attached itself to the political process which came to be filled with the uneasy jealousies and discontents of a variety of different sections of rural society.

Citizens disenchanted with a government no longer seen as impregnable—this then is one mark of the third period. It is important to note that it reflects the expanding political universe, the arrival of new actors: the younger generation, the regional bosses, the rural faction leaders. It is also important to recognize that in some aspects it has introduced changes which probably have come to stay. Agitational protests of great intensity which have featured fairly prominently in various parts of the country need not increase in importance or even remain at the levels of recent times. But an awakening citizenry confronting times of change and challenges to adjust constitutes a somewhat volcanic political soil and from that there appears little prospect of retreat. The task of governing the country has become one of increasing difficulty. Protest agitation on some issue in some area is therefore likely to be a normal feature difficult to avoid in a country of subcontinental size. But the size and the consequent variations of social patterns from area to area make it probable that the eruptions will be sporadic and unco-ordinated, that what puts Punjab into turmoil today causes no echo in Bengal and that tomorrow's storm in Madras leaves Bihar unaffected. Herein lies some hope that the political system can absorb the shocks and continue its work of combining adjustments with containment.

The other clear aspect of the period of challenge is the enhanced rivalry and competitiveness of the political forces. This will be discussed further in Chapter 5 but certain general points may be briefly made here. An initial point is that in indicating competitiveness as a distinguishing characteristic of the third phase of post-independence development one is drawing attention not to something completely new but to a change in degree. Independent India has never been a one-party unitary state, it has been in some measure federal and in some measure multi-party. What is here suggested is that a consistent trend in Indian politics over its first quarter-century is a movement from a system in which the competitive or 'market' element was rather limited to one in which it has become predominant and decisive—the emergence of a 'market polity'. By this is meant a system in which decisions are highly multiple and widely dispersed, arrived at by a process of bargaining in which partnership and terms of trade change continuously. It is an untidy system and such coherence as it possesses derives from the fact that the gains are distributed and calculations of profit dictate to the separate interested parties that they should stay in rather than get out. There are some rules of market behaviour and although groups of political traders are constantly tempted by prospects of quick advantage to evade or bend these there is some consensus or general perception that they have to be retained if the process is to continue. Some operators, for instance those on the extreme left, do indeed withdraw but there are many who are only too happy to gain admission.

The extension of the scope of market politics can be seen if we consider the relatively specific operation of choosing a prime minister over the three separate occasions of 1964, 1966 and 1967. On the death of Nehru the competitive element was small. By several moves Nehru had pointed to Shastri and although there was an attempted challenge from Morarji Desai the consensus against him was established without great difficulty. Moreover, the whole operation was firmly controlled by Congress President Kamaraj and the participants in the decision-making process were limited in number to the party's working committee and to an inner group of its members in particular. On Shastri's death, a larger element of competition was manifest, no doubt because the suddenness of the event had prevented careful preparation of consensus and the choice did not at first point very clearly to any one person. The conflict was resolved not by consensus but by vote in the parliamentary party. Kamaraj's management of the affair was again evident but the number of participants was expanded by virtue both of the importance achieved by 'the Chief Ministers' Club' and of the fact that the final choice lay with the parliamentary party. However, since the MPs were substantially marshalled in contingents by states, there was not in fact quite the decentralisation of influence that appeared on the surface. The third succession struggle was occasioned not by the death of a leader but by wounds inflicted on the leadership as a whole in the elections. While the setting was thus different, the problem for the party was similar and it is instructive to see how it was handled. The conflict narrowed down, as on the previous occasion, to one between Indira Gandhi and Morarji Desai; but the conflict was resolved, not as in 1966 by voting, but by consensus as in 1964. Nevertheless there were important ways in which the 1967 succession differed from both its predecessors, ways which seem best summed up in terms of an increasingly market situation. In the first place there was no single manager of the operation; Kamaraj was again a key figure but mainly as mediator. In that capacity he may indeed have been able to recover for himself and his office some of the ground lost by his electoral disaster in Madras. But he was not in a position to control and impose a solution; if he came out of the affair rather well, it was because he understood the changed situation and adjusted accordingly to a reduced role. It was not only Kamaraj who was diminished; other key figures—Atulya Ghosh and S. K. Patil certainly, Sanjiva Reddy and Nanda in some measure—were less powerful, and some, like C. B. Gupta, who might have expected to come into prominence, were checked. In the absence of directing giants, all the actors in the drama had to feel their way towards their proper parts; there was introduced all the tentativeness of a market situation. More than that, there was scope for some players to move into stronger positions and also for some fresh entrants to come into the game. Thus, the Chief Ministers of those states where Congress had survived the storm were well placed; Mishra of Madhya Pradesh and Nijalingappa of Mysore were in no way cut down, while B. Reddy of Andhra, Sadiq of Kashmir and Naik of Maharashtra (somewhat concealed behind Chavan) come into the game rather from outside. The group of younger MPs who formed around Dinesh Singh and Asoka Mehta as a pressure group for Mrs Gandhi was a further novel feature indicating considerable dispersal of influence. Above all, however, the enhanced market quality of the third succession was revealed in the intense and unprecedented degree to which it was bargaining that dominated the proceedings, through 'an extraordinarily free and open inter-personal network'.

That illustration apart, the spread of market competition can be best observed in two of the main areas of Indian politics: centre–state relations and the party system.

As already indicated in Chapter 1, the form of political structure handed over at independence was, for a country of India's size and diversity, remarkably centre-directed. To those who had watched the shift from decentralization in 1909 to devolution in 1919 and incipient federalism in 1935, the centre no doubt seemed less impressive than before. It still possessed great formal and informal power even though its erstwhile monopoly had come to an end. When the Constituent Assembly deliberated on the future, there were a few voices which argued in effect that the clock be put back and unitary government restored. But they belonged to a tiny minority; the larger part envisaged a continuation of shared power between the Union and its component units. Shared power, however, did not mean competitive relations. First, it was anticipated that centre and states would have their separate and distinct arenas, the concurrent powers being a residual category. Each would get on with its own job. Second, certain reserve powers retained by the centre permitted even the sharing to be rescinded if need be, for certain periods and areas. Above all, the facts of the informal power structure, Congress dominance in all parts of the country, and the concentration of its top leaders at the centre, weighted real relations heavily on the side of New Delhi. India called itself not a federation but a union and observers felt the need to term it a quasi-federation.

Almost from the start these expectations went somewhat wrong. The neat distribution of powers was upset by the realities of social and economic policies whose ramifications refused to observe the constitutional boundaries. The Planning Commission and Community Development Administration are only two principal examples of central inititatives that powerfully shaped state government activity. But the connections thus established were not one-sided; initiatives were one thing, implementation another, and in that respect the dependence was that of the centre on the states. The terms of a market relationship came dimly into view. Within, and sometimes beyond, the limits of federalism as constitutional, financial and administrative structure, there emerged federalism as political bargaining. The former might be so centrally biased as to be labelled quasi-federalism, but it remained to be seen where political strength lay.

The reorganisation of several states along linguistic lines in 1956 is reckoned by many to be the critical juncture from which flowed irresistible centrifugal tendencies. Some of the monolingual units (e.g. Maharashtra, Madras) certainly developed a greater cohesion (in others sub-state regional differences remained or were even accentuated, as in Andhra and Gujarat) and this might have served to improve their bargaining strength. Quite apart from this consideration, however, politics at the state level attracted the substantial talents and energies of a fresh layer of home-made political leaders. Delhi's vote was often, not always, decisive in settling who should get in as chief minister, but once in the saddle it was not Delhi but his own management of the local situation which determined his term of power. Some state leaders—B. C. Roy, Kamaraj, Kairon— achieved almost impregnable positions. Of course, Nehru was happy to have such men in convincing control of their parts of the country and it is a mistake to imagine that the centre could consistently prefer weak state governments. Nevertheless such men would come to the central conference tables very conscious both of their value to Delhi and of the degree of their independence of Delhi's support. Even with Nehru at the helm these were encounters of negotiation and compromise, not of orders to agents.

Under Shastri the market style of centre-state relations became more obvious. The terms of political trade may not have changed as much as many observers imagined; the central team were still the seniors of the party with a great deal of knowledge and indirect influence in state politics. However, it did mean something that the headmaster, complete with special personal status and ready temper, had given way to the negotiator. Not even the Pakistan war could obscure the settled fact of bargaining federalism. Indira Gandhi's coming to power made less difference than had been expected, thus demonstrating that the new style had been institutionalised to a degree that made individuals, even at the top, of less moment. Her various teams of ministers and planners went about their business of handling the states according to the rules of the traditions which had been growing steadily over the previous decade: initiatives have to be sold and implementation has to be bought.

Mention may be made of three awkward policy issues which confronted the central government in relation to the states in this period. In each case a resolution of the problem came with painful slowness, the outcome of a patient inching towards the settlement which seemed least unacceptable to the parties concerned. Tara Singh's reluctance to die a martyr's death in the cause of Punjabi Suba (p. 100) damaged his political career but did not remove the item from the agenda of the central government. The Sikh community set about finding a leader made of sterner stuff and by early 1965 Sant Fateh Singh had emerged as their man. All did not go smoothly: after a little preliminary skirmishing the Sant proclaimed that he would undertake a fifteen-day fast and if he was still alive and if the demand for a separate state had not been conceded he would burn himself; but even he found a reason—the government's setting up of a Cabinet committee to look into the matter—for calling it off, and was promptly expelled from his party. In the following year when Mrs Gandhi had taken over from Shastri, the Congress Working Committee, without waiting for another martyrdom campaign to start and presumably satisfied that Congress could never keep Sikh support unless it gave in, suddenly announced that a new state of Punjab with Punjabi as its language would be formed, with the Hindi-speaking areas called Haryana becoming the second state. There was still the difficult problem of the Le Corbusier capital, Chandigarh, which did not belong unambiguously to either new state. An enquiry commission's recommendation that it belong to Haryana was turned down by government which took the middle course of making it a union territory. Although the two states came into existence on that basis in November 1966, Fateh Singh in the following month began another fast to burning death. Mrs Gandhi refused to concede any demands under such threats. At the last moment as the pyre was being prepared the Sant was persuaded to break the fast on the PM's agreeing to arbitrate. Not until 1970, by which time Fateh Singh had begun another fast and the government was presumably convinced after two elections and several changes of state government that the issue was not going to die away, was the decision finally taken to give Chandigarh to Punjab and various compensations to Haryana.

The second instance provided less drama but was equally drawn out. For many years the hill tribes of Assam, very distinct from the plains peoples, had expressed their grievance that the Assam government failed to understand them and at once neglected and dominated them. Already in Nehru's time they had come to formulate a demand for a separate hill state. Nehru evidently had some sympathy with them but having just conceded Nagaland in the North-East was reluctant to fragment further and therefore suggested some imitation of the Scottish model of devolution. Even this was anathema to the Assam government while it looked insufficient to the All-Parties Hill Leaders' Conference (APHLC). For three years commissions and committees sat and there were lengthy negotiations with the Assam government and the APHLC. At the end of 1966 a cabinet committee moved towards the idea of a solution going beyond the Scottish and other variants of mainly administrative devolution but still short of a separate state: the idea of a sub-state within Assam. It took a further two years to work out the details and sell them to both parties, but by 1969 the constitution amendment was passed and in 1970 the novelty of Meghalaya, a state within a state, became reality. The device is ingenious—the area has its own assembly and ministers and responsibility for most of the subjects dealt with by states, but Assam still retains law and order and police functions and the Governor, High Court and public service commission are common. With regional restiveness evident in some other states—Saurashtra in Gujarat, Telengana in Andhra—it may be a model whose imitation, while further complicating governmental processes, will ease certain troublesome tensions.

The Punjab and Assam problems are similar in that they concerned the identity of particular units. A more general problem which raised questions of national integration and centre-state relations is that of the official language, to which reference has already been made (pp. 101–3). Here too the centre found itself caught between rival pressures from the Hindi states of North India on the one hand and Tamil Madras on the other and at the same time obliged to determine an all-India policy on the language to be used in nationwide official communications. Some may have expected that the Official Languages Act of 1963 would solve the problem. But the language issue is unlike the problems of Punjab and Assam: in the latter cases a more or less permanent solution can be envisaged and may indeed have been found; in the former it is necessary to think merely in terms of moving tentatively and perhaps over a long time through a number of different staging points each of which can supply no more than temporary accommodation. For the positions of the two sides can change: when the South—especially its students, potential competitors for civil service jobs—gets gripped by a fear of being penalized by Hindi-speakers, it resists furiously, but given time and adequate guarantees it may well be more accommodating and quietly resume as an insurance policy the study of Hindi. The government statement in December 1964, called for in view of the approach of the constitutionally appointed day for the introduction of Hindi, had seemed reasonable and reassuring: central circulars and documents would issue in Hindi and English, the Hindi states' correspondence with each other and with the centre would be in Hindi, but that of the non-Hindi states would remain in English as long as they wished. But there was no trust and Madras for some days went mad. Not until the government gave assurances about 'equitable shares in the services' and followed this up by agreeing that civil service examinations could be taken in all regional languages was some calm restored. These terms were by the end of 1967 embodied in a further act of Parliament. The DMK in power in Madras (now called Tamilnad) still takes the view that the only satisfactory measure would be a constitutional amendment to remove the Hindi sword that hangs above their heads, but the possession of secure power in the state government makes them and their public less nervous and fearful than before.

Mention of the DMK takes us over at once to the other zone of increased competition, that of the party system. Indeed it is impossible to consider centre-state relations and the whole position of 'national integration' in the post-1967 period without reference to the changed party situation. But this at once takes us into the heart of Chapter 5, while other more administrative aspects of centre-state relations are discussed in Chapter 4.

4

GOVERNANCE

The first three chapters have been aimed in different ways at preparing the ground for a more analytical account of the political system of modern India. That system is to be presented as a dialogue between two inherited traditions, 'governance' and 'movement', a dialogue taking place within a 'mediating framework' of parliamentary and judicial processes which can properly be regarded as a third tradition.

The traditions have all undergone great changes. 'Governance' has changed least—partly because administrative processes are substantially dictated by factors which change slowly—whereas, 'movement' has, in appearance at least, been transformed from a coherent single national front into a variegated pattern of political forces. The framework continuously influences the conversing elements; they, by participating in the regulated conversation, make their own contribution towards moulding the framework.

All three elements are of course 'ideal' and separated only for exposition. The patterns of behaviour and the processes to which they refer are in practice mixed; one institution therefore partakes of more than one element. The chapter headings have a tidiness which must be denied to the contents of the chapters. 'Cabinet' must thus appear in all three places, 'party' certainly in 'framework' as well as in 'political forces'. This is only to say that the whole is a system, an affair of permeating interactions.

We begin at the beginning, with 'governance'. While some parts of this complex—notably the cabinet—are at the same time constituents of the 'framework' and even reflections of 'forces', other parts are more isolated. Within the field of governance in India, it will be best to start with those latter parts, the relatively still centre of administrative life. It is a relatively still centre in two senses: it does not undergo the kaleidoscopic changes of party politics; further, it is less open to outside gaze and less disturbed by public intrusion. But the emphasis is heavily on the words 'relatively' and 'centre'. For one thing the area of administrative activity has been expanding continuously and quite fast; this poses problems for the administation itself as well as for its place in the political system. Moreover, in periods of political fluidity 'vacuum' areas develop in decision-making and into these the administrative organs tend inescapably to be drawn. Politics and administration, never easily separable, are in fresh ways closely interwoven in the new states where the development of politics is so largely the politics of development. Administration is no piece of 'mere' machinery suitably handed over to the technicians to explore and explain; it is a key growing point in the political process.

The civil servants

As already explained in Chapter 1, it was neither possible nor necessary for India (nor indeed even for Pakistan) to start from nothing in making a system of administration. The task was at once easier and more difficult, one of discriminating adaptation. This has been done piecemeal and minimally, not by comprehensive review and radical reform. This is itself a remarkable fact. Among politicians at all levels and of all parties there has been almost continuously a great deal of talk about the need for a completely new kind of administration to meet the fresh needs of a planning and welfare state. But Indian administration seems resistant to change, while non-administrators are not easily able to produce practicable proposals for reform. (The conservative character of even the upper levels of the Indian bureacracy may be in contrast with what is found in some other developing nations. Their British predecessors, of course, were hardly innovators.) Certainly at the constitution-making time there was, despite the evident concern of some politicians, no sufficient opportunity for major overhaul of the civil services. The Constitution in its 'Part XIV: Services under the Union and the States' is content to state the outlines of the *status quo*. Union and state legislation is to lay down regulations for recruitment and conditions of service for union and state services respectively. Civil servants hold office during the pleasure of the President (or, in the case of state services, Governors)—a provision whose effect is to give security of tenure, especially when read along with other articles prohibiting arbitrary dismissal. Independent Public Service Commissions (for the Union and for each state) are established with members (half of whom must be civil servants of ten years' service) appointed for six years by the President (or Governors). The Commissions are responsible for conducting the examinations for admission to the services and have to be consulted on disciplinary matters and all questions relating to recruitment, promotion, transfers and demotion.

Reference has already been made to the fact that India has not a single civil service but instead three sets of services: those of the states, those of the Union or Centre and those known as all-India services. The Constitution recognized the IAS (Indian Administrative Service) and IPS (Indian Police Service) as the only two all-India services common to Union and states (and regulated by Parliament), but it provided that others could be established by Parliament if so resolved by a two-thirds majority of the Council of States. This reference to the upper house of Parliament signified acknowledgement of the states' interest in this matter. And here came 'politics' at once into purest administration: State governments have been determined in their opposition to the creation of new all-India services. When, between 1920 and independence, certain areas of administration were transferred to the provincial governments, several all-India services were disbanded and replaced by provincial services; government medical and forestry officers for instance were switched into state services from their previous all-India cadres. Today's states are reluctant to see this process reversed. They do not wish to share control with the centre over their bureaucrats; they want to avoid high salary scales (and perhaps the difficulties of dealing with prestigious civil servants) which tended to go with all-India services; they may also prefer to restrict intake to their own people. At the same time, the case for more all-India services has become gradually stronger and more evident: only thus can minimum standards be secured everywhere, all talent well used regardless of area and origin and local political pressures minimized. Above all, the all-India services have come increasingly to be seen as a great force for national integration, in many respects more reliable for this purpose than all-India political parties. When the States Reorganization Commission bowed in 1956 before the demand for linguistic states, it sought to counter any tendency therein towards disintegration by recommending new all-India services. The campaign developed strongly behind the scenes and won a victory when advantage was taken of the 'national integration' movement to force a concession out of the states: their chief ministers, at a special 'integration' conference in August 1961, agreed to the creation of three new all-India services—engineering, forestry and health and medical—while resisting the proposal for a fourth, for education. In the wake of the 1965 war with Pakistan, the states surprisingly agreed to all-India services for education and agriculture. The crisis over, they soon changed their minds and these two proposals were dropped. However, the Indian Forest Service and the Indian Medical and Health Service have been constituted and the Indian Service of Engineers is on its way.

If almost any account of civil servants in India begins with the IAS it is because this service has inherited much of the prestige of its predecessor, the ICS. In mere number it is insignificant: the total authorized strength in 1969 was about 3,000 (already increased from only 800 in 1948) and its actual strength about 2,600. Many of these have been recruited by special procedures called for by the fairly sudden disappearance of the ICS (already by 1949 the British members numbered only 22; by 1953 Indian and British numbers together were down to 373, by 1958 to only 146) and the growth of government responsibilities, and the shortage is still marked. The normal recruitment has been less than 100 persons a year, about 25 per cent by promotion from other services and the balance by competitive examination. The direct intake rose fairly steadily from 33 in 1947 to 73 in 1959 but the Krishnamachari Report (1962) made it clear that the annual figure needs to be near 100. The competitors are graduates of twenty-one to twenty-four years (by typical concession, twenty-nine for scheduled castes) and the test is frankly academic with no preference for particular subjects except that Essay and Language (still English) papers and General Knowledge are compulsory. Enthusiasts for Hindi would have liked to see English displaced as the medium of examination; when this proved totally unacceptable to the south, Congress and the then (in 1967) government were forced into accepting that any of the regional languages could be used. An implementation delay followed; not surprisingly, for the prospect of regional examiners for regional candidates went some way to making an all-India merit scale impossible. A start was made in 1970 in that the option was offered to candidates. Interestingly, few chose anything but English. Even more significant, the Union Public Service Commission made it clear that it would not depart from a single examining board; the multi-lingual danger was at least held off for a while by the use of translators. For a period it was the rule that a candidate could be failed on personality test alone, but the interview mark is now simply added to those of the eight papers. The rush at this entrance to the élite corps is considerable: there are still over 5,000 hopeful men each year—this is a decline of some 1,500 compared with 1959—competing for the 250-

E

odd places available for the superior services (comprising the IAS, IPS and a few others). It is often said, especially by older civil servants, that the quality of the service is going down on account of the relative lowering of the prestige and attractiveness of the career. It is a fact that while the numbers of first-class graduates nearly doubled between 1959 and 1967 from 6,434 to over 11,000, those of them seeking this career decreased from 818 to 604 and among those successful the percentage of 'firsts' went down from 52 to 36. Of course, the class of degree may not be the most important criterion of relevant qualities and the entrants do not seem to be lacking in talent. Whether government attracts too much or too little of the best people is a matter of unending argument. What is clear is that a growing proportion of able students are drawn to technological work (the new institutes of technology have attained a high level in a short time), but while this may withdraw them from entry into the IAS it by no means takes them from government service. As the range of government activity and enterprise expands, the need for highly qualified specialists also increases. The problem then becomes less one of a tussle between public service and other employment, more one of the relative qualities and status of specialists and generalists within government service.

Social factors reinforce the select character of the IAS. Of 350 appointees over a few years, 200 were sons of government officials and a further 100 were from professional families. Nearly 100 had a 'public school' education in India or abroad. Only 15 per cent came from rural areas. The predominance of certain universities—and, even more, of certain old-established colleges—is quite marked. The regional distribution, too, is uneven: between one-quarter and one-half of the successful candidates regularly come from Madras; UP with Delhi accounts for a similar proportion; some states provide no more than one or two.

The chosen few are made further aware of their position by the remarkable training period. Each batch of successful candidates, the 'probationers', spend nearly a year at the National Academy of Administration at Mussoorie (from 1971, at Delhi). Originally the IAS had their own training school; at the Academy, exclusiveness is modified by the presence of cadets from a few other superior services who join them for a common 'foundation' section of the course; but the IAS is still the core. The course seeks to avoid a too strongly vocational emphasis but has to reckon with the wide field of degree subjects previously studied. The examination at the end of their training year consists of two parts: Qualifying Tests in a regional language, in Hindi (but those who take it as their regional language are not required to take any other language—a nice illustration of Hindi's favoured position) and in Riding (a quaint survival, even though there certainly are some rural areas where jeeps cannot go); written papers in General Administrative Knowledge (including social and political history of India, elements of economics and public administration), Indian Criminal Law (with a view to the magistrate functions of district officers) and the Constitution and the Five Year Plans. The last item is the most obvious concession to the new world. The politicians, often still haunted by fear of civil servants out of sympathy with national aspirations, have further ensured that the young men receive lectures in Gandhian Philosophy. During the course they may spend as much as three months on visits and short periods of attachment to various governmental institutions— community development training centres, magistrates' courts, a river-valley project, a steel plant, and so on—all over India. Their placing in the final examination, taken together with their performance in the competitive entrance examination and their course record, determines their seniority within their 'batch'. (It may here be mentioned that some other services—railways, postal, etc.—have their own training establishments, as do certain states, where immediate post-entry training is given. There is little or no institutional training for 'executive' and 'clerical' civil servants).

No one who has met a class of probationers can fail to be impressed by their keenness and awareness. The valuable part of the ICS 'ethos' has been astonishingly preserved. Their job is honest administration without fear or favour; to be part of an élite corps is to be given a heavy responsibility; they are 'guardians' of the highest purposes and protectors of the meanest person; India cannot do without their devoted contribution of intelligence and energy. At the same time, they know that the facts of political life are new. Their predecessors were themselves the government; the IAS are servants. Their masters are politician-ministers, often innocent of administration and its requirements, responsible to an elected assembly and sensitive to all kinds of pressures. They know that even as district officers they will now be confronted by new classes of local politicians not without power. The young IAS seems to accept the challenge: they see their role as still crucial but to be played in a new style; they go from the Academy willing to learn that style.

Adjustment of style comes more easily and gracefully at the start of a career than at mid-way; the deeper forms of cynicism tend to prevail among a few of the more senior officers who have found the new style too repugnant. Whether the new entrants have less

sense of dedication to their 'calling' than their predecessors is difficult
to assess, for here we are in a world of 'golden ages' where fact
and fantasy are closely interwoven. In so far as a sense of a calling
is a function of status and the status of top bureaucracy while still
high is lower than before, it is likely that today's cadets enter the
service in a cooler frame of mind, appraising this career among others
as very good but not out of this world, not a lone pinnacle above the
clouds. Meanwhile, the status of the all-India civil servants is still
too high for the liking of some politicians: the move in 1970—
unsuccessful in the event—to abolish the constitutionally guaranteed
service rights only had the disappearing ICS as its target and in any
case was simply part of a radical wave against survivors of the
ancien régime such as the princes, but it nevertheless illustrated the
hostility that can still be excited by rhetoric about the bureaucracy
as a towering bastion of privilege and reaction.

Although the IAS and IPS are all-India services, they consist of
state cadres. Each entrant into the service is allocated to a particular
state cadre and in that cadre he stays for his career. The initial
allocation is influenced by the officers' own wishes, the top probationers having more choice than others. But these wishes may not be
decisive, for they may not fit in with the states' needs. Moreover, it is
deliberate policy—for the purposes of furthering integration (even
before that word became a slogan) and securing impartiality and
greater freedom from local influences—to ensure that at least half of
each state's cadre shall come from outside the state. The result is that
the entrant from, say, Orissa or Assam stands a good chance of
being allotted to his home state if he so wishes (quite a number of the
men are happy to have a career away from their own home state);
his fellows from Madras are so much more numerous that many of
them will be allotted elsewhere.

To become a member of, say, the West Bengal cadre is, however,
not necessarily to spend one's whole service in that area. In the
absence of any central cadre of these all-India services, the Union
government relies for the staffing of most of its senior posts on a
system of deputation from the state cadres. It calls upon the states to
supply men on deputation. The states draw up panels of names from
which the Centre has to choose. The young entrant will normally
begin in district administration within the state to which he has
been allotted. For the first eighteen months (there have been wide
variations of period in different states, but this is both an average
and a recommended period) he is regarded as still continuing
training and indeed his period of probation extends for one year
beyond his passing out of the Academy. (From 1971 it is planned to

reorganize the training into a sandwich pattern: four months Academy, one year in a district and six months back at the Academy with an examination at the end. This scheme further underlines the training character of the district year. It should also enliven and make more meaningful the latter Academy stage.) This on-the-job training involves the performance of some duties as well as attachment to more senior officers; apart from quite a short period at the State Secretariat, the work will normally be in all the parts of district administration—collector's office, treasury, land settlement and survey, police, magistrates' courts, sub-divisional offices and, increasingly important, all branches of development work. Variety of experience continues to be the keynote even after this eighteen months; by the time he is ready for a senior post (e.g. as district collector) after six of seven years' service, he will have had perhaps two years in charge of a sub-division and two as Under-Secretary in the State Secretariat.

During these early years of a man's career, his progress is in some measure watched by the appropriate personnel division of the central Home Ministry, but the postings will have been the concern of the state government. (For the all-India services the division of powers between centre and state is that the former has the last word in the service matters of discipline, dismissals and promotion, the latter controls postings within the state.) Thenceforward, his career movements are more variable. Although central secretariat posts are not reserved for the IAS (they were for the ICS), the central ministries expect to be able to rely on filling a substantial number of key posts from IAS. In 1961, 404 out of 1,419 senior IAS posts were centre posts filled by deputation from state cadres of the IAS. The factors which determine the career movement of an IAS man between centre and state are several, and evidence regarding their relative strength is not easy to assemble. Some force attaches to the old notions of mobility, still guarded by the services division of the Home Ministry: spells at the centre should be followed by a return to the state to whose cadre he belongs, the rounded officer of an all-India service being one who carries with him always the viewpoint of district and state as well as of New Delhi. But sometimes it seems that the establishment chiefs can only preside over a real tug-of-war between central government departments and state governments, each wanting the best men. It is alleged that movement is frustrated in that many who go to the centre stay there while others remain always within their states. Personal and quasi-political factors are also believed to play an important part. State ministers are said to develop favourites among the senior civil servants; there is a suggestion that weaker ministers prefer local men or men of their own community or political viewpoint, while stronger ministers like to have men from outside the state as impartial top administrators. The wishes of powerful state premiers carry some weight even against central ministries and service opinion. This is true even when one party is involved; when, as in 1967, Congress was displaced by others several senior officials were rapidly shifted by incoming ministers who identified them with the previous government or for other reasons wanted their own men.

Outside the IAS and IPS, complexity reigns in the central as well as the state civil services. It was not helpful of Nehru to hurl the epithet 'jungle' in the direction of the administration while showing little interest in its reform, but the description as applied to services structure was not inappropriate. The central services alone number more than twenty, of which the Foreign Service, Audit and Account, Customs, Income Tax and the Central Secretariat Service are the main non-technical ones; the technical services include Geological, Archaeological and Zoological. The establishment of separate services, each with its own pay scales, conditions and rules is usually justified in terms of the distinctive requirements of each of these groups of functions: they can lay down their own recruitment standards and procedures and offer satisfactory career ladders to their members. The plea is sometimes made for a rationalized integration into one single civil service of all the 'fragmented' central services—or even of the all-India services too; or, failing that, at least the bringing together of all the technical services into one Scientific Civil Service. To this the reply is given that if this was to be more than a very superficial tidiness it would necessarily entail the loss of these advantages of specialism. The present complex structure no doubt shows the marks of *ad hoc* response to emerging needs, but its 'fragmentation' is inherent in the variety of tasks to be performed. If it tends to produce petty inter-service jealousies these are mostly harmless and may even have their useful aspect in service pride and loyalty. Just how far this reply is adequate is difficult for an outsider to judge, but three comments may be offered. First, the fragmentation of the technical services is more easily defended than that of the non-technical ones. Second, the case for some all-India services, belonging exclusively neither to central nor to state and distinct from the central and state services, is on general political grounds very strong. Third, the pride and loyalty of members with regard to their own service has not only an administrative usefulness, it serves also an important political purpose by supplying a stiffening and independence of spirit to a bureaucracy which in the Indian situation might have swung too violently and too far from its original position of domination to one of subservience.

If various civil services remain unintegrated, then it has to be recognized that new administrative needs will from time to time suggest either the creation of new services or some breaking down of barriers between established services. This question has arisen on a few occasions in recent years. Already in 1938 a breach in traditional service structure had been made with the creation of the Finance–Commerce Pool. The introduction of provincial autonomy with the Act of 1935 had substantially separated central and provincial subjects and this, together with the increasing complexity of financial and trade problems to be tackled by the centre, had suggested the need for change. The old idea of the generalist top administrator of the ICS with district experience having a tour of duty at the central secretariat seemed not quite to respond to the call for expertise now being heard from certain central ministries. About sixty key posts were incorporated in the new cadre which was to be filled by officers with appropriate qualifications not only from the ICS but also from such central services as Customs, Audit and Income Tax. By 1950 this Pool had become depleted, yet the need was even greater. After much deliberation within the top administration, eventually at the end of 1957 a Central Administrative Pool was established into which the Finance–Commerce Pool was merged. At an initial strength of 120 these posts were to be filled by men selected (by a committee of senior secretaries) from the IAS, the central services and the top class of state services on the basis of their capacity and experience in 'economic administration'. In addition, a small number of men with economics qualifications were to be directly recruited from business or academic life. A third example of the 'pool' device is the Industrial Management Pool also formed in 1957. This too was a response to a call for expertise. A number of state enterprises had come into existence and new ones were appearing each year. In view of the seeming difficulty of finding (for what were in many cases industries new to India) suitable persons from the field of private enterprise, government had naturally entrusted this important sphere of activity to its valued and experienced generalist administrators of the ICS/IAS. But running a steel mill was conceded to be a novel line of activity for a civil servant and the need for more deliberate provision for such management posts was acknowledged. The problem was considered for several years. Parliamentary and other voices called for a new Industrial Management Service and after much hesitation a decision in favour of such a new *service* was in fact announced in 1956; within a year it had been altered to the 'pool' idea. The pool was a compromise between a full new service to staff management posts throughout the public sector and separate staffs to be recruited independently on its own lines (though perhaps subject to certain general governmental rules) by each enterprise. The abandonment of the idea of a special service was the result of pressure from the enterprises desiring no restriction on the field of their recruitment; it was perhaps also the result of pressure from existing services, especially IAS, who saw an area of valuable employment being taken too firmly away from them. In the event the compromise got the worst of both worlds. The enterprises, not bound to take their staffs from the Pool, often went their own way and had to be bullied. The recruitment into the Pool was sluggish (there were great delays in the working of the scheme, which did not help), both from the other services as well as from the private sphere, and in fact out of a total of 212 men eventually (1959) selected (for an initial establishment of 200) by the Special Recruitment Board, only 131 actually got as far as accepting definite offers of pool posts. By 1963 the size of the Pool was diminished; the scheme, though far from worthless, had made several enemies; another reappraisal began. The pool compromise has persisted—and even spread, as in the Scientists and Technologists Pool—but it lacks enthusiastic support. The creation of quite new services is still found to be a more congenial device despite its tendency to introduce fresh boundary lines; the Indian Economics Service and the Indian Statistical Service, both central services, have come into existence and in 1968 had strengths of over five hundred and three hundred respectively.

Just as the idea of a 'pool' is designed to overcome rigidities as between parallel services, so of course promotion arrangements are the main device for countering 'horizontal' cleavages of grades and classes. Almost as much is heard of the sinfulness of Indian administration on this score as on that of the vertical inter-service divisions. It is, however, debatable whether the degree of mobility is out of keeping with the country's social ideas. (There is evidence from other places that if a bureaucracy becomes a leading avenue for social mobility in a country with an otherwise rigid social structure, there is some tendency for the bureaucrats to develop independent political ambitions.) It is true that these ideas are changing but it is a mistake to exaggerate the distance so far covered. As already noted, even the élitist IAS is drawn to the extent of 25 per cent from other services by promotion and there is pressure from the state services to increase this to 33 per cent or even 50 per cent. The proportion of posts filled by promotion in the other services is even higher. In the states' civil services the position on paper is that in some states and for some grades the promotion proportion is 70 per cent—while in practice it has been 100 per cent since the examinations for direct entry have simply not been held.

It is true that promotion is not everything, that much depends on the gaps between grades or classes in terms of pay, conditions and status. It is further true that these gaps have been considerable in India—in part a legacy from the days when the top administration was British—both between some services (significantly termed 'superior') and others and between classes within services, such as the central secretariat service. India is a country in which most men speak enthusiastically of equality but, in spite and because of this, cultivate distinctions with loving care—and nowhere more as-siduously than inside the civil services. It we add to this the difficulty of man-to-man imaginative sympathy in India—to say nothing of superior–inferior relationships—we can see a situation readily damaging to good morale. That all is far from well in this connection was shown by the threatened strike of certain central government employees in 1957, called off only by the setting up of the Second (Das) Pay Commission. (The first Pay Commission of 1947 had recommended a reasonable closing, from both ends, of the gap between the highest and lowest salaries.) The Das Commission report, a 700-page result of careful delving, turned up much informa-tion about the facts of material life inside the bureaucracy. The number of central government employees was 1,770,000 (since then risen to about two million), an increase of 23 per cent over nine years. (Since the great bulk of these are employees of railways, posts and telegraphs and ordnance factories, it is not surprising that the workshop and manual element is two-thirds of the total.) The 1947 Commission had recommended 156 pay scales but the 1957 Commis-sion found 517 different scales still flourishing and proposed a simplification down to 140. It resisted the demands of the unions for a substantial rise in the basic minimum, rejecting the 'model employer' notion: while the government should not betray the principles it preaches to private employers, it would impose unfair burdens on the taxpayers if it acted as pace-setter in wages. The need-based minimum was worked out at Rs. 80/- per month (as against the Rs. 125/- demanded), an increase of Rs. 5/- only. They also proposed that the maxima required no reduction; only forty-seven men were getting over Rs. 3,000/- per month and the disparity between bottom and top starting salaries had already been reduced from 1:43 in 1939 to 1:7 in 1948 to 1:5 in 1957. The five-day strike of the employees in July 1960 was the outcome partly of disappoint-ment with these proposals, partly of annoyance at the slowness of the government in implementing even the increases of which it had declared its acceptance. Most important perhaps was the Commission's firm exposure of the unsatisfactory nature of the Staff Councils as machinery for consultation and negotiation (their powers being limited to advising the ministers) and strong recommendation that government should go ahead with genuine Whitley Council arrangements (as indeed already suggested in 1947) together with compulsory arbitration.

Payment which is regarded as fair, conditions of work felt to be reasonable and a machinery through which grievances can be met—these are basic to good bureaucratic morale. But there are other factors. One of these is the pattern and style of working dictated mainly by the structures and procedures. Paul Appleby's controversial survey, *Public Administration in India*, at least did well to press the analysis of administration faults beyond the too-sweeping popular complaints. It will indeed not do to say simply that the bureaucracy is too large (when in fact there are at some of the higher levels too few for the increased work to be done), that it is inefficient and corrupt (when these terms are too vague to be helpful in indicating what is needed for improvement) or that there is 'red tape' (when some of what is covered by this phrase is an essential part of the business of running a responsible public service). Nor is it much more than a starting point to record the impression of impregnable indifference and massive sloth which assails a visitor to the clerical levels of government offices. It seems agreed, however, that the well-ordered bureaucracy left by the British has not yet been replaced by an equally well-ordered one more fitted to the needs of the new planning and welfare state. One trouble seems to be the curiously elongated shape acquired by most hierarchies in Indian secretariats—tending to further the purposeless passing of paper. The original fairly simple pattern has been stretched and this seems to have afforded increased scope for weaknesses perhaps present in pre-independence administration: distrust of the man below, excessive zeal for collecting even faintly relevant opinions before reaching decisions and a preference for co-ordinating and advising the actions of others rather than undertaking direct execution. The usual levels nowadays are: Secretary, Additional Secretary, Joint Secretary, Deputy Secretary, Under-Secretary, Section Officer (Class I and II), Assistants-Clerks (Division I and II); efforts at streamlining by eliminating Additional and Joint Secretaries and Assistants have been allegedly defeated less by work requirements than by status needs. On the other hand, Organization and Methods units have been steadily at work for a decade and conduct a continuous battle against duplication and delay. (The O and M Directorate was placed, after a tussle between Finance and Home, in the Cabinet Secretariat, with units in each ministry. There is within Finance a Special Reorganization Unit also concerned with economy and efficiency but concentrating on work study; it too has trained officers from other ministries for this purpose.) They are up against strong enemies—old habits of more leisurely days, the tendency for status-consciousness to kill team-working and the dilution of quality (perhaps particularly at the 'executive' level) consequent upon massive expansion of numbers, little direct recruitment and over-rapid promotion at certain middle levels. No one doubts that there is a substantial number of most able and dedicated top administrators, nor that the young entrants into the superior services are of as high a quality. But although it is tempting to say that the pity is that their efforts are spoilt by the time-wasting ways of those below them, yet they themselves cannot escape blame for this position. A high administrator cannot be in a full sense good at his own job if he is failing in the leadership role which is an essential part of that job. It is unfortunately only a few of these able men who have the ability to inspire and guide their staffs as a team.

The spirit and temper of a bureaucracy is also influenced greatly by its general standing in the eyes of society; a people gets the bureaucrats it imagines. The civil servant of independent India is regarded generally as less powerful, less impartial and less honest than his predecessor. Whether there was real ground for such opinion is difficult to say, but such opinion tends to make itself valid; former civil servant A. D. Gorwala, in his *Report on Public Administration*, pointed out that 'the psychological atmosphere produced by this persistent and unfavourable comment is itself the cause of further deterioration, for people will begin to adapt their methods, even for securing a legitimate right, to what they believe to be the tendency of men in power and office'. Gorwala's concern—manifested in his making the chapter on 'Integrity' the longest in the Report—has been widely shared. Several explanations of increased corruption have been offered: the wartime decline of standards in the area of war contracts; the increased scope for corruption which comes from growing regulatory activity by government; certain new forms of political pressure—and several variants of the kind of analysis offered in Chapter 2. Explanations as to why stories of corruption are bound to be exaggerated can also be offered. Measurement of the facts of corruption, however, proves as elusive as ever; even a steadily rising graph of successful prosecutions might only reflect greater vigour and skill in detection. Such counter-corruption measures have in fact been taken in the civil services. Between 1956 and 1964 over 80,000 complaints were registered with the Administrative Vigilance Division in the Home Ministry acting as clearing-house and headquarters for 490 units located in departments and other government offices. 63,000 of these were found worth investigation and as a result of cases taken up, major penalties were imposed on 6,449 government servants including 178 gazetted officers and minor penalties on 61,639 officials including 1,661 of gazetted status. These figures unfortunately do not speak for themselves. Perhaps they tell us no more than that counter-corruption absorbs considerable energy. In 1964 the vigilance organization was altered following the Santhanam anti-corruption committee report of that year: the new Central Vigilance Commission enjoys some measure of independence of government and some probing power—though both are less than recommended—and works with the Central Bureau of Investigation. In recent years there has been a decline in the numbers of cases whether sent to court or reported for departmental disciplinary action, but it is uncertain how far this reflects a real improvement. Detection and punishment apart, it is, of course, possible to devise procedures which tend to the prevention of corruption by making it difficult. Unfortunately, much skill is necessary if what is thus gained on the swings of corruption is not lost on the roundabouts of further delays.

Many civil servants would say that it is a pity there is no vigilance division to spot corruption among their political masters. The demand has indeed been voiced frequently—and notably by a former Finance Minister—for the establishment of a standing inquiry tribunal charged with the investigation of accusations of corrupt or improper conduct brought against ministers. The suggestion has not found favour with the government, who fear that such an institution would be exploited for base personal and political motives, resulting in the throwing of mud in public in the hope that some of it would stick. Instead they regard as adequate on the one hand official machinery for setting up tribunals for specific investigations, and on the other the Congress Party's own machinery for handling allegations against members of the party in office. However, following the publication of the Santhanam report (and the removal of Nehru's over-protective hand), a further drive began and even Chief Ministers were not spared. Santhanam in fact recommended a regular procedure: any allegation of corruption brought against a minister by not less than ten members of the legislature should be automatically referred to an independent investigating committee of three persons including one judge. The government declined to accept this.

Instead, two announcements were made: the Congress Parliamentary Board approved a scheme whereby charges against a central minister would be investigated by the PM, those against a state minister by the chief minister of the state, those against a chief minister by PM and Home Minister; hardly more reassuring was a government statement introducing a code of conduct according to which ministers on assuming office and annually while in office will disclose to the PM their own (and their families') assets, liabilities and business interests. It has not been easy to detect the operation of either procedure.

This raises at once the question, so important for bureaucratic morale and the inner harmony of government, of the relations in general between politicians and civil servants. Nowhere easy, these relations in India have been subjected to peculiar extra strains. The transformation of politician from seditionist to responsible minister and of official from ruler to servant did not have to take place in a moment; experience of co-operation, in 1937–9 and again in 1946–7, had been brief but valuable. Nevertheless the gulf in ways of thought and behaviour between the new ministers and their senior officials was considerable, and relations were not eased by the frequent public declarations made by some politicians expressing hostility and distrust towards the bureaucrats and a determination to clip their wings. Several forms of distortion from a fruitful relation can be distinguished. One form is that where the politician abdicates his task out of weakness and becomes a creature of powerful officials. This is not spoken about as common in India; the officials are not thus aggressive, and most ministers, centre and state, have been either strong enough or, if weak, sufficiently 'covered' by colleagues. (Even the influential and independent-minded staff of the Planning Commission makes no exception: they have been able to over-power individual Commission members and ministers but only by putting themselves behind the Prime Minister.) In the recent years of governmental instability in several states, ministerial tenure has of course been so brief and insecure that officials must have found themselves playing bigger roles than previously in the making of policy decisions. Three other forms are at least much talked about and must be present in significant measure. First, there is the aggressive politician who approaches his officials in posture of war and destroys any partnership quality in their relation. Such aggression may be ideologically motivated: the official is supposedly reactionary and needs to be bullied into executing the policy. Or the politician may be moved by a determination not to allow officials to stand between him and the exploitation of even the details of administration for political-cum-personal ends—benefits and concession for 'clients' of one kind or another. Second (and this form, like the third, may come as responses to the first or may be independently inspired), there is the official who distrusts the politician and fears the damage he can do to the administration. He feels himself to be the guardian of the machine, and in order to shield it becomes emphatically professional, secretive and uncommunicative. Moreover, the attempt to separate policy and administration which is then entailed can lead to sabotage of the one for the sake of protecting the other. Thirdly, the official may over-adjust himself to the new regime—to the extent of being willing to do and say all that will please and nothing that will displease his political master. This abdication of role from the official's side may produce immediate harmony but only at serious cost in terms of the quality of government. The 'courtier' official ends by not even serving his master well, for he deprives him of independent advice; at worst their properly distinct roles get blurred and each may abet the other's corruption.

   In this realm it is not easy to proceed further than impressions and each observer has his own to offer. The chief one to be put forward here is that, while no doubt over the several hundred minister–official relations in states and centre governments things have gone seriously wrong at times, the worst in terms of hostility and distrust is past and a remarkable improvement has taken place in the last few years. If true this would not be wholly surprising. The old days are by now old enough; for most of the direct entry members of the IAS, the struggle between government and movement is a tale told by the elders; the preoccupations of the present close the political gap for all except those with little but long memories. The cultural gulf between official and politician has also narrowed; both the Westernized and the home-spun are less insistently so now than formerly. Many of the IAS have learnt brilliantly the new art of understanding and then handling the politician, and they combine this with a zeal for development work which rivals that of the most ardent political leaders. The differences remaining between them are not much more than those required for the maintenance of distinct roles and a desirable modicum of tension. The remaining anxiety is indeed that harmony may not always be of the right kind—that the official, disheartened by lack of appreciation from ministers for outspoken, independent advice, has very often turned courtier. The disowning of a senior civil servant by the Minister of Finance in the Life Insurance Corporation case (the Mundhra affair) was particularly depressing in its effects on officialdom's morale; the minister's resignation was accepted with obvious reluctance and within a few years he was back in the cabinet, while the civil servant's career was brought to an end. But harmony for good reasons is also happening —in which politician and administrator come to respect each other's distinct contribution to a partnership of government. It is reasonable to hope that the new generation of officials will be able to arrive at this position more easily than their predecessors.

The machinery of government: at Delhi

We have taken some views of the administration from within. We now need to move towards a larger picture in which the administration is seen in its relation to the rest of the political system. This is a picture in three main parts: the organization of the government of India; the nature of centre-state relations; the emerging character of India's new local government.

The government of India began to have departments in 1763: it started off with two, frankly designated Public and Secret. Such simplicity did not last long; the increase in departments was steady up to and even including the Second World War. In 1946, when Congress and Muslim League were at last brought together to form the last government of undivided India, there were eighteen departments, each with a secretary as permanent official head. The politicians who took office as members of the Viceroy's Executive Council were fourteen in number, as dictated by the painfully negotiated ratio of the elements of the coalition, 6:5:3. The grouping of some departments to form a member's portfolio was not new but the political compulsion on the size and composition of the 'ministerial' group was; both features continue into the post-1947 executive.

During 1947–50, under the constitution of the suitably amended Act of 1935, the place of the Executive Council was taken by a Council of Ministers and it is this designation which has continued under the new Constitution from 1950. The Council (or 'Ministry'), in fact, never meets; the cabinet was almost from the start a smaller body, and apart from cabinet ministers there are 'ministers of cabinet rank' though not in the cabinet, ministers of state and deputy ministers. The last category is unambiguously junior and assistant, but ministers of state (often confusingly described as of 'cabinet rank') have been variously used—to hold separate but lesser portfolios, to be responsible for a department within a ministry and even to have duties not easily distinguishable from a deputy minister. In 1949 Gopalaswami Ayyangar, a member of the cabinet, was charged with the job of being a one-man commission to report on the organization of the central government. He was content to let alone the minister of state ambiguity but advised a clear training role for the deputy ministers not unlike that of the British Parliamentary Secretary. In practice both categories have continued to be very mixed, considerations of status, convenience and influence combining to put tidiness out of reach. (That matters less than the use of elderly loyalists to fill deputy ministers' posts. And that in turn matters less than that of the few young deputy ministers fewer still have made the grade upwards.)

The Ayyangar Report contained an interesting 'Basic Plan of Reorganization'. On the basis that a minister's job is different from that of a permanent secretary it was proposed that although most ministries should consist of one department (a secretary's charge) only, four should be multi-department. Thus an increased number (twenty-eight) of departments would be consistent with no great change in the number (twenty) of ministries. In order to facilitate inter-departmental co-ordination, each multi-department ministry was to be given a central administrative office for 'functions of a common house-keeping nature'. Moreover, thirteen other ministries were to be grouped in four bureaux, each with a similar central office: Natural Resources and Agriculture; Industry and Commerce; Transport and Communications; Labour and Social Services. This was seen to have the additional advantage that the cabinet could be small—one representative of each bureau might suffice. It was also proposed that co-ordination should be furthered by a rather formal establishment of four standing committees of the cabinet (Defence, Economic, Administrative Organization, Parliamentary and Legal) which should have their own secretariat organizations and 'authority to give binding decisions on most of the matters entrusted to them'. Ayyangar attached special importance to the Economic Committee, furnishing it with support from cabinet sub-committees, a 'Council of Economic Administration' (consisting of secretaries of ministries concerned) and an Economic Wing of the Cabinet Secretariat—all for the tasks of economic intelligence and integration.

This last proposal was partly implemented but partly overtaken by the creation of the Planning Commission. The other ideas were mainly set aside. Certain cabinet committees have proved to be more permanent and powerful than others but the advantages of flexibility and the influence of personalities have precluded uniformity. The 'Basic Plan' itself has not been followed and the subsequent two decades have witnessed frequent changes in the structure of departments and ministries. The fluctuating fate in particular of portfolios such as Industry, Commerce, Works, Production and Supply has been the consequence of trying in various ways to accommodate new areas of governmental activity; the need to secure harmony of personalities and political balance has of course also been evident. While indignant pleas for 'logic' and 'reason' are a little naïve, it does seem as if some of the shifts betrayed indecision or insufficient attention. In 1970 the cabinet numbered 16, there were 4 ministers of cabinet rank, 16 ministers of state and 16 deputy ministers. The number of parliamentary secretaries has been steadily declining and it appears that the position is on the way out.

A continuous problem of any government is the unity of its parts. Stature of leadership must count for much in this and, clearly, having the same leader for eighteen years induced a tendency for unity to be shaped in terms of personal control. Nehru's relations with his cabinet, however, were seldom those of a commander equidistant from a number of inferiors equal among themselves. For when Nehru was strongest there were other strong men like Patel capable of forming subsidiary centres of power, and by the time the great names had vanished Nehru himself (especially after the punch from China) was less able to have his magic way. This is to say that tussles between ministers have never been absent and their resolution has seldom been a matter of simple dictate from the top. This is particularly true of the post-Nehru period. Shastri's cabinet worked as a team of near-equals out of whom a consensus had patiently to be constructed. But Shastri's stature was growing fast towards the end of his brief tenure as PM, suggesting what became clearer later—the fact that Nehru had passed on some of his personal magic to the office itself. Indira Gandhi was less than dominant when she came to the political throne in 1966—a situation reflected in the revival then, after a lapse of sixteen years, of the office of Deputy Prime Minister which had to be given to her rival Morarji Desai— and although she largely escaped blame for the shock to Congress fortunes at the 1967 elections her position remained difficult. Indeed, it worsened in 1969 as those tensions developed which brought about by the end of that year the split in the party. For although the strain was mainly visible as between PM and stalwarts located in the party organization, it naturally cut into cabinet coherence, eventually culminating in the dismissal of Desai as Finance Minister (he then resigned his place as Deputy PM) and thus accelerating the split. But the point to note is that it was throughout quite evident that the office of PM carried with it outstanding power: it was to protect that legacy that Indira Gandhi struck out against threats to confine her; it was the reality of the legacy which helped her to survive the confrontation; it was the office of PM that emerged undiminished, perhaps even enhanced, by the battles.

Cabinet committees and informal ministerial groups naturally play an important part in the task of maintaining coherence and co-ordination in the ministry. Of the former there will normally be about 10 or 12 at any time, some like foreign affairs and defence corresponding to ministries, others like appointments and parliamentary affairs cutting across; all may vary in importance according to personalities and occasions. The reign of flexibility here is illustrated by the domination exercised for a considerable period by the emergency committee of six set up in 1962. Informal groups of ministers can also prove important: neither Nehru nor his daughter is an exception to the rule that a PM makes some ministers more equal than others when it comes to friendly consultations, and when the Congress storm developed in the post-1967 years many were the references to Mrs Gandhi's 'kitchen' cabinet. In the internal politics of the cabinet, certain ministerial positions, notably Finance and Home, tend to have special influence, almost (but not entirely —there have been exceptions) regardless of personality. Apart from the intrinsic importance of the portfolios, their holders would usually be tall men in party terms and also well placed in relation to committees and informal groupings. The Home Ministry is a peculiarly important power point since it has general responsibility for the administrative services and for internal security, the latter entailing especially vital roles in relations with the states; an impressive succession of Home Ministers including Patel, Pant, Shastri and Chavan have known how to appreciate the situation.

On the official side co-ordination is sought by a variety of instruments. There are a number of committees of secretaries only in part parallel to those of the cabinet. From its position of responsibility for the management of cabinet business, the Cabinet Secretariat headed by a very senior civil servant is well placed to patrol areas of overlap and impending conflict. It has under its wing the Central Statistical Organization which has co-ordinating functions as well as an advisory role and its own allotted tasks. The Cabinet Secretariat also contained until 1964 an Organization and Methods Division but this was then incorporated in a Department of Administrative Reforms with wider responsibilities which was set up in the Home Ministry. But if the influence of the Cabinet Secretariat has declined it is probably for a different reason: the Prime Minister's Secretariat has acquired special influence. This particular centrally placed office was set up at independence but under Nehru assumed no great prominence. Its later rise tends to be associated with Mrs Gandhi's premiership but in fact it was already under Shastri that it began to emerge as important. It can be suggested that while Nehru needed no such special instrument to express and convey his authority, his successors have found it useful. Its role appears quite significant in the more manœuvring politics—within the central government and between centre and states—which have characterized recent years. The existence of this little group of officials in the personal service of the PM also bears on another aspect of co-ordination. It is worth remembering that in spite of the rapid expansion of New Delhi and of the administration, the two top circles, of civil servants and of ministers, still form intimate groups. On the whole the social life of the capital has tended to consolidate each rather than bring them close to each other. But the PM's Secretariat are among the bridge-builders.

The central government comprises ministries, departments within them and a host of subsidiary offices and bureaux and all this is set out in any organization manual. But on any realistic view this is not the whole story. In accordance with Industrial Policy Resolutions in 1948 and 1956 the government has set about creating a large public sector of industry. There are now no fewer than some 75 state enterprises or public sector undertakings. These are various both in their area of operation and in their form of organization— but whereas the former matter has been widely debated on the basis of Industrial Policy Resolutions indicating the boundaries of public and private sectors, the latter has had little public discussion and government policy has received no clear expression. Broadly, it can be said that a few industrial undertakings of a kind associated closely with a particular central department have been simply made additional departmental responsibilities; the locomotive and coach factories under Railways are the main example. The bulk of industrial enterprises are managed through private limited companies in which the government is chief owner; these include Hindustan Aircraft Ltd, Sindri Fertilizers and Chemicals Ltd, Hindustan Steel Ltd, Hindustan Machine Tools Ltd. The third form is the public corporation, which has been used for air transport, life insurance, river valley development projects and industrial finance and credit. The company form has been defended as convenient for the inclusion of foreign capital and management but it seems likely that its chief attraction was its supposed greater flexibility and independence. Against this it has been attacked, notably in the mid-fifties by the Auditor-General, as a 'fraud on the Constitution and on the Companies Act', preventing adequate parliamentary control over public money. The question of parliamentary control raises several issues, but here it may be remarked that ministerial control is not precluded by the company form; it is only forced to operate in unobtrusive and informal manner. This is in any case one of the valid criticisms offered to ministerial relations with the public corporations. The Life Insurance Corporation case illustrated how ill-defined can be the scope of ministerial influence and how casual its character. Fuller public reporting and more explicit (but not necessarily increased) ministerial directives seem to be the chief needs whether with the corporations or companies.

The impact of the Planning Commission (PC) on the constellation of ministries and departments has undoubtedly been an important and controversial matter. Any examination of it should begin with acknowledgement that the problem of integrating a planning machinery into an established administration and accommodating it within an open democratic political system is one that has nowhere yet been satisfactorily solved—least of all in Britain. Of the two extreme accounts of what happened in India, one insisted that the PC had acquired such power as to make nonsense of ministerial responsibility, the ordinary machinery of government and even the democratic Constitution. The other view presented the PC as a helpless victim of frustrating resistance from the established administration and of distorting pressures from politicians, the adviser no one listened to. Since 1966, however, the argument has been killed by events. There is still a PC, but it is no longer what it was in Nehru's reign. It is with that, however, we should start.

When a PC was first spoken of, in 1946, it was envisaged as a small, independent, non-political, advisory body of full-time members. Under Nehru the advisory role remained at least in form; the PC's scope of work was wide—not merely the formulation of the plans to ensure an effective utilization of resources, but also the statement of priorities, stages and allocations, the detection of barriers to development and the appraisal of implementation—but all this was in principle by way of recommendation to the Cabinet. However, the composition of the PC clearly moulds its relations with the Cabinet. As at first set up, it had five full-time members who were not ministers, but even then the Prime Minister was its chairman. In the course of a few years a strong ministerial element was introduced, and from 1956 the five full-time non-ministerial members were 'balanced' by the PM plus three ministers (Finance, Planning and—inexplicably except on personal grounds—Defence), together with the influential statistician–ideologue, Professor Mahalanobis, confidant of the PM. This pattern survived Krishna Menon's departure in 1962. In mid-1963 the PC consisted of Nehru as chairman,

Nanda (Minister of Planning) as deputy chairman, two other ministers in Desai (Finance) and T. T. Krishnamachari (Economic and Defence Co-ordination, from 1962), Professor Mahalanobis and five full-time members. Of the last, two had political careers, Sriman Narayan notably as Congress Secretary, T. N. Singh as MP and Public Accounts Committee chairman, while three—Trivedi, Thacker and Tarlok Singh—had mainly official careers, Tarlok Singh as a senior member of the PC staff. The task of balancing rested, up to his retirement in 1960, on the diplomatic skill of the deputy chairman, V. T. Krishnamachari, and neither he nor anyone else in possession of information has so far revealed evidence that would enable judgement to be passed on the nature of the balance.

It is clear, however, that in the making of central planning policy four parties had substantial place: (a) the expert staff of the PC; (b) the full-time members of the PC; (c) the ministerial group on the PC; (d) the Cabinet and its Economic Committee. The obvious and important point is that these four were intimately linked, so that hard divisions between PC and Cabinet were rendered unlikely: (c) was contained in (d), (b) and (c) were members of the same body, while (a) and (b) had close affinity. (Members of the PC attended meetings of the Cabinet and its committees when PC papers were under discussion.) Moreover, there were certain key official links: the Cabinet Secretary was PC Secretary; the Secretary of the PC's Committee on Plan Projects (which sets up efficiency investigation teams) was Director of O. & M. in the Cabinet Secretariat as well as Joint Secretary in the Ministry of Finance; the Economic Adviser to the PC held the same position in the Ministry of Finance. Experience here seemed to confirm the rule that such multiple and overlapping divisions reduce the chances of grave friction and deadlock. (There were also interesting and probably useful disagreements within these groups—for instance between 'generalist' and 'technocrat' elements on the PC staff itself.) Overall views in mainly physical terms were formulated by the PC staff; overall views in terms of resources and finance were presented by Finance and the Economic Committee. At all except perhaps the earliest phases of planning, representational pressures could be exerted by individual ministries (Agriculture, Commerce, etc.) through the Cabinet, its committees and the PC itself. Furthermore, since planning is a continuous activity there was permanent contact between ministries on the one hand and the subject 'divisions' of the PC; each PC member had a grouped portfolio and each division a 'chief', and thus irrigation for instance engaged the attention of the minister and his staff in conjunction with the appropriate PC member, division chief and staff. The outcome was not uniform; in practice so much depends on the strength of personality and argument behind the pressures and on the direction of the 'casting votes' of the key figures—deputy chairman, Minister of Finance and Prime Minister. For this reason it was easy for opposite tales to contain truth—that of the PC pushed by a powerful minister out of its rational course and that of the minister whose voice is not heard in the high-pitched hum of the planning machine.

That paragraph has been put in the past tense. Whether that indicates excessive caution is difficult to say. As already stated, the PC continues to exist but some would say that it is withering away, along with real planning itself. This is probably too extreme a view; as to its lately reduced status and influence there can be no doubt. This has been the result of at least three factors. First, the PC was one of Nehru's favourite children; as such it grew to rely on his protection and it also created envious enemies. While there were a few political leaders opposed to vigorous planning as such, there were many more—in ministries, in state governments—who resented the directive power of the technocratic economists who through Mahalanobis had the ear of the PM. When the shielding and encouraging hand was removed, they were poised to cut the PC to size. Second, the country's poor harvests and economic setbacks in 1966 caused disruption and virtual suspension of the regular planning process; in the prevalence of *ad hoc* emergency measures the PC was vulnerably placed. Finally, the move away from a clearly dominant-party leadership over the whole country exposed the difficulties of planning without a solid political consensus. The steps that were actually taken are described below (pp. 160–1.)

Bargaining federalism

The role of the PC has been controversial in relation also to centre-state relations. Here again contrary stories were told, presenting the PC as victim of federalism, or as its killer. What is clear is that the formulation and implementation of the plans has become one of the major areas of centre-state relations in practice. On this, as on the wider political relations between state leaders and those of the centre, the Constitution is naturally almost silent. In this sense the Constitution may be said to have been by-passed, but in this sense every constitution is by-passed. This does not make it unimportant, indeed it still carries much of the political traffic. The unitary emphasis built into the federal Constitution has already been mentioned (in Chapter 3). The impact on this of the planning process is by no means simple.

A fast-growing and by now very substantial part of state budgets is geared to the plans. The planning initiative comes from the centre but the state governments are the main instruments through which development is pushed. (The large public undertakings are of course owned by the centre.) Everyone wants to see development, but there can be differences of interest and opinion as to the type and location of development and as to the manner of its financing. State governments will each attempt to maximize benefits and minimize costs. Each will stress its own needs and, even more, its potential for development, while hingeing this firmly on to central aid. The PC and the centre generally will be endeavouring to induce development by offering assistance. In doing so they encounter two major problems. First, there is a choice to be made between maximizing immediate returns on investment and securing development which is geographically and socially 'balanced'. Second, assistance must be given in such a way as to stimulate rather than discourage the fullest mobilization of resources on the part of the states. On both issues interests are engaged which find several points at which to press on the planning process.

The interchange between centre and states in this process is as continuous as between PC and ministries, and the running assessment of the current plan is meshed in with the formulation of the next. The interchange is at both official and political levels. The former has tended to manifest an unbalance in favour of the centre—partly because the PC has no equivalent at state level. State planning boards in some cases exist but they are usually no more than committees of department officials. The main links tend to be specialized along subject lines, a centre transport working-group, for instance, being associated with transport working-groups in the states. Centre-state tussles can thus be overlaid by sector rivalries, and the more technocratic the officials the more important this can be. Much will depend, too, on the degreee of attachment of the state officials to their own state as against all-India sentiments. (This may in turn depend greatly on their relations with state ministers.) The official who identifies himself mainly with the state he serves will less readily team up with his corresponding centre colleagues. Very important in the Nehru period as co-ordinators and checks on such divisions—and also as agents of central influence—were the PC's Programme Advisers, each in close touch with a group of states.

The political level is no less complex. Each state minister will of course have official dealings with the appropriate minister at the centre and some will be more effective than others in pressing their claims. But in most states the Chief Minister is the key figure in relations with the centre. His officials and ministers will be to and fro to Delhi often enough but their difficulties and unfinished business of importance will be gathered up in the chief minister's file for discussion with the capital. While much of the discussion will be individual and informal, the National Development Council is a regular meeting place for states and centre. Its sessions are only for two days and about twice a year (this alone rules out 'super-cabinet' as a label for the NDC), and no doubt the real pressing of claims is done outside. Moreover, NDC meetings are clearly great occasions for the PM to preach the centre's view of general policy. Nevertheless, they also serve the states; here one Chief Minister can follow another in hammering home their common needs and difficulties. Neither centre nor states can impose decisions on the other. Nor must it be forgotten that these men were until 1967 (with minor exceptions such as that caused by the Communist government in Kerala, 1957–60) members of the same party, many of the Chief Ministers meeting the PM and other central ministers as members of the Congress Working Committee and other party bodies. Another strand in the politics of planning in a federal state is the role of MPs. They are associated with the planning process not merely by the fact that the plans are submitted to Parliament for debate and final approval but more significantly by committee consultations. For the third plan, at least, a large all-party committee held a series of meetings even before the preparation of the draft outline, while five more specialised committees later examined particular aspects of the outline. It is probably true that sectional representations are more prominent than regional ones in these discussions (the opposite might be true of the more rundimentary MLA committees in states) but state blocs of MPs can have some influence.

The upshot as regards plan formulation seems to be a convincing form of co-operative federalism—so long as we understand that phrase to include hard competitive bargaining. This is indeed the character of Indian federalism throughout. Whereas the emphasis in the Constitution is on demarcation, that of practical relations is on co-operative bargaining. One illustration may be given from procedures on legislation. The Constitution prescribes that bills passed by state legislatures may on submission to the Governor be refused assent or returned for reconsideration or reserved for the consideration of the President, and further that bills dealing with public acquisition of property must be so reserved. By convention, however, states send such bills to the centre for examination and comment in advance, so that the reservation procedure when reached is merely formal; some states go further and submit in this way most bills which deal with subjects on the concurrent list.

The same is true of financial relations. As already mentioned, the Constitution sets out the sources of revenue for states and centre, distinguishes sources to be collected by states from those collected by the Union but to be distributed to the states, and prescribes an independent Finance Commission, set up every five years, to lay down the distribution of these shared taxes and the principles for making grants-in-aid from the centre. However, since the second plan both these tasks have declined in relative importance as compared with the rise of a system of 'matching' grants scarcely envisaged by the Constitution (they are made under Art. 282 which simply states that 'the Union . . . may make any grants for any public purpose'). These have become by now the backbone of federal planning finance. The attractions of this form are obvious but criticisms have been voiced as to its effects. Apart from the partial eclipse administered to the Finance Commission it has been said that the system gives rise to an undesirably pronounced atmosphere of dependence and irresponsibility in the states. The particular charge that states indulge in competitive importuning, putting up scheme after scheme to attract funds, and then happily run up big deficits by failing to collect their own share of the costs was partly met by some procedural improvements introduced in 1958. Nevertheless, politically sensitive state governments will always be tempted to barter away the responsibilities of freedom for the comfort of support, even with controls attached.

The loss by Congress in 1967 of its pre-eminent position on the political scene clearly has great bearing on the relations between centre and states. To be confronted with non-Congress governments in half the states was a shock and a novelty that might be expected to reveal just how far single-party dominance had previously served as a lubricant to the practical mechanisms of federalism. Some would say that co-operative federalism had never existed, that under Nehru there was irresistible central direction and that since his death and especially since the fourth elections the balance of power had been reversed leaving the centre at the mercy of the states. This is over-simple and misleading. First, by presenting a picture of states' subservience to Nehru, it fails to acknowledge the strong bargaining position, even at that time, of certain chief ministers—as has already been pointed out (p. 122). Second, it misses important distinctions between the non-Congress governments. Only of governments led by the Communist Party (Marxist) which have been in power for periods in West Bengal and Kerala can it be said that there was a relationship of basic conflict. This can be said neither of states ruled by area-based parties—DMK in Tamilnad, Akali Dal in Punjab and Ganatanta Parishad (dressed as Swatantra) in Orissa, all of whom are ardent localists but willing to come to terms—nor of the coalition groups who have at different stages formed the governments of UP, Bihar, Madhya Pradesh and Haryana. The latter have been too internally torn to present effective challenges to the centre. Third, that kind of situation, however, has not been confined to the states. Indeed it makes good sense to argue that centre-state relations have been affected less by the rise of opposition parties in 1967 than by the internal dissensions in Congress culminating in the splitting of the party in 1969. The centre is not so much at the mercy of the states as it is the victim of its own unsteadiness. In so far as centre-state relations have a tug-of-war aspect the situation is not that the states team is pulling the centre to defeat nor that the rope is about to break but rather that both sides are so busy with team-control difficulties that the rope often lies limp in their hands.

There have, however, been times of tension. These have arisen around four kinds of general problems. (Some particular policy issues which proved tricky have been mentioned on pp. 122–5) Large questions of constitutional change have been raised by some state leaders and other public figures. The suggestion is that what was put together as a framework in 1949 no longer fits the changed political realities. A new constituent assembly, it is argued, would fix the point of balance between centre and states very differently. The position of the state should be improved by a fresh division of financial resources, so that the strings of the expanding purses should no longer be held in Delhi. The allocation of subjects as between union, state and concurrent lists should at the same time be adjusted in favour of the states. And those parts of the Constitution which permit the invasion of state automony in certain circumstances should be revised so as to confine Delhi's powers more narrowly. While there is certainly some support for such notions, there is more widespread feeling that in a phase of political instability such changes are the last to be encouraged. A more purposeful rather than a further enfeebled centre is the general sentiment. It is also to be noted that the Jan Sangh, the party which over the last decade has made the most consistent progress, is in doctrine the most centralist. A second general problem concerns the respective roles of centre and states in the preservation of law and order. While this is in normal circumstances unambiguously a state subject, it may also become a matter of concern to the centre. The communist-led governments of Kerala and West Bengal were during 1968–9 at odds with Delhi in this regard on a number of occasions—mainly because they resented the deployment of the Central Reserve Police, an armed force of the union government, without orders of the state authorities. West Bengal adopted a confrontation posture of particular truculence, even calling for a state-wide *bandh* (strike) against Delhi.

Thirdly, there have been bitter centre-state disputes about the centre's handling of problems of instability in state governments—in particular its imposition of President's Rule (see p. 82) from the centre on its being 'satisfied that a situation has arisen in which the government of the state cannot be carried on in accordance with the Constitution'. The discretionary powers of the state Governors have been central to the controversy; it is they who have had to judge—in situations of rival claims and rapidly shifting allegiances on the part of legislators—who can command a majority and whether, if it appears that no one can, a fresh election should be held or a period of President's rule imposed. It is clear that the Constitution envisaged the Governor as in one aspect responsible to the centre; it is also evident that he can be faced with genuinely difficult decisions; unfortunately, it is clear too that in some cases—a small minority of those that have arisen, and notably in West Bengal, U.P. and Rajasthan—decisions were taken which proved unwise and open to criticism as not being impartial between the parties.

Finally, while the view that relations between centre and states over the area of planning and development administration have been transformed by political upheavals must be rejected, it must be admitted that they have been affected. Even if the main change has been a loss of coherent purpose at the centre, it is also true that some states have stood in the way of a nation-wide carrying through of all-India plans. With two it has been a matter of ideological hostility; this for instance goes some way to explaining the unprecedented rejection by Kerala and West Bengal of the draft fourth plan. With some it is a non co-operation born of exclusive devotion to local interest. With many it is a combination of political opportunism and sheer lack of commitment that makes them unwilling and unable to do their share of the mobilising of resources that implementation requires.

Within this section belongs some mention of the Zonal Councils. Invented (see above, p. 101) at the time of the linguistic reorganization of states in 1956, they were envisaged as a countervailing device against excessive provincialism on the part of the newly created states. States were grouped into five zones; Northern (Punjab, Eajasthan, Kashmir), Southern (Andhra, Madras, Kerala, Mysore), Rastern (Bengal, Bihar, Orissa, Assam), Western (Maharashtra,

Gujarat) and Central (Uttar Pradesh and Madhya Pradesh). The insertion of a third tier between centre and states would serve both to bring those two main levels closer and at the same time to smooth relations between neighbouring states. Although some observers expected great things of the new bodies, in fact their purely governmental character tended to indicate that no more than an administrative co-ordinating mechanism was intended. Each Council consists of the Chief Minister and two other ministers from each of the state governments of the zone, and the body meets under the chairmanship of the central government Home Minister. The Southern Zonal Council, which has been the most active and effective of the five, has met about twice a year. Matters dealt with include the formation of a zonal police reserve, water supplies for irrigation and power development schemes in which more than one state has an interest. A signal success for the Southern Zonal Council was its satisfactory handling of the problems (mainly educational) of linguistic minorities such as Telegu-speakers now in Tamil-speaking Madras. Apart from administrative co-ordination and the negotiation of solutions to certain kinds of common problems, Zonal Councils may also serve as a convenient channel for broad regional representations to the centre.

At the local level

It has already been explained (pp. 113–14) that the 'somewhat inconclusive (pre-1947) experience of marriage between local self-government and centralized bureaucracy' was quickly followed by the double impact of Community Development (CD) and Panchayat Raj (PR). There can be little doubt that the third stage of reforms has been the most important in modifying the character of governance at the local level.

The pre-1947 district boards and constituted village panchayats (the latter being distinct from caste panchayats and informal village leadership groups, both of which could have real power in their own fields) were significant in local administration mainly perhaps as additional factors requiring to be managed by the appropriate local officials. The situation changed already with the coming of CD. The effect was to create in local government a kind of 'dyarchy': while the 'negative', law-enforcement side (together with older environmental services) continued to be the responsibility of the regular district staff under the supervision of the collector, an expanded 'positive' or welfare side was developed by the new CD staff. The two structures were not exactly parallel, for although District Development (or Planning) Officers were introduced, the key CD unit was the block, of which there would be more than one in each district. They differed too in that while the district administration was firmly linked with appropriate departments of the state government, that of CD tended to look beyond the State Development Officer to the bustling new CD ministry at Delhi. Above all, the ethos of the CD was to be quite distinct: if it was to be by strict definition a bureaucracy, it was to be perfectly unbureaucratic. In its procedures, red tape would be banned; its staff would be found in the field, not in the office; its purpose was to be not control but service through guidance and assistance and inspiration to self-help. (In drawing its own image, CD liked to point the contrast with the ordinary district administration, but the outcome was sometimes a caricature of the latter as absurd as it was ugly.) Although CD was to work 'with' the people, it was largely left to the village level workers to discover how this was to be done. There were established Block Advisory Committees, but in the absence of statutory powers —and even with the best will in the world on the part of the BDO— these usually became as ineffective as the still existing but mainly decrepit district boards.

Dyarchy of this kind required much skill and understanding for its working. The two rocks between which it had to steer were near and fatal: insufficient distinction (between the two operations) and insufficient co-operation. The regular district staff were not to be indifferent to CD but were to help in every way. The CD staff were to set up not as rivals to the ordinary administration but as an additional albeit novel arm. It proved very difficult to hit on the right course. If CD men acted in new ways they pointed a contrast which was irritating to the regular bureaucracy and seemed to 'weaken administration'; if they followed established attitudes and procedures, they failed in their purpose and seemed to add little to local administration beyond confusion. If the collector showed enthusiasm for development work, his high status would dominate over all; if he and his staff stayed aloof, they could hinder work. In addition to these difficulties, it was soon reported that relations within the CD structure were far from smooth. The 'team' ideal readily disintegrated partly because status-consciousness demanded superior–inferior distinctions, partly because of pressure for quick results. BDOs more often than not found release from their own double subordination (to the higher CD levels and to the collector) by turning their own block specialist staff into subordinate assistants and by bossing the VLWs. This was rather the last straw for the latter, already encountering enough difficulty in understanding and dealing with the traditional power relations in village life.

However, it was not these administrative creakings which led to the next stage so much as the disappointing response of rural India to the CD programme. Reports by the Project Evaluation Organization, by individual investigators and finally by the Balwantray Mehta study team all agreed that although it could be said that CD was in demand, it was sought for wrong reasons. So far from stimulating self-help, CD seemed only to have increased the proneness to look to government. There were also accusations that CD had been efficiently exploited by dominant sections of the rural community in such a way as to strengthen their own positions relative to the less fortunate. The remedy for these ills was to be a grasping of the nettle of local politics by the thoroughgoing introduction of democratic local bodies with real powers. Many thought that this Panchayat Raj (PR) would simultaneously resolve the administrative tensions.

It is not easy to understand the widespread enthusiasm with which in the years 1959–62 state governments all over India set about a reconstruction of local government. The panacea-like quality of PR owes something to Gandhian memories and their revival by J. P. Narayan; the latter's teachings tended to present PR as indigenous and traditional—'communitarian democracy'—and at the same time as more modern than the West—'participating democracy'. Hard-headed civil servants and staid parliamentary draftsmen laboured to produce schemes and bills for rapid implementation. Rajasthan and Andhra were eagerly away by the end of 1959. The general idea, taken from the Mehta Report, was for three levels of representative bodies, all turned out in Hindi titles: Gram Panchayat (village), Panchayat Samiti (block) and Zila Parishad (district). (Even the BDO became Vikas Adhikari.) While the gram panchayat was to be directly elected, the higher two levels were to consist of members indirectly elected from the tier below, together with co-opted parliamentarians, co-operative movement officials and others. The legislation of some of those states which took more time to think about the implementation of PR has in fact shown variations from this general pattern, some (e.g. Maharashtra) preferring the old district to the newer block as the basic unit and introducing direct elections for that level. There is also no strict uniformity as to the powers of these bodies and the controls which are retained by the collectors and state governments.

It is by now possible to assess the consequences for governance of the introduction of PR—the interesting political consequences are considered later—and it is clear enough that the foundations of a new and lively system of local government have been laid. This is not to say that it is everywhere running smoothly and in democratic fashion. But it does mean that the officials—both regular and CD—are now confronted for the first time by a co-ordinated network of popular bodies endowed with considerable powers and protected by political support. This will not at once end administrative tensions, nor will a single body of local government 'servants' be born overnight. But already the Panchayat Samitis, where (in most states) power is concentrated—Village Panchayats are mainly agents and Zila Parishads mainly co-ordinators—are feeling this power and exercising it. It will always be possible for a skilful official to exert great influence over lay representatives—but to speak in these terms is already to speak of a transformed situation, one akin to that of ministers and civil servants.

Administrative reforms

The subject of governance cannot be left without reference to an extraordinary examination of the whole system which was undertaken in the post-Nehru period. This was something wider in scope than the Fulton Commission in Britain, more akin perhaps to the earlier Hoover investigation in the United States. The Administrative Reforms Commission (ARC) came into existence in January 1966. Its terms of reference covered consideration of the machinery of the central government and its procedures, planning machinery at all levels, centre-state relations, financial, economic and personnel administration and the redress of citizen grievances. It must be supposed that the decision to launch such a thoroughgoing enquiry was taken by Shastri. He may have sensed that an era had ended and that the time was ripe for a hard look at the inherited and vastly expanded apparatus of government. He may have been pressed by people with particular axes to grind—such as ministers anxious to demote the PC. He was almost certainly most impressed by the thought behind the last item in the above list of the terms of reference: administration had to be, and be seen by citizens to be, clean, effective and responsive. The Santhanam Commission had looked at the question of corruption but had seen that it was part of a wider problem; this would now be examined.

The ARC was a body of five under the Chairmanship of Morarji Desai. This had been decided before Shastri's death. It was an interesting choice: for one thing it gave a worthwhile job to an energetic but frustrated man who had been thrown out of high office by Nehru under the Kamaraj Plan and had been unable to mount a successful challenge to Shastri on Nehru's death; for another, it endowed the ARC with great prestige and vigorous leadership. Desai, having contested and lost to Mrs Gandhi at the second succession, displayed his restiveness by trying, again without success, to get the post of Chairman given high place in the official order of precedence. He stayed in the job until the 1967 elections; when Mrs Gandhi was forced to make him Deputy Prime Minister he was able to pass it over to Hanumanthaiya, a former Chief Minister of Mysore, already a member of the ARC and one of Desai's backers against Mrs Gandhi. When the Congress split took place in 1969, it was believed that the ARC's days of influence or even life might be numbered. By then, however, its work had been virtually completed. The question was how many of its recommendations would be put into effect. For scholars in any case there was already great value in the descriptive analyses which had emerged from the extensive investigations, for each of the separate Report volumes is matched and preceded by a more detailed series of studies completed by 'study teams' appointed for each range of problems.

The ARC made a considerable impact by producing two somewhat dramatic interim reports. The first which appeared in October 1966 addressed itself at once to the redress of citizens' grievances. It boldly recommended the use of the 'ombudsman' device. There should be created independent authorities at centre and state levels to be appointed by the President on the recommendation of the Chief Justice: a Lokpal whose duty would be to investigate complaints against ministers and against senior officials and whose status would be the same as that of Chief Justice, and a Lokayukt for the area of all other officials. The recommendation was accepted and at the moment of writing while the bill has been passed appointments have not yet been announced. All that can be forecast with confidence is that they will need and acquire large staffs to deal with the representations.

In March of the following year the second interim report appeared and dealt with the machinery for planning. It sounded the death knell for the Nehru PC which if never a super-cabinet had developed at least some of the marks of a super-ministry. The ARC sought to put a firm stop to its imperceptible invasion of the executive sphere by stipulating that the PC should be in no way engaged in executive functions and decisions; it was to be an expert body with a purely advisory role. Its essential task was to formulate in broad outline the long-term perspective plan and the five- and one-year plans and conduct continuous evaluation. As such it required no large staff; the existing staff should be reduced by half. The detailed planning which is necessarily difficult to separate from executive work should be left to the central ministries and the state governments. To underline the change of role, ministers (including the PM) should disappear from the PC which should consist of seven full-time experts. Within a few months the PM announced broad acceptance of the ARC's view and the consequent reorganization of the PC. The decisive change was the replacement of Asoka Mehta as Deputy Chairman by Dr D. R. Gadgil. The former, while not inexpert in economic affairs, was a political leader, previously at the head of the PSP; the latter, a widely respected elder economist, was strictly an expert with no special ambitions or influence in political or administrative life and known to be hostile to the mixed roles of the earlier PC. There were other changes too, all tending to reduce the leverage of the PC on the government machine. (One of these, in itself small but significant, had happened earlier—the separation of the offices of Cabinet Secretary and Secretary of the PC.) One point the PM was unable to accept from the recommendations: she and the Finance Minister would remain members of the PC. But from that time the PC certainly receded from the limelight. This is only partly due to its now more limited role. It was also a result of the setbacks suffered by the plans following the war and famine years of 1965–6. It was a consequence too of the absorption of leadership energy in the new intricacies of market politics.

Soon after the interim reports of the Desai period, the regular reports of the ARC began to appear; they continued through 1969. One of these was on the machinery for planning and it put the finishing touches to the proposals of the interim report on this subject. The Planning Commission's strictly advisory expert role was underlined not merely by the recommendation that it should work as a commission and not as a secretariat and not only by the view that it should be cut by half in size but also by the proposal that it should be organized simply in three 'wings': one for plan formulation (where the use of working groups with ministries and states would continue); one for evaluation of plan progress in which the existing Programme Evaluation Organization and the Committee on Plan Projects would become integrated and more closely related to each other; and one for establishment matters. Since the PC was not to engage in future in the details of planning, the report stressed the need to ensure that this work would be done effectively by those responsible: every ministry should have its planning cell and every state must have a real planning board. An important recommendation was that the prevailing general use of a matching pattern of grants to states (i.e., centre grants to be forthcoming for given projects on condition that there is a given state contribution) was to end. Instead this device would be reserved only for a limited number of 'schemes of basic national importance' while the larger balance of grants would be

F

made available to the states for spending (though only on approved projects) in an order of priority which the states themselves would determine.

The report by the ARC on the machinery of the central government and its procedures is a curious document in that it contains pronouncements of such very different kinds. In the sections dealing with the Cabinet and with relations among ministers and between them and their civil servants, it probably went beyond its area of 'administration'. It boldly laid down the right size for both Cabinet (sixteen) and full Council of Ministers (40–45), insisted that there should always be a Deputy Prime Minister and said the PM should not hold any ministerial portfolio. It also laid down a structure of cabinet committees and proposed the elevation (to check the growth of the PM's secretariat?) of the position of Cabinet Secretary from 'co-ordinator' to 'principal staff adviser to the PM, the Cabinet and its committees'. It even pronounced on the points which should determine the PM's selection of ministers. These matters have an admitted administrative relevance but one would imagine that political convenience, as judged by the PM, must outweigh other factors. To those unfamiliar with the fact that in India the habit of taking a holiday as a rest is little practised, the report's recommendation that ministers should take at least two weeks off for 'reading, reflection and relaxation' sounds sillier than it is. Relations between ministers and civil servants were handled mainly by homilies: ministers should make a point of giving decisions in writing, they should encourage frank and impartial advice and there should be discouragement for 'unhealthy personal affiliations to individual ministers among civil servants'. These sentiments at least indicated some of the worries but it is doubtful if they did a great deal to change the position. Rather more useful was the ARC's discussion of ministerial accountability, undertaken no doubt with some of the *causes célèbres* in mind; even here, however, there were difficult and perhaps unavoidable ambiguities, as when the report said that ministers should not be held accountable for an act of an official which is 'by implication prohibited by policies already approved by the minister'. Very different was the tone of the report when it moved on to the organization of ministries. Here it had before it a highly technical and sophisticated report by the study team which had carried out a fascinating detailed analysis of the type of work done in the ministries. The ARC accepted only in part the study team view that policy-making and executive functions should be separated but it agreed that there should be certain 'staff' offices in each ministry: for planning and policy formulation, for personnel matters and for finance. The heads of these, together with those of the subject-wise wings of each ministry and those of the executive organizations integrated into each ministry, should form a policy advisory committee in the ministry. The report also added that there should be a central department of personnel, directly under the PM and located in the Cabinet Secretariat, which would concern itself with broad personnel policy, not with the administration of any particular service. Other recommendations included detailed re-organization and reallocation of departments within ministries, support for the setting up of parliamentary standing committees on the main fields of government work and the creation in place of the administrative reforms department within the Home Ministry of a separate department to be placed directly under the Deputy PM and working through a special cell in the Cabinet Secretariat, charged with the implementation of the ARC's recommendations.

Space does not permit description of all the reports. That on public sector undertakings, for instance, important though it was for management problems, is too elaborate for effective summary here. It must suffice to mention that in its search for greater efficiency it recommended the grouping of some forty-five of the existing corporations under 'sector corporations' (e.g., the ten different engineering undertakings under an engineering corporation), each unit retaining operational autonomy but the overall sector corpora-tion being responsible for promotion and development in the field as a whole and for common services. More must be said, however, on two further reports—on personnel and on centre-state relations.

The report on personnel clearly set out to professionalize admini-stration and to enhance the status of the specialist. The ARC took the view that the 'generalist' administrator's reign should be terminated or at least substantially modified. Analysis of the tasks carried out in the central ministries persuaded them that many posts required more subject-matter specialism than had been hitherto recognized. Each of these specialisms should have its own service where it did not already exist. But when this had been done there would still remain at the top what could only be described as general policy level positions. These too required particular skills, described as 'conceptual and managerial', but the important point in the ARC's eyes was that these skills were liable to be found among the officers working in any specialist service. Therefore a way had to be found for locating and transferring such men: there should be a special examination open to all officers of the higher services who had 8–12 years' experience and the policy posts would be filled from the best. This recommendation left no place for the prestigious IAS man but the ARC discovered a way of avoiding abolition of that service. It should be retained, but instead of being the service specially seen as equipped for the top posts it should be placed in the position of all the specialist services; it would in fact become itself a specialist service, its specialism being revenue and magisterial work at the district level, from which its abler members would be able to compete with all other services in the mid-career examination. Needless to say, this recommendation ran into substantial opposition, not merely from the IAS men themselves but also from anyone still persuaded that good general administrators are best discovered at graduation rather than in their thirties. Less controversial but not necessarily any easier of implementation were the ARC's recommendations for lateral entry into government service from university teaching, industry and commerce, a unified grading structure (with only 20–25 different grades in place of the hundreds existing) and a special emphasis on training to be reflected in a training wing of the department of personnel and a fresh stress on mid-career and middle management courses.

Finally, the report on centre-state relations was important for its attempt to recognize the way in which political changes since Nehru called for changed administrative relations between Delhi and the states. It insisted that no constitutional change was required and that nothing would be proposed that was damaging to the unity and integrity of the country as a whole. Nevertheless, experience suggested that adjustments were called for in the sense that administrative arrangements which had perhaps worked at an earlier stage were now conducive not only to political conflict but also to inefficiency. Thus the report stressed again the greater scope for state freedom offered by its proposals on plan grants to states; priorities would not be dictated from Delhi. It further recommended that the central government should confine within fairly narrow limits its activities, previously grown quite extensive, in those fields which the Constitution had made over to the states. On the other hand the report came out unambiguously with a restatement of the centre's rights in the crucial and lately troublesome matter of law and order: the right to use the armed forces of the Union (including the Central Reserve Police) in any state of the Union does not require a request for help from a state but may be exercised by the Union government on its own initiative. Some conflicts be-tween centre and states might be unavoidable; what was important was to minimize their number and provide means for their resolution. In this connection the report recommended a new relationship between the PC and the Finance Commission, enlarging the role of the latter: it should be its task to recommend the principles which should govern the making by the centre of even its plan grants to the states. The effectiveness of the Finance Commission, an independent and not a centre body, would be enhanced by ensuring that its work would not be by-passed by the PC; it should be appointed only when the plan outline is available and one member of the PC should be a member of the FC also. Finally, for the resolution of conflicts the dormant constitutional provision (Article 263) for an Inter-State Council should be brought to life. Composed in such a way as to give the states security—Prime Minister, Home and Finance Ministers but also five representatives from the Zonal Councils and the leader of the opposition—it was envisaged as taking over much of the work otherwise dispersed over the NDC, the National Integration Council, conferences of chief ministers and other (e.g., food) ministers. This new Council should have as an early task, the report added, the establishment of guidelines for the conduct of Governors and in particular the use of their discretionary powers.

Although it is impossible to give any account of how far all these recommendations have been effectively accepted, it has seemed worth describing them at some length because they indicate, at least on many questions, the broad directions in which the administration is likely to be changed. Some of the changes may be gradual; this is probably the case with the revision of planning procedures, which may indeed have been altering even before the ARC reported. Other changes may meet some of the ARC's points without going all the way with the specific remedy proposed; the creation of a special career development section in the Home Ministry is perhaps an example of this kind. So long as the uncertainties of political marketing persist it is only to be expected that the pace of change will be determined less by the political leaders than by the current administrative leaders. (However, the possibility that marketing may bring surprise is provided by the curious twist to the ARC story contained in its end: it was wound up in 1970 whereupon its chairman, Hanumanthaiya, erstwhile backer of Mrs Gandhi's rival Desai, was promptly taken into Mrs Gandhi's cabinet.) But even if rapid change is unlikely, this cannot detract from the considerable achievement which the ARC's review represents; it is not a bad system that can take such a long hard look at itself.

5

POLITICAL FORCES

Any political system in which free citizens are enabled in various measures to participate will contain parties. The nature and arrangement of the parties will normally be a key middle term in the relations between society and politics already discussed in brief (Chapter 2). The party system is shaped and coloured by the interests and ideas of groups in society and in turn contributes significantly to the character of the whole political system. Since the relations are never merely in one direction, we have equally to remember the ways in which the total complex of political institutions influences the party system contained within it, as also the capacity of that party system to mould the social patterns. Also to be borne in mind is the already mentioned peculiar situation in post-colonial regimes where the 'gearing-in' of politics with society, delayed by foreign rule, comes late and suddenly—and therefore often with severe jolts and much noise. (Crashing through the gears of social change is fairly typical of new states but not peculiar to them. At the same time, some new states, of which India is the outstanding example to date, may be said to have either installed synchro-mesh systems or at least secured drivers who manage to double de-clutch.)

Parties are said to receive and express the notions and wishes of their supporters. Such a passive, conveyor-belt view is of course incomplete, especially in a new state. The particular segment of the political élite which forms the leadership of parties is indeed engaged in listening to the cries that come up from below. But the cries are not simply to be echoed; they need to be translated, related, worked into a choral harmony which permits an act of ordered performance. Or, to try putting it another way, it is part of the contortionist posture of any political leader that while he lifts his eyes to the hills he must keep his ears close to the ground; and the ground is always moving and the hills change shape as they move in and out of the mists. This is universal; yet there are features of the process, aspects of the activity, which are by and large peculiar to new states. The degree to which the ground keeps moving is especially marked; the politician of a new state works on shifting sands. For all that has been said, and rightly, in criticism of the concept of political development, it is unwise to deny that in regard to those parts of a political system which handle the initial processing of the opinions and interests of the public—the 'demand' or 'input' side according to one's model—new states do constitute a valid and useful category. (It would be almost equally foolish to deny that there are some very important differences within the category, so much so that for some purposes the category would best be set aside permitting one to see more important similarities between a new state and one long established.)

The key to the distinctiveness of new states as regards the working of the political forces within them has perhaps already been suggested by the discussion in Chapter 2 of the nature of the linking of politics to society. There we spoke of the very wide gap in political culture between the apex of the pyramid and its base. But we also stressed the fact of change as leading to a closing of the gap and the prominence of political activity as an agent of this process. Spelling this out now in relation to the organization of public preferences and prejudices as part of the political system, the points can best be set out under two broad, superficially contradictory but essentially complementary heads: new states are made distinctive by the disparity of the 'levels' of politics and also by the rate of change in the direction of reducing that disparity.

From the contrast of levels there follow a number of consequences for the organization of political demands and desires. The tendency in any political party or similar body will be for the leadership to be somewhat removed from the rank and file, to be confronted therefore with continuous problems of communication and coherence within the organization. This point is of course reinforced by the separate but related consideration that in the case of a federal polity like India's, where the units are not simply a consequence of size but also correspond to regional languages and cultures, nation-wide political organization has to learn to rely on loose reins. Along with the obvious disadvantages which this brings, there are advantages of which the most notable is that quite diverse groups can be held together in the party's confederation, providing support as well as tensions. It must also be remembered that in such a society there will be, in addition to the sections of society already at least partially mobilized in party organizations, other sections still lying outside, unmobilized; such sections, awaiting and even seeking incorporation, provide a challenge to party chiefs, a prize to be won if the right approach can be found and if—here is the rub—the new entrants can be accommodated without hurting the established members and followers.

The social distance between leaders and led tends to give the former more scope than their opposite numbers in more established polities enjoy. They are not so much delegates with mandates from below as manipulators using support for the tussles against their rivals, whether these be within their own party or in other parties. The leaders of all parties in this sense have more in common with each other than they have with their own 'mass base'. This is often helped by the fact that they tend to come from the same social milieu. It will often appear that rival leaders compete in framing appeals that bear relation solely to support they may gain, hardly at all to what their organization purports to stand for in terms of general outlook or policies. This rivalry flows in part from the great importance of political power in these societies. This in turn is to be explained by the paucity of alternative foci of power and the saliency of government over the whole range of social decisions. But the rivalry flows too from the extent to which members of the political élite themselves feel and respond to the loyalties of the partial communities within the state. We are after all talking of societies where community divisions of one kind or another—religion, language, caste or tribe—run very deep. At the same time, it is a consequence of rivalry within the élite that despite the leader-follower gap, élite coherence is continuously undermined and difficult to sustain. We have to say that the tendency of the élite to fragment is a reflection of the fluidity of political affiliations. This is evidently a paradoxical situation: if social divisions are hard one would expect political affiliations to follow suit.

Here indeed is a tension which is a key to much of the politics of new states: on the one hand, the tendency for social divisions to dictate the lines of political cleavage—caste parties, tribal politics, linguistic and communal movements; on the other, the tendency for political rivalries within the élite to create formless opportunism, devoid of pattern and permanence and inhibitive of institution-building. Both tendencies are usually present in some degree and the question arises as to what factors lead one to prevail over the other. The answer seems to lie in what might be called 'the arithmetic of the arenas'. That is, with any given arena of political conflict the number, relative strengths and arrangements of the ready-made, socially-moulded blocks will determine whether political lines follow or cut across the social divisions. But to this very general statement must at once be attached two vital qualifications. First, arenas are not irrevocably given, except in the short run; by boundary changes or by alterations in the allocation of powers among the units of the state, the arenas can be shifted—as they often are by the efforts of groups who otherwise see no future for themselves. Second, and relatedly, no situation is ever of the blank slate variety; there is always a history and this may impose patterns which persist against the persuasions of arithmetic. And there has been no single historical 'shaper' more potent than imperial rule; long after the transfer of power its legacies remain, not merely in the definition of arenas but also in the institutionalized patterns of political collaboration.

The complexity engendered by the contrasts of levels is further developed when account is taken of the second broad head, the speed of change in the direction of reducing these same contrasts. It must be emphasized at the outset that the process here referred to is not the same as egalitarianism. The gaps between rich and poor and between city and rural areas may or may not be closing; most often they appear to get wider. Our levels however are of political culture and style. These shift rather independently of simple economic levels; they respond more readily to factors such as education, urbanization and communications. New states start their lives with a dual (or indeed multi-level) polity. With the spread of education, the growth of towns, the breaking down of isolation and remoteness through transport and communications, above all by the expansion of political activity, a single political culture comes to be formed. This entails not the simple victory of one style over the other but a steady, albeit confused, act of political creation in which a new culture, containing the transmuted elements of its parents, is born. The politicians are the agents of this change, its beneficiaries if they manage to adjust, its victims if they fail.

The process presents different aspects according to the point from which it is seen. To the villager it may well appear as a disturbance to familiar patterns of power; the horizon of influence is extended and there are new routes to be navigated towards the old goals of security and improvement. Seen from outside it is a picture of an expanding political universe. In an established polity the universe is mainly constant; it may stretch a little when, for instance, the age of political consent is lowered from 21 to 18. In a new state political life seems to spiral outwards from the original centres of activity towards the silent, 'unpoliticized' periphery. (This was not in reality without politics; it merely had its own different politics. Moreover, it is not one unchanging politics that moves thus outwards; it changes as it touches each outer edge.) With each twist of the spiral—occasioned by a general election or some particular mobilizing campaign—fresh social layers are 'tapped' and incorporated, simultaneously offering support and gaining access. This may take the form of new kinds of voters; also, and more important, it will be former voters voting in a new way and with a new meaning. Beyond the ballot box, there will be new kinds of men as candidates for elected office and even newer kinds as applicants to parties for the candidature tickets. There will be an invasion of any new avenues of influence which open up, especially local councils and co-operative societies. And with each widening sweep of the political circle there is also a movement of persons inwards towards the centre, new recruits to the political leadership—from village into district, district towns into state capital and to some extent from states to national capital.

In all this movement party is central and the party system a more or less sensitive indicator. The underlying trend would be rising competitiveness, a struggle to build more stable party institutions and above all the expanding political universe. In each particular country these features would be present in differing degrees.

The preceding paragraphs have been expressed in general terms but may not have such general application for they are written with India above all in mind.

The nature of the party system

Yet even for India they may not fit very easily. Or, rather, if they do there is still much to be explained, in particular how the party system has changed so little during the first twenty years after independence. That system came to be known as that of the one dominant party. How did it come into existence, what were its characteristics, how far and in what way did it eventually change? Of the three trends just mentioned, India clearly displays the expanding political universe, has manifested party competitiveness only in recent years (unless, as will in fact be suggested, it was growing unobtrusively rather sooner) and has entered a phase of diminishing rather than increasing institutionalization in her party politics.

The twenty-year supremacy of the Congress Party, lasting up to the elections of 1967 and the split in the party in 1969, is a massive fact of Indian politics not likely to be speedily erased in all its effects and needing to be understood. Now any bare and simple form of 'legacy' explanation will only go part of the way. That Congress was already there in command could perhaps tell us why it dominated when the

new state began its life. But more seems required if we are to explain
its scarcely diminished stature as much as twenty years later. It is at
least necessary to remind ourselves of some of the distinctive features
of this legacy. The great age of Congress is a factor, no doubt—habit
and loyalty having great importance in political behaviour—but one
of the implications of age is skill, and age itself is an achievement
which requires explanation. The sixty-two years of pre-independence
continuous development indicates from one viewpoint the near-
equilibrium of forces on the two sides of imperial power and
nationalist aspiration. It also indicates, given India's heterogeneity,
a capacity for political management, for it is not as if there were not
several threats to coherence (of which the Surat split of 1907 was
only the most dramatic). That capacity in turn must be related to
many considerations. One point must be that Westernization was
not only profound in some places but also that the degrees of
Westernization were infinite, the slope to the shallow end very
gradual. This meant that there could be found a set of leaders at once
accomplished in the modern art of political claim-making and not
too isolated from at least a substantial body of followers. (This is not
to deny that there were vast non-political sections, or, more precisely,
sections confined to the tiny worlds of traditional politics.) Another
point may be that despite the Western impact, sufficient remained of
the refinement and sophistication of the former cultures to provide a
basis for a high level of political maturity. The tradition of learning,
the habit of disputation and argument preserved in Brahmin
families may have had some shortcomings when regarded from the
standpoint of Western intellectual character—indeed, the same
shortcomings as medieval learning, from which that Western
intellect was born! But it did combine a fineness of mind with a
familiarity with leadership in a manner which made a political
asset.

Age is a cause as well as an effect of skill. The art of managing men
and their ideas became developed by being exercised within the
confines of the Congress. A Jawaharlal inherited not only from
Motilal and Gandhi but from the earlier past of the movement, not
only from a few generations of Western influence but from many
more of cultivated living and leadership. But the inter-war period
alone was a great school of politics for Congressmen. Here were
tried all the techniques of persuasion and pressure, here were
encountered all the forms of resistance. Almost it becomes a
rhetorical question to ask: What experience could independence
bring that had not already been met in some not too dissimilar form
in the years of struggle? Congress did not embrace all sections of the

Indian people with equal thoroughness, but membership of its Working Committee or even of its lower organs at provincial and district levels was an excellent introduction not simply to nationalist agitation but to many of at least the higher constituent elements of Indian society and therefore of Indian political life. These elements had to be reconciled and adjusted. It is true that differences of interest and attitude on social and economic matters could be submerged for periods by the more pressing questions of nationalist strategy—but only submerged, not resolved, and only for periods. Radicals and socialists were always trying to translate ideology into policy and independence into terms that would appeal to the masses, thereby alerting and even alienating the establishment sections of the movement. The Karachi Congress of 1931 was an occasion of sharpening discord. Gandhi himself was frequently upsetting some section by his opinions, though he took care to distribute his irritants evenly on all sides. As already mentioned earlier, significant indications of divergent opinions were given by the formation of inner groups such as the Congress Socialist Party (1934) and Bose's Forward Bloc (1939).

All this is to say that Congress long ago learned that it had to be an Aristotelian party, a party of the middle way, if it was to survive and succeed. And the Congress political leader became moulded as a man of the centre, normally permitting himself the luxury of only a shade of emphasis on one side or the other. (Was Nehru not a very big exception? Yet it must be remembered that he never joined the Congress socialists. Also, the political centre of India and of Congress has on many matters, such as planning, an inherent left bias. Further, Congress, like the British Labour Party, can perhaps be more easily led from slightly left of its own centre than from slightly right.) Most nationalist movements are ideologically electic; Congress, no exception, was able to make good use of this for maintaining its political supremacy. By any normal definition of the political spectrum there was almost as big a range to be found within Congress (Krishna Menon to S. K. Patil) as within India. It was thus difficult for anyone outside Congress to voice opinions which would not be echoed, or at least silently endorsed, by some members of the great party— or, after the split, of its two successor organizations. At one end it is, of course, unlikely that any Communist Party members are Congress members and no Marxist could feel at home in Congress. Similarly, at the other end, the more blatant and bigoted forms of communalist and social reactionary are no doubt absent. Thus, while the majority of Congressmen are men of the centre, right and left minorities extend far, though the requirements of harmony dictate a certain discretion in the expression of views too far from the middle. (Krishna Menon's position was peculiar: his background of London exile and the protection of Nehru combined to afford him special licence.)

These explanations, 'from the top', do not go all the way. There needs to be added a dimension of depth. Briefly, a party like Congress has enjoyed special advantages in conditions where a sudden expansion of franchise and political involvement invades hitherto unaffected social levels. Quite evidently the main electoral strength of Congress is, with a few exceptions, in rural areas rather than in the large cities. There can be little doubt that if the franchise had been kept narrow and restricted to mainly urban and educated groups, Congress supremacy would have been secured with much greater difficulty. To say that this is because the villager is more easily manipulated polling-fodder is to put the matter too crudely to be true. It is rather that the 'interests' and approach of the peasant and middle-class city dweller are different. For the latter is better able both to grasp the notion of alternative policies and to be influenced by the power of general ideas or ideologies, and on both counts his allegiance to Congress would be more precarious. The illiterate villager is in a very different frame of mind. He has understood (if not in 1951, then certainly by 1962—and not merely because of general elections but also because of local elections) that he has a new importance and that men come from away to seek his vote. He has also understood that there is competition for his vote, that in some sense he therefore has a choice. But there is still a large gap—though one that has been closing more rapidly since 1967—between his approach and that of the educated city voter. In so far as he understands only the traditional language of politics he will have to grasp 'party' in terms of groups with which he is more familiar. He may simply follow the advice of his caste leaders; he will certainly find it difficult not to act as a member of a traditional group. But, above all, he will tend to see the competition not as between parties to become government but but between government and others. This is a big difference. What the villager expects of government tends to be very tangible, material, local—a school, a well, a road. (What he fears from government has the same quality of particularity.) He has therefore needed very good reasons not to give his vote to government. Even if he is displeased with what government has done, who else but government is in a position to do things for him? From this point of view, the question turns out to be, not why the Congress collects many votes, but why anyone else collects any.

To these considerations must be added others linked with the arguments of Chapter 2. The translation of caste from social and local unit to political and regional unit operated to strengthen the tendency to the dominance of Congress. In this respect there is a significant difference between caste and the larger religious community—such as Muslims or Sikhs. Caste is a component element of a complete traditional society; when the traditional world is disturbed, caste can compete for position, but it cannot be separatist. Caste seeks to be accommodated. When caste moves upwards into the modern political structure—when, that is, caste affiliation acquires significance in supra-local politics—it looks for effective means of improving its position within the established order. On occasion such means have seemed to present themselves in the form of distinct political organizations. Thus behind the small Commonweal and Tamilnad Toilers Parties in Madras in the 1950s were the aspirations of certain specific local non-Brahmin castes. Rather different are the instances of more generalized anti-Brahmin sentiment and pressure to be found already before independence in the Peasants and Workers Party (PWP) in Maharashtra and the Justice Party in Madras. The Dravida Kazhagam (DK) and Dravida Munnetra Kazhagam (DMK) Parties which succeeded the Justice Party have retained the anti-Brahmin theme but have added to it a southern hostility to North India and the Hindi language, and it is this latter aspect which has given rise to separatist programmes. These cases are, however, all less typical than the formal or informal organization of caste as a pressure group. To form a caste party is a bold move, but it is very likely to cut the group off from access to influence in government—unless the party can get into some kind of coalition. Even quite highly organized caste associations such as the Nair Service Society in Kerala have therefore sought to avoid translation into a separate political party, preferring to work through the existing political parties. But if they are to do this, what party should they concentrate on if not the party of government, in most cases and unambiguously until 1967, the Congress? It is true that castes in some areas (Ezhevas in Kerala, Kammas in Andhra) seem to have been captured fairly solidly over certain periods by (and/or committed themselves to) the Communist Party. But these are the cases that demand special explanation rather than the general impregnation of Congress by caste influences.

Congress thus acquired a consolidation of its domination because it operated in a political society in which nothing succeeded like success and in which there is almost every reason why the pendulum should not swing. It should be noted that this existence of a dominant party has helped to achieve smoothly the integration of political styles. It seems likely that in the absence of such a party traditional social groups would have been more tempted to form their own political bodies. (It has often been the case that in regions where Congress is relatively weak, caste support in rather explicit form is given to other parties. But cause and effect are not easy to separate here.) So long as such parties operated within the modern idiom, it is true that the process of integration would go ahead. But it would be less thorough. For one thing, such parties would tend to be at most regional in scale. For another, their style would be less clearly modern: leadership would tend to be ascriptive, authoritarian and only minimally policy-oriented. Congress by contrast has been a great educator: its eclectic ideology and shifting centrist policies have proved not handicaps but aids to the performance of its task as the instructor of new recruits to the modern political process. Thus a dominant party is a unifying agent not merely in the obvious 'horizontal' sense in which it holds together a range of opinions and interests but also in the important 'vertical' sense that it brings into contact and interpenetration all levels of politics from the most sophisticated to the most simple and traditional.

Before considering the changes of the late sixties, there are questions to be put regarding the situation of non-Congress parties. The first which suggests itself is why they remained so weak for so long and why they have continued to be so divided. To some degree this needs no special treatment: since their position has been the obverse of that of Congress, the factors that explain the persistence of Congress's strength also explain the delay in the challenge to its dominance. It must also be noted that when one speaks of other parties' weakness it has never been one manifested in terms of combined electoral votes, for even before 1967 non-Congress candidates polled regularly more than half the votes in the Lok Sabha elections: 1952, 55 per cent; 1957, 52 per cent; 1962, 55 per cent. In the state assembly elections the figures were: 1952, 58 per cent; 1957, 55 per cent; 1962, 56 per cent. Non-Congress parties do better in the contest for state assemblies than in the Lok Sabha elections because constituencies are smaller, non-Congress candidates more numerous and local personalities and issues more important. With a first-past-the-post electoral system the distribution of 'opposition' votes over several parties and groups naturally gave Congress a clearer advantage in seats: at the centre, non-Congress members constituted, in 1952, 26 per cent; in 1957, 25 per cent and in 1962, 28 per cent. Congress's relative weakness in the state assembly elections gave non-Congress strengths as follows in all the assemblies taken as a whole: 1952, 32 per cent; 1957, 35 per cent; 1962, 40 per cent.

If the weakness of other parties has thus been substantially a consequence of their multiplicity this in turn is closely related to the nature of Congress. It has been so adept at shifting its position so as always to occupy the centrist area that it has left only a host of diverse peripheral positions for others. These positions are, by definition so to speak, difficult to combine; from circumference to centre may be a shorter distance than from one circumference point to another, left and right opposition groups having more in common with Congress than with each other. Indeed, all they can consistently share with each other is dislike of being excluded from power and determination to hold on to it if it comes their way; the motions of no confidence in the government which from time to time in opposition they have jointly endorsed obscure the even less confidence they have in each other. It is a question, however, whether their mutual distrust does not exceed what would be expected from their political position alone. As already mentioned above (p. 63), opposition fragmentation is furthered by the general social difficulty of co-operation and by the preference of the party militants for the little unit even without power rather than the larger group. Real prospect of power has after all seemed remote to most parties most of the time before 1967; in these circumstances the delights of good companionship become all the greater and the incentive to co-operation minimal. To all these explanations should be added the general consideration that in a heterogeneous society party fragmentation outside the dominant party cannot be regarded as odd; as already suggested at the start of this chapter, when there are sharp social divisions one strong tendency will be for each so far as practicable to seek its own political organ; and from this standpoint it is the achieving of any containment within a dominant organization which appears as striking. All these points become clearer on reviewing the non-Congress political groupings.

The non-Congress groups

It is not easy to find any classification of India's other parties which is significant and watertight. There are several useful distinctions which can be drawn, but none avoids great overlapping. While some parties present themselves as all-India parties, others are by definition regional in scope and activity. In this way it is possible to distinguish between, for instance, the Communist Party (CPI) and the DMK; while the former takes the whole country as its audience and fights in every state, the latter has meaning and aspirations only for a limited area. (The DMK was born and lives in Madras or Talimnad, though it tried for a while without success to speak for the whole of the Dravidian south.) The Election Commission has indeed given formal recognition to this distinction by compiling for each general election a list of the parties entitled to all-India status. At the same time, this distinction should not obscure the fact that an all-India party may have strong regional bases and indeed be most unevenly represented over the country as a whole; this would be true, for example, of the Swatantra Party. Nor should it be taken of course that an all-India party will work in the same way in different regions; on the contrary, local factors may be so important as to impose on a party a character in one area quite different from what it bears in another—a feature which tends to produce strains on the all-India coherence of the party and bitterness in the relations between party HQ and the regional bosses. The special caste bases of the CPI in Andhra and Kerala might be instanced, as also the aristocratic colour taken by the Swantantra Party in Bihar and Rajasthan as compared with its more popular complexion in Andhra, or the special features of the Praja Socialist Party (PSP) in Assam (stress on Assamese fears of Bengalis) and Kerala (close association at times with the Nair community). These reservations regarding the all-India character of some parties would of course apply in some measure to Congress itself.

Most political parties have modelled themselves on Congress in structure, but useful distinctions could be made between them in terms of the manner of their internal working and the character of their internal mechanisms for arriving at decisions and policies. At one end might be placed the rather genuine constitutional democracy of the PSP; the party has its influential leaders but their differences have helped to ensure a relatively large role for the rank-and-file members. At the other extreme are parties whose membership is extremely vague and whose constitution is either non-existent or a dead letter, leaving the way open for authoritarian dictates from the leading personality or personalities at the top. This is partly a matter of size and most of the clear examples would be found among small parties: the Jharkhand Party, mainly of tribals in Bihar, was created and sustained by the colourful Jaipal Singh in whom it had its being; Ram Rajya Parishad (RRP), an orthodox Hindu party of the fifties, might be another case, though without a single widely known leader. Size apart, what a party stands for has some influence on its internal working. We may bow towards Michels' iron law of oligarchy but still see that some can be more so than others. Parties whose creeds are conservative and traditional will contain men most respectful of authority and they will accept and prefer strong rather than account-able leadership. The RRP, besides being small, was this kind of party.

Even the substantial Jan Sangh seems to be somewhat thus inclined. In terms of this distinction, the communists are of course *sui generis,* seeking to combine a membership of none but active militants of an anti-traditionalist disposition with an exceptionally tight discipline. The communists have in fact not found this easy and their discipline has been very poor by international communist standards. This stems from a combination of regional and doctrinal tensions and has nothing to do with the constitutional changes introduced in 1948, when, in order to emphasize a switch of emphasis to the parliamentary front, the CPI insisted that 'cells' become 'branches', and replaced the familiar Politburo (of 9) and Central Committee (of 39) by a Central Executive Committee (of 21) and a National Council (of 100).

Traditionalism, an element in the formation of authoritarian style parties, can be made the basis of a further distinction; reference is often made to the two types of modernist and traditionalist parties. There are no doubt some fairly clear examples of both—the communists and the RRP might serve as the two opposites—but there are far more cases in which substantial elements of both are combined. Swatantra, for instance, has a strong and clear modernist aspect: it expresses boldly a conservative policy of defence of the private sector in industry and the rural establishment in agriculture against 'socialistic' measures of state ownership and controls and radical land reforms, and no figure in Indian public life could be more unambiguously modernist than its secretary Minoo Masani. On the other hand, the party's founder and leader, C. Rajagopalachariar, is an ingenious and perfect combination of both worlds, and a great deal of Swatantra publicity is couched in traditional terms—from prayers and the blowing of conch shells at meetings to a heavy stress on the idea of *dharma* (approximately, a 'natural law' concept of duty, individual and public, with religious sanction). Sometimes the lines have got prettily crossed: reportedly it was beef-eating Parsi Masani who had to persuade vegetarian Brahmin Rajaji that, modernist or not, Swatantra if it wanted votes would in some constituencies at least have to campaign energetically against cow slaughter! The truth is that modernism and traditionalism are the twin interacting features of Indian political movements, the proportions of the mixture usually varying with the level of the organization. Traditionalism in style and even 'content' will tend to be strong at the base; the top leaders will tend to be modernist, if not by background and training then by political experience itself.

In practice, modernist-traditionalist is close to another distinction, that between 'communal' and 'ideological' parties, and on this latter, too, there are difficulties in avoiding the domination of hybrids. If 'communal' is taken in its narrower sense of political concern with the claims of a distinct religious community, there will be a few parties which clearly declare themselves communal: the remains of the Muslim League, surviving only in South India and strong only in Kerala on the basis of the Malabar Moplah community; the Akali party of the Sikhs, operating only within Punjab; the Hindu Mahasabha, in principle all-India but mainly prominent in Madhya Pradesh and neighbouring areas. Of these, the last may perhaps be regarded as less than wholly communal; the Mahasabha has made a slight attempt to broaden its appeal to rather more than a defence of the rights of the majority community against excessive secular impartiality, and it has produced programmes on general questions of social and economic policy. The position of the Jan Sangh is delicately intermediate. The views and motivations of many of its adherents would be difficult to distinguish from those of the Mahasabha, but its being a newer party, less burdened by memories of the past and more geared to an electoral struggle, has helped to make its adumbration of policy and programme rather more than a top dressing for a communal base. At the same time, so long as the fanatically inclined RSS, combining Hindu cultural zeal with militant training, works assiduously in the shadows of the Jan Sangh, providing it with its best workers and proving a school for its leaders, communalism remains one important aspect of that party. If communal is, on the other hand, taken in the broader sense of relation to any socio-religious community even within the Hindu fold, then this is a brush with which all parties are at some level and in some measure tarred, Congress itself not least of all. (Congress in Kerala has been so linked with the Christian community there that it has been called communal even in the narrow sense.) Even the communists, as already noted, have cultivated the communal field to some purpose in a few areas. Perhaps the PSP would of all parties be the most willing to undergo examination to prove absence of traces of communalism. The Republican Party (formerly Scheduled Castes Federation) is perhaps the only expressly caste political party. It may be added here that linguistic community became for a while and in some regions a dramatically successful basis for the organization of *ad hoc* political groups such as Mahagujarat Janata Parishad and Samyukta Maharashtra Samiti, whose campaigns presided over the formation of Gujarat and Maharashtra out of Bombay state.

In describing Congress as occupying a centre position, reference was made to the hallowed categories of 'right' and 'left'. And certainly it is in these terms that much of the urban discussion of

Indian politics takes place. Already before independence, 'right' and 'left' were popular as descriptions of wings of the national movement, but although the reception of Western ideas was indeed profound on the part of some of the leaders, the terms had nevertheless a local (or at least a 'colonial') significance; leftists were distinguished at least as much by the impatience of their nationalism and their willingness to use extra-constitutional means as by their socialism. Today, too, the terms stand in need of special Indian interpretation, though now the greater awkwardness attaches to 'right'. Both 'right' and 'left' in fact contain sub-divisions which might be argued to be more important than the general label.

The left of course sub-divides into communist and non-communist. That this should be true in India may seem to indicate mismanagement on the part of the CPI. Certainly some of its past policies— logical though they were in terms of its doctrines—have made the establishment of a united front under their influence very difficult. Even if some of the bitter and sectarian attacks on the Congress during the inter-war period could now be forgotten, the approval of the war as a 'People's War' (and consequent opposition to the climactic Quit India movement in 1942) and the sympathy shown to the Muslim League's Pakistan demand as a legitimate aspiration of the Muslim people were still near enough to make barriers, even before the party's initial hesitation and eventual split on the Chinese issue placed it at further disadvantage. But even if the CPI had been spared these compulsions of international loyalty and marxist doctrine, united fronts would have met two substantial obstacles: the presence of a sufficient few among the socialist leaders who were adequately versed in the history of communist handling of other left parties and familiar enough with marxism not to be intellectually put off course; second, the existence of a separate, Gandhian inspiration for social radicalism. Marxist thinking among socialist leaders in fact decreased after independence and this served not only to keep socialist and communist apart but also to bring together the socialists with Kripalani's Gandhian KMP after the 1951–2 elections.

The Praja Socialist Party formed by the merger did not flourish as much as expected. The distance between its Gandhians and the rest was not easily bridged. There was almost an *embarras de richesses* so far as leaders were concerned; they did not make a team while in the party, yet their subsequent withdrawals made for further weakness: J. P. Narayan moved into the Bhoodan movement from 1952; Lohia, after fighting from within for some years, formed his own Socialist Party of India in 1956; Kripalani preferred increasingly to make complete and explicit his ever-independent role; Asoka Mehta in 1963 became Deputy Chairman of the Planning Commission (and later gave up opposition by joining Congress with some followers). The PSP thus divided itself in three directions during 1963–4: apart from those who went with Mehta, there was a sizable proportion which reunited with Lohia to form the Samyukta Socialist Party (SSP) and others who remained to keep the PSP alive. The Mehta line that the 'compulsions of a backward economy' entailed a modification of the opposition role displayed high conscientious responsibility, but it failed either to bring in the vote or to offer a rousing battle-cry for the faithful. (Nor was it always observed by regional branches of the party; in UP and other states, PSP groups broke loose into noisy agitations on linguistic and other similar issues.) Congress's own proclamation of the aim of establishing a 'socialistic pattern of society' dulled the image of the socialists further. More fundamentally, it could perhaps be said that while the 'haves' of Indian society were not prepared, for all their love of socialist talk, to go further than Congress would take them, the 'have-nots' were not ready for an independent political role. The socialists' failure at least up to 1967 to unlock the political energies of the poorer peasantry and landless labourers (still closed in village worlds) and of the industrial workers (still unorganized and essentially rural or, if organized, contained within Congress or communist control) does not mean that the socialist parties are finished, only that they have had to play a waiting game. This may have made political life less lively than it might have been but it has helped the political system as a whole to take shape and it has spared economic development some awkward pressures.

The sub-divisions of the 'right' are no less profound, though they are less clearly reflected in party terms. 'Right' in India can mean what it means in the West, but it can also mean communal. These two senses are combined in different proportions among the rightist groups. In contrast with the situation on the left, there is, one supposes, no logical difficulty about being 'right' in both senses, but the two have in fact by no means merged completely. There is also the third sense of 'right' as traditionalist which can be distinct from both communal and modern 'right'—'Tory' rather than 'conservative' perhaps. Thus we could say that the Mahasabha is primarily communal right with strong traditional and slight modern elements, RRP was primarily traditional with some communal element, Jan Sangh is a blend of the three in equal proportions, and Swatantra is primarily modern conservative with elements of the others mainly in localities where it has linked up with previously existing groups. The more specialized communal parties (such as Akali) and regional parties (such as DMK) may or may not be 'right' in the traditional or modern senses. The DMK tends to be anti-traditional (because the dominant South Indian traditions are Brahmin-tainted—but they work hard, especially through films, to revive non-Brahmin Tamil lore), while the colour of its social and economic policies has been a subject of dispute between its leaders, with at least one wing favouring radicalism as being most likely to appeal to its under-privileged sections. The Akali Sikhs, on the other hand, tend to be more traditionalist and conservative. Enough has been said to make it plain that unity of the right is hardly easier to achieve than unity of the left. Of the rightist parties, Swatantra is certainly the most flexible and the most realistically power-oriented, and it is noteworthy that it did in 1962 achieve some success in joining up (in varying degrees extending from electoral arrangements not to compete to fuller integration) with the Akalis in the Punjab, Ganatantra Parishad (a party of mixed princely and popular character) in Orissa, and the Krishak Lok Party (a Kamma caste, Congress breakaway of 1951 created by Ranga, who later became a Swatantra leader).

The tables on pages 184–93 show the electoral achievements of all these parties in the four general elections

NOTES ON THE ELECTORAL TABLES

1. Abbreviations: CPI=Communist Party of India; PSP=Praja Socialist Party, formed after 1952 by merger of the Socialist Party (formerly Congress Socialist Party) and Kisan Mazdoor Party; SP=Socialist Party, a new Lohia-led breakaway from the PSP; JS=Jan Sangh; HM=Hindu Mahasabha; RPI= Republican Party of India, before 1960 the Scheduled Castes Federation; RRP= Ram Rajya Parishad; DMK=Dravida Munnetra Kazhagam; GP=Ganatantra Parishad; ML=Muslim League; PWP=Peasants and Workers Party; PDF= Peoples Democratic Front; DNC=Democratic National Conference; APHLC= All-Parties Hill Leaders Conference.

2. All figures have been taken from the official *Reports of the Election Commission*. Other sources (such as *Asian Recorder* and the year-books) give slightly different distributions of seats and votes between parties; this can happen because candidates' labels can be differently interpreted (see the very important case of Note 6 below) and because some sources (not the official *Reports*) classify candidates under the labels adopted *after* election. Votes per candidate for Congress are slightly underestimated since they take into account uncontested winners.

3. State Assembly elections (Tables II and IV) are normally held at the same time as Lok Sabha elections, but circumstances have sometimes prevented this. The Andhra elections of 1955 have been included in the 1957 figures, the Kerala elections of 1960 and Orissa elections of 1961 have been included in the 1962 figures.

4. The seats and votes percentages of the one-state parties have been calculated on two different bases; in the Lok Sabha election (Table III) their performance has been shown in proportion to the all-India totals to bring out their relative insignificance on the full scene; in the State Assembly elections (Table IV) their performance is given as a percentage of the totals of seats and votes in the state in which they fought, thus showing their sometimes large place in their chosen areas. In this Table, the figures in brackets in the 'Seats gained' and 'Votes polled' columns are the totals for the particular state (not constant over the period owing to states reorganization) and the percentage columns express this relation. The Forward Bloc (or, more accurately, the several local Forward Blocs) contested in several states in 1952 but the bracketed figures in this case are the West Bengal totals, for it was only there that the vote impact was significant. Sometimes, and especially in the case of the 1952 election before states reorganization, the figures still conceal a party's regional importance. Thus the Muslim League appears weak in Madras in 1952, but it was not unimportant in the areas it contested which were later to become Kerala. Again, the PWP appears not very important in Bombay in 1952 but it had significant strength in the Maharashtra areas to which its appeal and efforts were limited.

5. The distinction between 'all-India' and 'one-state' parties is of course far from tidy, for there are several 'some-states' parties. Of the parties usually thought of as all-India, both Swatantra and the HM left some areas uncontested. The RPI and RRP might have all-India claims but they too failed to contest in more than a few states after 1952. Parties like the PWP and the KLP have operated within a single area but the area has itself fallen into different states at the three dates as a result of changing state boundaries. (It is this which makes extremely difficult any comparisons for individual states over the period.) Certain parties have been wholly excluded: KLP (Kriskak Lok Party), a congress breakaway which fought in Andhra areas with some success but which has since 1960 disappeared into Swatantra; the two parties of Kashmir State, National Conference (until 1967) and Praja Parishad, the former approximately equivalent to Congress and providing the government and the latter, a Hindu-minority group, favouring speedy integration with India; the Praja Party in Bihar; the Revolutionary Socialist Party and other very small 'leftist' groups, mainly of Kerala or Bengal.

6. The official statistics underestimate the Communist vote in 1952 (Tables I and II) because the party's candidates contested as independents in Travancore–Cochin and as People's Democratic Front in Hyderabad. *Asian Recorder* gives 5,299,095 as the total CPI vote for Lok Sabha, 23 as the number of seats gained.

7. The SCF Lok Sabha vote of 1957 (Table I) is given by *Asian Recorder* as 2,430,324 and the number of seats gained as 7. This would imply that some 'independents' were in fact SCF men. Again, the same source gives the SCF (RPI) vote in the 1962 Lok Sabha elections as only 1,059,886.

8. The 18 Swatantra seats in the Lok Sabha in 1962 (Table I) were those gained by the party under its name at the elections. Subsequently (see Note 2 above) their strength in the House was increased to 28 by the merger with Ganatantra Parishad and the accession of independents.

9. Blank rows have been left for parties which temporarily did not contest even though they existed.

TABLE I
ALL-INDIA PARTIES—LOK SABHA

Parties	Candi-dates	Seats gained	% Seats	Votes polled	% Votes	Votes per Candi-date
1952						
Congress	472	364	74·4	47,665,875	45·0	100,987
CPI	49	16	3·3	3,484,401	3·3	71,110
SP	256	12	2·5	11,216,779	10·6	43,816
KMP	145	9	1·8	6,156,558	5·8	42,459
JS	93	3	0·6	3,246,288	3·1	34,906
HM	31	4	0·8	1,003,034	0·95	32,356
RPI	27	2	0·4	2,501,964	2·36	92,665
RRP	55	3	0·6	2,151,603	2·03	39,120
Other Parties	215	35	7·2	11,739,244	11·1	54,601
Independents	521	41	8·4	16,778,749	15·8	32,205
Total		489		105,944,495		
1957						
Congress	490	371	75·1	57,579,593	47·78	117,509
CPI	108	27	5·4	10,754,075	8·92	99,575
PSP	189	19	3·8	12,542,666	10·41	66,363
JS	130	4	0·8	7,149,824	5·93	54,999
HM	19	1	0·2	1,032,322	0·86	54,333
RPI	19	4	0·8	1,812,919	1·5	95,417
RRP	15	—		460,838	0·38	30,723
Other Parties	73	29	5·9	5,804,873	4·81	79,519
Independents	475	39	7·9	23,377,805	19·39	49,216
Total		494		120,513,915		

Table I (cont.)

Parties	Candidates	Seats gained	% Seats	Votes polled	% Votes	Votes per Candidate
1962						
Congress	488	361	73·1	51,809,080	44·72	105,556
Swatantra	173	18	3·6	9,085,252	7·89	51,938
CPI	137	29	5·9	11,450,037	9·94	83,577
PSP	168	12	2·4	7,848,345	6·81	46,716
SP	107	6	1·2	3,099,397	2·69	28,032
JS	196	14	2·8	7,415,170	6·44	37,832
HM	38	1	0·2	747,861	0·65	19,681
RPI	68	3	0·6	3,255,985	2·83	47,882
RRP	41	2	0·4	688,990	0·60	16,805
Other Parties	89	28	5·7	7,318,956	6·35	82,235
Independents	480	20	4·0	12,749,813	11·08	26,562
Total		494		115,168,890		
1967						
Congress	516	284	54·9	59,402,754	40·7	115,135
Swatantra	179	44	8·5	12,659,540	8·7	70,825
CPI	110	23	4·4	7,564,180	5·2	68,765
CPI(M)	58	19	3·7	6,140,738	4·2	105,415
(CP Total	168	42	8·1	13,704,918	9·4	87,086)
PSP	109	13	2·5	4,456,487	3·1	40,885
SSP	122	23	4·4	7,171,627	4·9	58,784
JS	251	35	6·7	13,715,931	9·4	54,645
HM						
RPI	70	1	0·2	3,607,711	2·5	51,539
RRP						
Other Parties	89	43	8·3	11,096,342	7·2	124,678
Independents	865	35	6·7	20,051,200	13·8	23,181
Total		520		145,866,510		

TABLE II
ALL-INDIA PARTIES—STATE ASSEMBLIES

Parties	Candi-dates	Seats gained	% Seats	Votes polled	% Votes	Votes per Candi-date
1952						
Congress	3,153	2,246	68·4	43,802,546	42·2	13,892
CPI	465	106	3·2	4,552,537	4·38	9,790
SP	1,799	125	3·8	10,071,211	9·7	5,598
KMP	1,005	77	2·3	5,306,219	5·11	5,280
JS	717	35	1·1	2,866,566	2·76	3,998
HM	194	14	0·4	848,415	0·82	4,373
RPI	171	3	0·1	1,751,294	1·68	10,241
RRP	314	31	0·9	1,260,049	1·21	4,013
Other Parties Independents	7,492	635	19·3	10,776,136 22,566,226	10·4 21·74	4,405
Total		3,283		103,801,199		
1957						
Congress	3,027	2,012	64·9	54,794,454	44·97	18,102
CPI	812	176	5·7	11,407,192	9·36	14,048
PSP	1,154	208	6·7	11,881,094	9·75	10,296
JS	584	46	1·5	4,380,638	3·60	7,501
HM	87	6	0·2	614,754	0·5	7,066
RPI	99	21	0·7	1,603,578	1·31	16,198
RRP	146	22	0·7	842,956	0·69	5,774
Other Parties Independents	4,863	611	19·7	36,317,487	29·81	7,468
Total		3,102		121,842,153		

Table II (cont.)

Parties	Candi-dates	Seats gained	% Seats	Votes polled	% Votes	Votes per Candi-date
1962						
Congress	3,059	1,904	61·3	50,624,462	43·65	16,552
Swatantra	1,038	166	5·3	7,788,335	6·54	7,433
CPI	866	186	6·0	12,418,294	10·7	14,339
PSP	1,094	179	5·8	8,832,712	7·62	8,073
SP	607	59	1·6	2,848,804	2·45	4,693
JS	1,143	116	3·7	6,376,170	5·41	5,578
HM	176	8	0·3	543,883	0·46	3,038
RPI	301	11	0·4	1,658,959	1·43	5,511
RRP	166	13	0·4	427,057	0·36	2,572
Other Parties	723	210	6·8	8,744,667	7·54	1,209
Independents	4,146	256	8·2	15,717,665	13·55	3,791
Total		3,108		115,971,958		
1967						
Congress	3,446	1,693	48·5	57,252,357	39·96	16,643
Swatantra	978	257	7·4	9,519,231	6·65	9,805
CPI	625	121	3·5	5,906,109	4·13	9,449
CPI(M)	511	128	3·7	6,579,652	4·60	12,896
(CP Total	1,136	249	7·2	12,485,761	8·73	11,173)
PSP	768	106	3·04	4,868,720	3·40	6,338
SSP	813	180	5·2	7,424,633	5·19	9,132
JS	1,607	268	7·7	12,567,918	8·78	7,821
HM						
RPI	378	23	0·7	2,188,973	1·53	5,791
RRP						
Other Parties	826	333	9·5	12,785,140	8·94	15,465
Independents	5,554	376	10·8	24,163,591	16·97	4,351
Total		3,487		143,256,509		

TABLE III
ONE-STATE PARTIES—LOK SABHA

Parties	Candi-dates	Seats gained	% Seats	Votes polled	% Votes	Votes per Candi-date
1952						
Akali Dal						
(Punjab)	8	2	0·4	569,973	0·53	71,247
GP						
(Orissa)	12	4	0·8	959,749	0·91	79,979
ML						
(Madras)	1	1	0·2	79,470	0·08	79,470
Jharkhand						
(Bihar)	6	2	0·4	601,865	0·57	100,311
Forward Bloc						
(W. Bengal)	8	—	—	425,971	0·40	53,246
PWP						
(Bombay)	12	—	—	899,489	0·85	74,957
Janta						
(Bihar)	6	1	0·2	236,094	0·22	39,349
PDF						
(Hyderabad)	12	7	1·4	1,367,404	1·29	113,950
1957						
Akali Dal						
(Punjab)						
GP						
(Orissa)	15	7	1·4	1,291,141	1·07	86,076
ML						
(Kerala)						
Jharkhand						
(Bihar)	12	5	1·0	751,830	0·62	62,653
Forward Bloc						
(W. Bengal)	5	2	0·4	665,341	0·55	133,068
PWP						
(Bombay)	6	4	0·8	868,344	0·72	144,724
Janta						
(Bihar)	11	3	0·6	501,269	0·42	45,570
PDF						
(Andhra)	8	2	0·4	1,044,032	0·87	130,504

Table III (cont.)

Parties	Candi-dates	Seats gained	% Seats	Votes polled	% Votes	Votes per Candi-date
1962						
DMK (Madras)	18	7	1·4	2,315,610	2·01	128,645
Akali Dal (Punjab)	7	3	0·6	829,129	0·72	118,447
GP (Orissa)	10	4	0·8	342,970	0·30	34,297
Muslim League (Kerala)	3	2	0·4	248,038	0·22	82,676
Jharkhand (Bihar)	11	3	0·6	467,338	0·41	42,485
Forward Bloc (W. Bengal)	6	1	0·2	615,395	0·53	102,566
PWP (Maharashtra)	10	0	0	703,582	0·61	70,358
APHLC (Assam)	1	1	0·2	91,850	0·08	91,850

Table III (cont.)/...

Table III (cont.)

Parties	Candi-dates	Seats gained	% Seats	Votes polled	% Votes	Votes per Candi-date
1967						
DMK (Madras)	25	25	4·81	5,524,514	3·79	220,980
Akali-Dal-Sant Fateh Singh Group (Punjab)	8	3	0·58	968,712	0·66	121,089
Akali-Dal-Master Tara Singh Group (Punjab)	7	0	0	189,290	0·13	27,041
Muslim League (Kerala)	2	2	0·38	413,868	0·28	206,934
Forward Bloc (W. Bengal)	6	2	0·38	627,910	0·43	104,651
PWP (Maharashtra)	11	2	0·38	1,028,755	0·71	93,523
APHLC (Assam)	1	1	0·19	112,492	0·08	112,492
Kerala Congress (Kerala)	5	0	0	321,219	0·22	64,244
Bangla Congress (W. Bengal)	7	5	0·96	1,204,356	0·83	172,051
Jana Kranti Dal (Bihar)	5	1	0·19	183,211	0·12	36,642
Jana Congress (MP)	3	0	0	136,631	0·09	45,543
Jammu and Kashmir National Conference (Jammu and Kashmir)	4	1	0·19	210,020	0·14	52,505
DNC (Jammu and Kashmir)	1	0	0	30,788	0·02	30,788
		(520)		145,866,510		

TABLE IV
ONE-STATE PARTIES—STATE ASSEMBLY

Parties	Candi-dates	Seats gained	% Seats	Votes polled	% Votes	Votes per Candi-date
1952						
Akali Dal (Punjab)	88	33 (126)	17·7	922,268 (6,333,058)	14·6	10,480
GP (Orissa)	38	31 (140)	22·1	741,887 (3,677,046)	20·2	19,523
ML (Madras)	13	5 (375)	1·3	186,546 (19,997,256)	1·0	14,350
Jharkhand (Bihar)	53	33 (330)	10·0	765,272 (9,548,840)	8·0	14,439
Forward Bloc (W. Bengal)	77	10 (283)	4·2	506,274 (7,444,225)	6·8	6,575
PWP (Bombay)	87	14 (315)	4·4	717,963 (11,123,242)	6·5	8,252
APHLC (Assam)	8	1 (105)	0·93	39,885 (2,448,890)	1·63	4,982
Janta (Bihar)	38	11 (330)	3·3	301,691 (9,548,840)	3·2	7,939
PDF (Hyderabad)	78	42 (175)	24·0	1,096,112 (5,178,593)	21·2	14,053

Table IV (cont.)/...

Table IV (cont.)

Parties	Candi- dates	Seats gained	% Seats	Votes polled	% Votes	Votes per Candi- date
1957						
Akali Dal (Punjab)						
GP (Orissa)	109	51 (140)	36·4	1,221,794 (4,255,915)	28·7	11,209
ML (Kerala)						
Jharkhand (Bihar)	70	31 (318)	9·7	726,983 (10,585,421)	6·9	10,386
Forward Bloc (W. Bengal)	26	8 (252)	3·2	425,318 (10,469,803)	4·1	16,358
PWP (Bombay)	60	33 (396)	8·3	1,186,169 (16,712,160)	7·1	19,770
APHLC (Assam)						
Janta (Bihar)	122	22 (318)	6·9	831,273 (10,585,421)	7·9	6,814
PDF (Andhra)	63	23 (105)	21·9	914,335 (3,603,585)	25·4	14,513
1962						
DMK (Madras)	143	50 (206)	24·3	3,435,633 (12,676,346)	27·1	24,025
Akali Dal (Punjab)	46	19 (154)	12·3	799,925 (6,739,223)	11·9	17,389
GP (Orissa)	121	37 (140)	26·4	655,099 (2,932,285)	22·3	5,414
ML (Kerala)	12	11 (126)	8·7	401,925 (8,104,077)	5·0	33,494
Jharkhand (Bihar)	75	20 (318)	6·3	432,644 (9,851,165)	4·4	5,769
Forward Bloc (W. Bengal)	35	13 (252)	5·2	441,098 (9,563,391)	4·6	12,603
PWP (Maharashtra)	79	15 (264)	5·7	818,801 (10,966,279)	7·5	10,366
APHLC (Assam)	15	11 (105)	10·5	134,591 (2,444,161)	5·5	8,974

Table IV (cont.)

Parties	Candidates	Seats gained	% Seats	Votes polled	% Votes	Votes per Candidate
1967						
DMK	174	138	58·9	6,242,695	40·8	3,699
(Madras)		(234)		(15,310,702)		
Akali-Dal-Sant						
Fateh Singh Group	58	24	23·1	870,663	20·6	15,012
(Punjab)		(104)		(4,257,113)		
Akali-Dal-Master Tara						
Singh Group	62	2	1·9	179,825	4·2	2,900
(Punjab)		(104)		(4,257,113)		
Muslim League	16	14	10·5	424,159	6·7	30,297
(Kerala)		(133)		(6,280,924)		
Forward Bloc	42	13	4·6	561,148	4·4	13,361
(W. Bengal)		(280)		(12,663,030)		
PWP	59	19	7·1	1,068,491	8·0	1,805
(Maharastra)		(269)		(13,371,735)		
APHLC	10	7	5·9	108,447	3·5	10,845
(Assam)		(120)		(3,105,481)		
Kerala Congress	62	5	3·8	475,172	7·6	7,664
(Kerala)		(133)		(6,280,924)		
Bangla Congress	80	34	12·1	1,286,028	10·2	16,075
(W. Bengal)		(280)		(12,663,030)		
Jana Kranti Dal	60	13	4·1	451,412	3·3	7,524
(Bihar)		(318)		(13,526,103)		
Jana Congress	33	2	0·6	138,982	1·5	4,212
(MP)		(296)		(9,115,360)		
Jammu and Kashmir						
National Conference	39	8	15·1	137,384	17·2	3,523
(Jammu and Kashmir)		(53)		(799,572)		
DNC	19	0	0	25,926	3·3	1,365
(Jammu and Kashmir)		(53)		(799,572)		
Jana Congress	47	26	18·6	542,734	13·5	11,547
(Orissa)		(140)		(4,028,258)		

G

The temptation, when confronted with tables, is to discern trends. Here the greatest caution is advisable. Even in Western elections, totals conceal unrepresentative, individual, 'accidental' events and influences; if trends can still have meaning, it is because on the whole the political language of the voter is the same as the leaders of the parties. But in India, as already suggested in Chapter 2, this is not the case, and what is concealed in the totals is not the merely eccentric but rather part of a different scheme of things. This can be expressed by saying that not for nothing is the term 'intermediary' crucial to an understanding of the Indian electoral process. Normally, candidates simply cannot speak to the electorate—not merely for physical reasons (state assembly constituencies have populations averaging about 150,000, Lok Sabha constituencies up to a million, and communications of all kinds may be poor) but because the electorate as a whole does not yet grasp their political language. (A local 'big man' is admittedly in a different position; he will not attempt to talk what we should call politics). This will be true even of urban constituencies though there the proportion of the 'inaccessible' may be smaller. Candidates will therefore rely on intermediaries and it is not too much to say that electoral success depends on getting the right intermediaries—men who themselves have a direct 'following' or 'clientele' and/or who can locate and persuade the leaders of sub-groups to hand over their vote-bundles. (Persuasion need not involve money but seems often to do so.) But there are still complexities and uncertainties which can defeat the best intermediaries and which keep the electoral process surprisingly 'open' and unpredictable. For one thing, 'leadership' in village India is not always unambiguous: the man who might be followed in his attitude towards new methods of agriculture may not be followed in electoral advice. Situations change over time, too, and last year's leader may be discredited today. Moreover, cross-currents can be bewilderingly numerous; caste leadership is not identical with village leadership and caste itself can be factionalized. Slips will therefore occur. Intermediaries may fail to live up to expectations, through inability or disloyalty. Success with one group may have astonishingly disastrous effects in pushing others into the hands of the opponents—just because of some local antagonism not sufficiently taken into account.

This said, however, certain tentative conclusions can be drawn from the figures. After all, purely local 'accidents' would tend to cancel each other out. In so far as they do not cancel out, there is something else at work: perhaps the intermediaries have scented a change in the air coming from above, or they may be responding themselves to even more subtly varying moods below them.

Moreover, as the political culture gap closes, it makes with each election more sense to attend to trends. This is certainly not to say that an all-India polity is more real or that national issues are more widely influential; rather it is to say that within each state or region there is somewhat less scope for purely local or personal waywardness.

Over the first three elections—it is better to take these separately—the position of Congress changed remarkably little. In the Lok Sabha elections its percentage of seats fell in 1962 from the 1957 'high' to below the 1952 figure, but its percentage of votes, while a little lower than in 1957, was still fractionally better than in 1952. The votes per candidate figure show a clear fall from 1957 to 1962 but to a point still above 1952. The poorer showing on seats is probably due to the greater use made in 1962 of anti-Congress 'electoral arrangements' and 'fronts'. In the State Assembly elections, Congress does less well, but so do most of the main parties; they all find more effective competition in these elections from independents and the smaller parties with local or regional pockets of strength. Over the three elections, the Congress position in the Assemblies changes in the same way as for the Lok Sabha, except that the seats position is more steadily eroded.

If Congress was losing a little, who was gaining? The CPI record is not easy to read for the reason given above (p. 183, note 6). Also it must be noted that with each election the CPI put forward more candidates. Now it is true that this policy will usually imply grounds for believing that there is increasing support for the party, but it still makes comparison of vote figures delicate. On the figures in Table I, it would seem that the CPI was three times as successful in votes in 1957 as in 1952. Even the alternative figure for 1952 (five million) would still mean a doubling of this vote. But they had nearly twice as many candidates in 1957. It is in cases like this that the votes per candidate figure is most useful. Here again, however, it has to be borne in mind that parties normally contest where they are strongest, and some parties (certainly CPI) have particular regional strongholds. Also, of course, to contest widely requires some constituency organization and a supply of candidates. Therefore one cannot suppose that if a party contests more widely it will always be able to sustain the votes per candidate figure. It seems fair to say that CPI's 1957 improvement was largely but not wholly a consequence of their wider coverage and their further 1962 gains in votes and seats were less than commensurate with their further extensions of effort (votes per candidate have fallen). Nevertheless, the party's proportion of seats and votes improved, though less rapidly in the second five years than in the first. The same pattern is reflected in the

State Assembly seats. The non-communist left clearly did less well. The Socialists and KMP together polled heavily in 1952 but these votes were gathered in by a very large spread of candidatures. In 1957 the PSP halved the area they contested and of course votes fell, but by much less than half. In 1962 the breakaway Lohia socialists made a significant effort, but the total socialist vote shrank further and so did the percentage. The State Assembly pattern is not dissimilar but the total decline is rather less marked.

The non-left parties' story is also uneven. Taking Lok Sabha and Assemblies together, while the Hindu Mahasabha declined in both effort and performance, the Jan Sangh increased its efforts, steadily improved its proportion of the poll (though not to an extent commensurate with the effort) and achieved a quite good proportionate increase in seats. Swatantra, making its first appearance in 1962, became at once the second largest opposition party. It obtained a better percentage of votes in the Lok Sabha elections than in the Assemblies (the influence of important top leaders perhaps) but the position was reversed for seats (more electoral agreements could be managed for the Assembly elections). It would seem correct to say that over the ten years the total all-India right has gained significantly, while the total all-India left has lost.

The tables do not reveal the large regional fluctuations of fortune which have taken place over the period. For example, Congress, while generally improving its position in 1957, lost heavily in Bombay solely because of the unsatisfied demand for linguistic states in that region; its less impressive 1962 general performance hides a complete restoration of its losses in that region (now Gujarat and Maharashtra). The 1962 figures for Congress also contain really dramatic losses in Madhya Pradesh, and to a smaller extent in Rajasthan and Bihar—largely due to internal dissension in the party and the ability of Jan Sangh and Swatantra to take advantage of this. Similarly, the Swatantra figures contain both substantial impacts in Bihar, Rajasthan and Gujarat and negligible support in some other regions; Jan Sangh recorded impressive gains in MP, Rajasthan and UP.

The smaller parties did not have an easy time over the first three elections. Those which are in principle all-India in scope have had to accept a shrinking of their area of effective effort. Indeed some like the Hindu Mahasabha and RRP can be said to have become negligible by 1962. Those which are by definition or history regional parties survive better, but even these may be faced by takeover bids. Ganatantra Parishad (Orissa) remained strong but nevertheless entered into an election deal and then merged with Swatantra.

Jharkhand moved inside Congress. KLP has been swallowed by
Swatantra. The more resistant small parties are the doctrinaire
groups of the left (Forward Blocs, Revolutionary Socialists, Revolutionary Communists, etc.), the Muslim League in its small Kerala
base and the DMK in Tamilnad. The Akali Dal (Punjab) made a deal
with Congress and went out of operation in 1957. It came back in
1962 and with the campaign for Punjabi Suba it flourished, though
not without internal feuding which eventually led to a split. Independents remained important but already by 1962 included a declining proportion of local 'big men' of genuine independence and a
growing proportion of Congressmen who failed to get the party
nomination but could still get the support of dissidents and those
parts of the party machine under their control.

To examine how far these patterns were varied in the 1967 elections, it is as well to begin with what changed very little; for although
in the fairly short-run effects it was the novel features of 1967 which
were striking, it could be that in the longer run the elements resistant
to change will count for a great deal. Of the latter none is more
impressive than the percentage vote share going to Congress: for the
Lok Sabha the figure which was 45 in 1952 and 1962 and had been
only 47·8 in the peak year of 1957 now dipped by just over four
points to 40·7; for the State Assemblies the figure which had been
42·2, 44·9 and 43·6 in the previous elections came down to just 40·0.
If this was scarcely dramatic, no more so was the performance of
several of the leading challengers to Congress. The communists
were by 1967 very firmly split into two completely separate and
increasingly hostile organizations, CPI and CPI (Marxist). Although
the break had focussed around attitudes to the Sino-Indian war and
the two parties came to be labelled pro-Moscow and pro-Peking
respectively this was less than the whole truth. Their differences,
stemming from conflicting applications of doctrine to the Indian
situation, lay principally in their views of Congress and Indian
nationalism; the CPI could contemplate collaboration with progressive Congressmen, for the CPI(M) they were class enemies.
The split divided the old CPI in fairly equal parts, with the important
difference that the new CPI strength was spread while that of the
CPI(M) was marked in the key communist areas of West Bengal and
Kerala. So far as the 1967 elections were concerned the two parties
fought each other bitterly—understandably so since they were competing for the same support—and this no doubt goes some way
towards explaining why the total communist vote share (divided
equally between the two) actually declined from the 1962 level.
The socialist parties, PSP and SSP, together fared no better; their

combined vote share, like that of the communists, declined in both the Lok Sabha and State Assembly elections. Nor was it that if the left failed it was the right in general which profited from the erosion of Congress. Swatantra, the leading right party in 1962, barely improved its vote share in 1967—and this in spite of taking over the successful Ganatantra Parishad of Orissa.

Wherein, then, lay the change-reflecting and change-producing nature of the 1967 elections? While still having regard to the vote-share columns, there are a few points to note. One is that there was in the whole country just one party which having made steady progress through the first three general elections registered its biggest advance in 1967: the Jan Sangh. Despite considerable efforts it was unable to make great impact outside the Hindi areas of north-ern India, but in the five states concerned it registered important advances, evidently consolidating support previously gained and conquering certain new sections of voters; it managed this, moreover, on the basis not of a wild and heavy investment in contests but of a moderate, carefully planned expansion of candidatures. Another point is that although the total socialist vote did not improve, that part going to the SSP certainly did; it became the major non-communist organization of the left and in these same Hindi areas in particular its combination of assiduous cultivation of the very under-privileged and its violent tone of chauvinistic radicalism enabled it to make gains along with the Jan Sangh and in preference to the communists. But thirdly and still more important is an exploration of what was happening to the two categories labelled 'other parties' and 'independents' on Tables I and II. These in fact conceal two signifi-cant developments. The first is the success of certain specifically state parties. Apart from the fact, already noted, that Swatantra in Orissa was virtually nothing but the Ganatantra Parishad of that state in new guise, there is (see Table IV) the revived prominence (with doubled vote share) in the new, smaller Punjab state of the Akali Dal, albeit in two factions, and above all the storming advance of the DMK in Tamilnad to 40 per cent of the poll there. The second development is concealed in both 'other parties' and 'independents' and consisted of defections from Congress. Some of these produced more or less formal organizations in competition with the parent party. These breakaway bodies were all firmly based in single states and arose out of internal dissension at that level; they therefore manifested and strengthened the tendency towards regionalization of parties already shown by Akali Dal and DMK, and the difficulty experienced since 1969 in trying to bring them together into an all-India organization only illustrates this. The most important rebel bodies were Kerala

Congress (created as early as 1964, largely on Christian community defections), Jammu and Kashmir National Conference (an old and honoured name appropriated by Bakshi to house his supporters when the bulk of the parent organization became Congress), Bangla Congress (resulting from a partly regional split against the domination of Congress boss Atulya Ghosh) and Bharatiya Kranti Dal in UP. There were in addition a substantial number of defections of smaller groups and of individuals. These led to a big revival of the previously waning independents; in 1967 very many, probably most, of the independents were men who failed to get the Congress ticket.

The importance of these dissensions and defections made it reasonable to say that the shock suffered by Congress in 1967 was administered by Congressmen and more on this will be said in a moment. But the other major feature of these elections is to be seen not by looking at the vote shares alone but by taking them in each election along with the seat verdicts. It will be seen that in the case of virtually every party or group other than Congress the ratio of seat-share to vote-share has increased; Congress's experience was the reverse as it saw its 40 per cent of votes yield not the 60–70 per cent of seats it had grown accustomed to but barely 50 per cent (rather more in the Lok Sabha, less in the State Assemblies). What happened was simple—though it was by no means easily attained. Although the number of candidatures (both absolutely and per seat) increased still further in 1967, in many states leaders of opposition parties had in the pre-election period been seeking ways of concerting their challenge to Congress and their efforts were rewarded. The negotiations were hard because the parties were unable to agree on which constituencies they should leave to their rivals. Eventually, however, there emerged a fairly solid united front in Kerala, two partly rival fronts in Bengal grouped around the CPI(M) and the CPI, and a variety of electoral agreements in half a dozen other states. In this move towards a straight fight situation, Congress as the government party could still hold the bulk of its vote share—indeed in terms of its votes Congress seems to do better as the number of contestants is reduced—but it could not retain the seats. This means of course that the agreements really worked and that votes were effectively transferred—that is, that when for instance Swatantra stood down in favour of Jan Sangh its voters performed as planned and voted Jan Sangh. This said rather more for the discipline of voters and/or intermediaries than might have been expected.

If this explains the shock in seat losses suffered by Congress, we still need to ask why on this occasion the concerting of opposition effort succeeded when it had failed in earlier elections. In part it was no doubt that the frustrations of twenty years in non-government wilderness had grown to match and occasionally to outweigh doctrinal antagonisms and personal distrust among the rival non-Congress parties. It was also presumably the case that opposition leaders sensed a new level of popular discontent and disillusion which could be exploited. But perhaps nothing so strongly worked to bring those outside Congress together than the sight of Congress tearing itself apart and lacking for the first time a towering leader who could both rally the party and exert a strong personal appeal to the electorate. In this way are the two causes of the Congress set-back—internal dissensions and opposition agreements—intimately related. To Congress therefore we must now turn.

Politics within Congress

In the earlier editions of this book it was said to be 'evident that for some time to come the movements inside the dominant party will have at least as great an importance as those outside' and this proved true even after the party ceased to dominate in the pre-1967 sense. It will be convenient to discuss first the situation prior to the 1969 split in the party and then enquire how much has changed as a consequence.

It was, of course, the interaction between internal Congress movements and movements of other parties which constituted (and may well continue to constitute in future) the core of Indian political life; tensions and factions within Congress both stimulated and were stimulated by the pressures of outside groups. The latter, awaiting no doubt with hope the eventual break-up of Congress, operated partly by weaning away disillusioned and frustrated elements and partly by giving confidence and encouragement to those of their way of thought who stayed within the ample fold of the Congress. This inter-action was active, genuine and open. One reason for this is the existence, along with great respect for those in authority, of a contrary tradition—more recent but real in politically active circles—of criticism and distrust of government. The dissident Congressman and the opposition spokesman are alike carrying on the noble work of denigration of government for long performed by the nationalist movement. The interaction is effective also because of the trained democratic sensitivity of the Congress politician towards (and increasingly his survival interest in) changes of force and direction in the currents of opinion. This is combined with the party's wise tolerance (or realistic acquiescence) towards fairly open dissent in its ranks short of explicit organization. To these reasons must be added that fluidity in electoral manœuvre referred to above (p. 195) which makes it possible for persons to make some political impact provided only that they can secure a number of the right backers.

The political movements within Congress operate inside the party's own constitutional framework, which must first be outlined. This constitution has itself been much altered since independence and some of the changes are themselves indicative of interesting features of Congress life. The main organs of the party as inherited on independence (see also pp. 35–7, 89–92 above) were (a) President of Congress, (b) the Working Committee, (c) the All-India Congress Committee, (d) the Annual Session of the delegates, (e) the Provincial and District Congress Committees. The body of delegates was historically and structurally the centre-piece: they elected the President who then nominated his own Working Committee; they actually constituted not only the Annual Session but also the PCCs and DCCs; from among them the AICC was chosen, by PCCs selecting one-eighth of their number to form the AICC. The delegates, themselves numbering some 5,000, were in turn chosen by the membership of the party. (It must be added that little is known about the membership and election situation in practice in the years before independence. The difficulties experienced in recent years suggest that when Congress was simply *the* nationalist movement procedures may have been extremely informal.)

Already before independence—indeed, as soon as the leaders were released from prison in 1945—it was realized that amendments were required, and after over two years' hesitation the first batch was produced in 1948. The process has continued and, as criticism concerning the vigour and harmony of the party has grown, so has the prominence of constitutional reform. The proposals and changes can be grouped under several heads. First, and of least importance, there had of course at independence to be a change in the objects of the party. The formula was introduced in 1948: 'The well-being and advancement of the people of India and the establishment by peaceful and legitimate means of a co-operative commonwealth based on equality of opportunity and of political and social rights and aiming at world peace and fellowship.' To the noun 'commonwealth' thus interestingly revived was added in 1957—following the 1955 Avadi Session's notable espousal of 'a socialistic pattern of society'—the additional adjective 'socialist'. Second, there has been much doubt and experimentation with the party's membership. In 1948 a three-tier membership was established: Primary—for which qualifications were minimal: to be over twenty-one and to believe in the objects of the party (even the old four-anna (4*d*) subscription went); Qualified—with a more exacting list of conditions including the wearing of *khadi,* teetotalism and non-communal beliefs; Effective—requiring the performance of given work for the party. Three years later the Qualified and Effective categories were merged into one Active group and the Primary qualifications changed to eighteen years of age and a one-rupee (1*s* 6*d*) subscription. This slight tightening coincided (see below) with an attempt to give primary members more weight, but was abandoned after only a year when the four-anna fee was revived for primaries, while actives were not only kept to the one rupee but had in addition to all their other commitments to collect Rs. 10/- for the party. In 1953, following shocking revelations of bogus membership in some areas, the rule that DCCs were to keep registers of members in their areas was tightened and enrolment, which should be restricted to a person's place of work or residence, was to be examined by specially revived Scrutiny Committees. Evidently some (presumably lesser) leaders had aspired to control blocs of delegates by creating 'rotten' party constituencies; that the danger has not been wholly removed was made clear in a party memorandum prepared several years later which spoke of falsified lists, 'lost' registers and financially engineered enrolment. Membership figures (1964: Primary 4,637,208; Active 65,494) should therefore still be accepted with reserve.

Thirdly, the party has struggled with the problem of creating effective lower units and integrating them in the party's electoral and decision-making structure. The basic local unit formed in 1948 was termed Congress Panchayat and on it was erected a system for the indirect election of the delegates: all members were to vote for the Panchayat but members of the Panchayat had to be qualified members of the party; all Panchayat members together with all Effective members were to vote for the delegates who had to be effectives; elections were to take place every three years and the number of delegates to be chosen was to be determined by the scale of one delegate per 100,000 total inhabitants of the given area. In 1951 this pattern was replaced by an attempt to get a unit to which *all* members belonged: this was called (from 1952) the Mandal Congress Committee (for a population area of about 20,000) and the total party membership organized in these units was to choose from among actives its quota of delegates. This apparently proved too unwieldy or subject to abuse, for in 1958 the process was reversed: the MCC was retained but itself made into an elected body chosen by general assemblies of primary members on the basis of one per 2,000 population. These MCCs were then to elect the DCCs and also the PCCs. By 1964 Panchayat Raj institutions of local government were being instituted in several states and it was very reasonably—though not so consistently in view of the rhetoric about keeping party out of local politics (see below, p. 228)—decided that the party structure should be adjusted to match and fit. Accordingly a new level of Block Congress Committees below the DCCs came into being. Then, in 1964, the Mandal unit having failed to produce the desired results, the main infra-district level unit became the Block Congress Committee, at once a larger unit (population, about 60,000) and one corresponding to a level of considerable PR activity.

Fourthly, the advent of Congress to power in government and the achievement of large majorities of Congressmen in Parliament and State Assemblies prompted consideration of means of integrating these persons with the party organization which had placed them in the legislatures. In 1952, therefore, following the first general elections, it was laid down that MPs who were members of the Executive Committee of the Congress Party in Parliament should be geared in by being made *ex officio* 'associate' members of the AICC and of their appropriate PCC and DCC; ordinary Congress MPs were to be associate members of their own PCC and DCC. Similarly, in the states, members of the Executive Committee of a (State) Congress Legislature Party were to be associate members of the PCC and their own DCC, while ordinary Congress MLAs were to be associate members of their own DCC. In 1958 integration was carried further when the parliamentarians ceased to be associate and became full members of these party organs. It may also be mentioned here that from 1955 provision was made for the inclusion by nomination on the AICC, PCCs and DCCs of a number of party members representative of special interests (e.g. women, communal groups) that might have been insufficiently brought forward through the elective process.

It may be appropriate to stress at this point that the Congress MP, like any other MP, can with difficulty have close direct relations with his constituents. There can be no equivalent of the week-end exodus from Westminster; neither as political educator nor as welfare agent does the MP appear regularly before his constituency. 'Nursing' a constituency is scarcely possible; perhaps the intimacy implied in the phrase requires a common political language for voter and member which is still to be cultivated. But, apart from that, distances and the length of parliamentary sessions make it necessary for him to rely on intermediaries. For the Congress MP these will naturally include men with positions on bodies such as PCC and DCC. Such men will get in the vote through their own village connections; they will also be able to use influence at the time when party candidature lists are being prepared for general elections. Clearly he must keep 'well in' with such people. (Since the lists have to be endorsed at Delhi, he must also have friends at that court—or at least no enemies.) The difference between a Congress MP and one of another party is that the former has a real party organizational network through which to operate; the informal links are still vital but they function within a formal set-up. Among the key inter-mediaries for the MP are of course the State Assembly members of his party whose assembly constituencies are contained in his own larger Lok Sabha constituency and who may well have been instru-mental in his own electoral success. The MLA's own position differs from that of the MP in that his constituency is nearer and smaller and he is not bound to be away at the state capital for so long. Even so, it is not that he will not use similar methods but only that he will be more easily an integral part of the machine in his area. He will be more region-bound than the MP, but even in his case 'constituency party' does not yet exist in the British sense of the term. The democratization of local government (discussed later in this chapter) may change this.

Finally, there have been some changes in the relations between the higher organs of the party. Dangers of some incoherence between the organization levels of the party were met in 1958 by making all Presidents of MCCs *ex officio* members of their DCC and likewise all DCC Presidents *ex officio* members of their PCCs. (These dangers could not arise before 1958 when all delegates were members of these bodies; from 1958, as already noted, these bodies were elected by MCCs, and it became possible for the head of a subordinate com-mittee to fail to be elected as a member of the superior body.) In 1948 formal constitutional recognition was given to party organs concerned with the supervision of the party's work in the legislatures and with the selection of the party's candidates for the general elections: the Parliamentary Board was to consist of the Congress President plus five men appointed by the Working Committee, while the Central Election Committee was to be composed of the Board together with five men chosen by the AICC. (While there are Pradesh Election Committees who prepare lists of candidates for approval by the Central Election Committee, there has been no state-level equivalent of the Board.) In 1960 a modest contribution to a diminution of tension between party organization and parliamen-tary party was made by a provision that party parliamentary and assembly leaders (i.e. Prime Minister and Chief Ministers) should be *ex officio* members of Central and Pradesh Election Committees respectively—a provision which had meaning in states where antagonism between Chief Minister and PCC President had resulted in the by-passing of the former in the preparation of lists of candidates. In some ways most interesting of all was the way the party met a challenging 'democratizing' proposal that the Working Committee, the 'High Command' of the party, should no longer be nominated by the President but elected by the AICC—a change that would have imposed on the party President the necessity of working more closely in conformity with the views of the party as a whole. After much hesitation it was agreed, as an experiment, to have one-third of the Working Committee chosen in this way.

These several changes did not silence critics within the party. The points on which concern continued to be felt—apart from the continuing and seemingly intractable problem of membership irregularities—are two. First, and less generally felt, is the question of whether a purely geographical basis of party organization is sufficient. Some Congress circles have been proposing an element of occupational or functional representation within the party. They do not go so far as to seek a 'corporate' structure (or the kind of 'sector' basis that is found, for instance, in Mexico's dominant party), but they would like to see Labour, the Professions, Peasantry, Industry, etc., represented alongside geographical units. Congress does, of course, already dominate certain section organizations (some trades unions —see below, pp. 221–3), but the suggestion is partly that it could advance its influence by organizing more explicitly its penetration into the occupations and partly that the workaday life of the country should be reflected more obviously in the form of party organization. The dangers (to a free society) as well as the convenience (to the party) of this suggestion should be obvious.

Second, and far more widespread, is concern with the divorce and continuous antagonism between party-as-government and party-as-movement, between the parliamentary or 'ministerial' wing on the one hand and the party organizers and 'constructive workers' (see pp. 88–9) of the party on the other. This problem has already been mentioned as having arisen even before independence (p. 37) and having become prominent subsequently (p. 90). The question has not been of pressing importance at the centre after 1951: Nehru's survival of the party crisis of that year, his combining from then up to 1955 the roles of party President and Prime Minister, a succession from that date of Congress Presidents willing to concentrate on party building leadership and leaving government alone, the considerable overlap of membership between the 'high command' and the government, the greater sense of responsibility among men at the centre, above all the unchallengeable position of Nehru—all these

kept the question in the background, at least until 1966. The position
in the States has been very different. It is not too much to say
that in the majority of states where Congress is faced by no serious
opposition threats, political life has been dominated by this kind of
intra-party conflict. Some observers have gone so far as to say that in
many states there is a two-party system, the Congress Party organization (PCC) constituting the opposition to the Congress Party state
government, offering itself (to the high command and to the state
public) as the alternative government. This is indeed a fair account of
events in such states as UP, Orissa, Mysore. In fact, in UP and
Orissa, this 'opposition', based in the PCC but working to undermine
the loyalty of Congress MLAs to their Chief Ministers, proved completely successful, Sampurnanand being obliged to surrender to
Gupta, Mehtab to Patnaik. In other cases, the pattern of conflict has
been more complex. In Andhra, for instance, it was said that the
line-up in 1960 was Chief Minister with some of his cabinet and the
majority of the Congress Legislature Party, assisted (untypically) by
the President of the PCC with some help from a member of the
central government, opposed by the Finance Minister backed by a
majority of the PCC, a minority of the Congress Legislature Party
and the President of Congress. This recruitment of allies from New
Delhi for state struggles was also reported from Gujarat.

These tussles of factions which have at times dominated the
internal life of Congress have their futile and even ugly aspects. The
disputes seldom seem to be genuinely about policy matters, even
though both sides will generally parade a few arguments for decency's
sake. Personal rivalry appears the central point, accentuated sometimes by community or sub-regional allegiances—as in Mysore
(Lingayat against Vakkaliga, and new against old areas of the state)
and Andhra (Reddy against Kamma and scheduled castes and conflict between the three sub-regions of the state). On the other hand, it
is not the case that these intra-party struggles are always quite
valueless. When strong opposition parties were absent, it was something to have a party opposition. It might manufacture grievances,
but it would also collect and express some genuine ones. This, however, could give little consolation to the party chiefs at the centre,
who saw the image of Congress becoming daily more tarnished: how
could the people see Congressmen as other than office-seekers without
scruple and office-holders without merit? How long could the party
live on its capital? Who could fail to be attracted by Vinoba Bhave's
plea for an end to party politics or by the arguments in favour of
strong presidential rule backed by a nominated ministry of all the
talents?

The Congress leadership did not remain idle in this matter. As early as 1949, a central circular instructed PCCs not to attempt control or interference in the conduct of state Congress government. In particular a firm prohibition was placed on the passing (as Rajasthan's PCC had done) of no-confidence resolutions against their own party's government. On several occasions, warring faction-leaders from the states have been called before the Working Committee and warned to put a stop to their morale-spoiling activities. At other times, emissaries from the high command (usually the General Secretaries, sometimes even ministers) have gone down to the state capitals, not so much to impose a decision in favour of one side but rather to initiate and supervise some procedure (e.g. full debate and vote in the Congress Legislature Party) for a resolution of deadlock. But this kind of intervention from above could have only limited success. That this was so was indeed an indication of some shift in the centre of gravity in the party which began to take place in the second decade after independence, a shift away from the centre leaders to the regional leaders. The party centre can only be most effective when the state struggles are between fairly evenly divided forces; it cannot easily discipline a man who has real backing in the state party machine and it cannot prevent the rise of new and younger leaders who use what means they can to oust the office holders.

The changes in the party constitution designed to break down the 'parliamentary'–'organization' tension by creating some *ex officio* membership of party bodies for parliamentarians signally failed to achieve the desired effect. (One cynical version had it that the effort to associate MPs and MLAs with party organs so that they should interest themselves in the work of the organization side was superfluous: the main work of the organization is the 'fixing' of its own elections, an activity which, because it indirectly influences the selection process for parliamentary candidatures, is already of absorbing interest for the sitting parliamentarians.) Some Congress circles accordingly advised more drastic reforms. One set of proposals simply sought a further substantial increase in the representation on AICC and PCCs of parliamentarians, so as to make it difficult, for example, for a PCC to consitute a separate force. Another idea, first put forward probably in 1959, suggested a systematic ten-year periodic switch of Congress leaders from ministerial to party office. This notion was endorsed by the Congress President himself in 1961 and was so much talked about in some circles that one Chief Minister, who in 1962 was being belaboured by rivals using the weapon of the 'ten-year rule', had to appeal to the Working Committee to declare that no such rule existed. The idea, however, persisted and blossomed strangely in the Kamaraj plan of 1963. The mass resignations (for the purpose of devoting themselves to the party) of six central ministers and six Chief Ministers of states in August of that year enabled Nehru to give Congress government a new face and served as a response to the first successful attempt to get a no-confidence motion against the government moved (not, of course, passed) in the Lok Sabha. It was also the kind of renunciation gesture which might have been expected, first, to restore the public repute of Congress in the face of Bhave–Narayan and general criticism about the sin of love for power, and second, to reassure the organization wing of their own importance and at the same time of their opportunities to reach the seats of power. In the event the plan failed in both respects and the slide towards low party morale and the defections of 1966–7 may be said to have begun.

The place of policy questions in these tensions and struggles inside the party has never been easy to judge because commentators have tried to find them when they did not exist and the participants have sometimes tried to hide them (for example behind constitutional wrangles) when they did. On the whole their importance was small, certainly less than that of loyalties and hostilities based on persons, places and power. This is not to deny that there have been in the party individuals, from Nehru downwards, with pronounced ideological leanings; Krishna Menon and S. K. Patil will serve as the extreme points of fellow-travelling left and right. This, however, is not the stuff of which the bulk of the party has been made; the great majority of Congressmen have been ambiguously spread over a blurred centre zone. This is not to say that there have not been informal organizations of groups among Congress MPs. These have usually been radicals of some kind and have been referred to as 'ginger groups'. But their composition and continuity have been uncertain and their level of organization minimal—though the group calling itself Congress Socialist Forum did get as far as publishing a few pamphlets such as 'Nehru Must Give the Lead' and later even a journal. The passing by the AICC and the Annual Sessions of advanced resolutions cannot be given any clear significance such as denoting a 'left majority' in the party. There is little evidence that either Avadi 1955 (the 'socialistic pattern of society') or Nagpur 1959 (co-operative joint farming, ceilings on holdings, state trading in food grains) was the result of any marked pressure from below. No doubt all who were somewhat left of centre were pleased, but the approval given to the resolutions does not indicate the relative weight of left and right in the membership. (Neither the plenary sessions nor even the AICC meetings have been great places for stirring policy clashes.) It is more than likely that centre and right merely acquiesced in a left lead from above, to some extent out of a suitable humility in face of a respected leader, to some extent on a calculated reflection that the Avadi slogan could harm no one except the PSP while Nagpur would in any case require to be implemented by state governments on whom appropriate pressure to go slow could if necessary be put in discreet manner and in due time.

It is one thing to suggest that matters of ideology and divisions on policy questions are not the prime movers of Congressmen. It is quite another to suggest that they have no importance in the party. To take the latter view would be to imply that Congress politics was unaffected by the campaigns of other parties and the general debate of politics in the country. This is unrealistic, as indeed are most of the extreme cynical views which are often taken of Indian politicians. It is not that there have been at any stage neat and solid left and right blocs within the party. It is rather that since these are for better or worse the seemingly inescapable oversimplified categories of modern political debate in India no less than elsewhere, the politicians themselves are affected in some degree. The currency of the talk in the town coffee shop is not to be lightly dismissed. For one thing, there are to be found the politicians' most immediate customers. For another the expansion of politics means that increasingly the currency of the urban centres becomes the coin of rural argument also. Left-right is not the sole ideological axis line—communal-secular would be another—but it is an essential element in the public language of politics and it is likely that more and more politics will become public. A centre party containing a variety of different opinions is often bound to subdue and muffle these divisions in order to try to preserve its fragile coherence, but when all the other parties are calling out loud in these terms this helps to encourage an imitation in Congress too. It is fairly clear that the appearance of Swatantra as a frankly conservative party in the sixties gave fresh courage and boldness to right-wing Congressmen. Certainly the advance of the left to governmental power in West Bengal and Kerala in 1967 pushed forward the more or less radical 'young turks' of the party. And that push had some role to play in the strains of following years which culminated in the clear split of Congress in November 1969.

Any understanding of the split must distinguish between the actual moves by which it came about and the more general undercurrents of tension which account for it. These latter were several but can be seen as related either to the familiar ministerial-organizational division or to broadly left-right attitudes. Congress emerged from the 1967 elections in a state of low morale and some of its senior leaders

were evidently in a state of severe shock aggravated by the fact that
several of them had suffered crushing personal electoral defeats.
Moreover, the post-mortem examinations which were soon conducted
at various levels in the party took place against a background of
mounting disorder as over several states in northern India governments proved chronically unstable as a result of numerous and
successive defections of MLAs. Prominent in such shifting movements
were the members of the recently established rebel Congress organizations as well as some Congressmen. The central leadership seemed
helpless to restore any semblance of nation-wide discipline. Even
state parties lost control; it seemed that discipline in situations of
dominance had been maintained because the alternative for the
individual had been the wilderness; now the defector could bring
down a government from which he was excluded and step into
ministerial office in its successor. Some younger elements in the
party began to see no prospect for the party's future unless there
were deep changes—a new policy image of radicalism, fresh faces in
the top leadership and a new style of disciplined party organization.
These questions emerged little by little during 1967–9.

The issue of relations between Congress ministers and the party
organization—already since 1966 chiefly in the shape of gossip
about coolness between Mrs Gandhi and Congress President
Kamaraj, a subject of public speculation—was prominent on the
agenda of a Working Committee meeting in April 1967 and the
seriousness of the problem was signalled by the decision to set up a
special liaison committee of four from each 'side'. The same meeting
also discussed whether Congress should be willing in certain states to
enter into coalition governments with other parties; the decision went
against such moves, but it was said that some leaders had argued for
such links especially with the right-wing parties. The Committee
reaffirmed the party's ten-point programme which included such
radical steps as 'social control' of banks, nationalization of insurance,
state take-over of import and export trade, ceilings on urban property
and income, curbs on monopolies, national control of foodgrain
distribution, prompt implementation of land reforms and removal of
the privileges of former princely rulers. All these issues cropped up
repeatedly at subsequent party debates. The AICC in June 1967
witnessed a revolt from the floor which succeeded in amending the
official resolution to abolish not only the general privileges but also
the privy purses of the ex-rulers. There was pressure too to go beyond
'social control' to complete nationalization of the banks and also to
implement an earlier agreed programme of party reconstruction.
Through 1968 the arguments raged on: those who may be termed

radical purists wanted a complete ban on company donations to parties (Congress itself being the chief beneficiary), no deals with other parties and no readmission to the party of those who defected; they were firmly opposed by others who could be called the establishment realists. By 1969 signatures were being collected among Congress MPs for a 'programme for socialist action'—bank nationalization, privy purses and the rest of the ten points—and the 'Forum for Socialist Action' within the party called for a reorganization based on 'cadres', replacement of the old party 'bosses', more rapid promotion for young leaders.

Thus there was considerable internal party ferment in a situation of growing political instability and the leadership, itself not firmly united, was riding uneasily. If to this picture is added the element of personal rivalries at the top and no prospect of any one person emerging readily as an unchallenged leader, it can be seen that not a great deal was required to produce a crisis. The precipitating event was the death in May 1969 of President Zakir Husain. In the pre-1967 party situation the scope for presidential intervention in political decisions was very limited. After 1967 the situation looked different, and if one thought ahead, as all concerned did, to 1972, it became clear that the President could have some vital decisions to take: if no party had a clear majority in the Lok Sabha it would be for the President to 'discover' who could form a government. The rival groups began to make their calculations: those opposed to Indira Gandhi saw the importance of placing one of their allies on the throne; the PM herself saw the need to ensure that this did not happen. The nomination power within the party rested in the Parliamentary Board and here the PM was defeated; having tried and failed to get support for either Giri or Jagjivan Ram, she agreed to sign the papers for Sanjiva Reddy, a member of the group of leaders known since 1966 as 'the syndicate' (including Kamaraj, S. K. Patil, Atulya Ghosh and Nijalingappa, by now Congress President). Reddy was backed on the Board by Morarji Desai. On the day following her defeat the PM suddenly relieved Desai of his post as Finance Minister. Although as Minister he was, with Chavan, one of her opponents on the Board against whom she could retaliate, the PM gave Desai's economic policies as her reason for the move. To underline this, she both invited him to remain Deputy Prime Minister (which he refused to do, resigning at once) and immediately nationalized the banks by ordinance. This step did something to avert a charge of vindictiveness and it also split the syndicate who were united against the PM but not at all agreed ideologically; it also put the PM firmly at the head of the radicals of the party. The somewhat spurious nature of the manœuvre—two of the syndicate favoured nationalization, Desai had reluctantly accepted it and Mrs Gandhi herself had only espoused the cause ten days previously —diminished but did not destroy its effectiveness. But Reddy remained Congress candidate for the Presidency, along with Desh-mukh backed by Jan Sangh and Swatantra, and Giri who entered as an independent but quickly gathered support from the two com-munist parties, SSP, DMK and Muslim League. Chavan, Home Minister, caught between the PM and the syndicate, tried without success to heal the breach; it widened irreparably when the PM not only turned down a request from party president Nijalingappa to call on all Congress legislators to vote for Reddy but actually declared that this should be a free, 'conscience' vote. The rest is quickly told. In August 1969 Giri was elected President on the second ballot, two out of every five Congress MPs having voted against their official candidate; the PM dismissed four junior ministers known to be syndicate supporters and launched a signature campaign to call an AICC meeting to elect a new party president; Nijalingappa responded by easing out two supporters of the PM from the Working Com-mittee so that he would have a clear majority of 11 out of 21 there; the PM's ten then met as a rival committee and called a meeting of the AICC; the Working Committee of 11 declared the requisition illegal and the PM was issued with a 'show cause' notice to explain why disciplinary action should not be taken against her; the PM dismissed the Railways Minister, a syndicate supporter; finally, on 12 November 1969, the Working Committee of 11 expelled Mrs Gandhi from the party. Thenceforward there were two Congress parties, Indira Gandhi being supported by three-quarters of the Congress MPs, rather more than half of the AICC members and most of the Congress chief ministers in the states. As with the two communist parties, each Congress became the other's chief rival and each began to build up its own network and strength against the other. The 84-year-old organization had broken; it remained to be seen which successor—the two were variously labelled Syndicate, Organization or Old Congress and Indicate (this did not quite catch on!), Ruling, Requisitionist, New or Mrs Gandhi's Congress— would be able to pick up the pieces and add new ones.

What did the split do to the party system as a whole? Writing close to the events (in 1970), it is not easy to be certain. It is clear that the trend towards a more competitive 'market' system, previously fairly well 'contained' by the dominant Congress but undermined by the 1967 elections, was further strengthened. Bargaining or coalitional politics with all its inconsistencies and uncertainties had already established itself among the non-Congress, rebel Congress and some state Congress parties during 1967–9; at different times and in different states, right and left parties would combine or oppose each other as advantage dictated. With the Congress split, both successors were now drawn into this politics of manœuvre. Kaleidoscopic changes and strange alliances came to be everyday occurrences. This, however, is only a part of the whole picture.

Alongside the politics of manœuvre, and opposite to it as a tendency, could be seen an enhanced prominence attached to ideological or at least policy stances. Indira Gandhi may, as her enemies insisted, have been concerned with nothing except the preservation and increase of her own power, but there seems little doubt that by her adoption of certain measures and attitudes she highlighted in particular the communal-secular and radical-*status quo* divisions in public opinion. Her opponents alleged that in this she was merely bidding for specific sectional support. She was certainly responding to two important changes which took place about this time. The first was an ugly increase in communal conflict; large-scale killings following Hindu–Muslim tensions took place in Bihar, Gujarat and Maharashtra. Reflecting the growing isolation and despair of Muslims and the renewed aggressiveness of Hindu cultural fanaticism, these outbursts of violence polarized opinion with new sharpness. Whether concerned to recapture the backing of Muslims and moderate Hindus or anxious to reinforce the principles and ideals of secularism and communal harmony, Mrs Gandhi declared her position in clear terms. The second change was that of increased radicalization of politics. Compared with the fairly muffled tones of the previous decades a new sharpness of positions on more or less class lines began to appear. Prompted in part by the coming to power of the communist-led front governments in West Bengal and Kerala, this was at a more fundamental level connected with the social impacts of economic changes. In the towns increased prosperity for some was accompanied as a result of some slowing down of industrial expansion by rising unemployment among the educated youth and growing anxiety regarding price increases. In the rural areas there were important consequences of the much-vaunted 'green revolution'. The impressive increases in agricultural productivity, achieved by the introduction of new high-yielding varieties of grain, accompanied by large inputs of fertilizers and irrigation water, may well have saved India from a choice between mass starvation and dependence on huge food imports, but the programme which brought about this 'miracle' increase had its social cost. The programme relied on concentrating the investment where it would bring the quickest and largest returns; this meant favouring the more advanced areas and within any given area allowing the richer farmers to forge further ahead. The result of these differential impacts was to create fresh tensions between areas and between agricultural classes. In urban and rural areas the soil was thus ready for the sowing of radical seeds.

Here again, there was argument as to whether Mrs Gandhi was by her statements and measures—bank nationalization, for example, was defended as necessary to provide cheap credit facilities for smaller peasants—merely trying to outdo the left in a bid to capture the discontented sections or really putting herself at the head of a movement for genuine reform of social injustice. Such argument often fails to understand politics as the art of the possible; the pure black of machiavellian manipulation is almost as rare as the pure white of obedience to principles, and most politicians are in the grey middle where considerations from both are well mixed. It is worth noting, however, that Indira Gandhi took up positions that were in line with those of her father. It is also to be noted that neither the pursuit of social justice nor the gathering of electoral support could be served by any one simple course. In any event, the mixing of the extremes of power and principle has become more vivid in Indian political life, the paradox of issue-orientation and the power-search going hand in hand has become more prominent.

Several observers hurried to declare that with the 1967 elections and the 1969 split the system of one dominant party had come to an end. In some obvious respects—the formation of non-Congress governments in several states and the replacement of what was formally one Congress party by two—this was true. But it may not have been the whole truth. Not all the characteristics that defined that system have disappeared. The 'centre' party has not dropped out of the system, it has become two. The kind of interacting relation between centre and circumference parties which existed prior to 1967 has not ceased; rather each of the two centre parties to some extent carries this on as before, and so do the non-Congress parties. The one dominant party system has been bifurcated. If the pre-1967 pattern was a 'Paul Jones' dance situation of two concentric circles, an outer circle moving around and periodically joining up with elements from the inner ring, then the post-1967 pattern began to look like a figure of eight with movement between as well as within each of the circles. Although the polarized party system ardently hoped for by many intellectuals did not really emerge, it was true that Mrs Gandhi's Congress became a kind of centre around which the left parties moved, while the Syndicate Congress related itself in a similar way to the right parties. These are not fronts so much as sub-systems.

One of the reasons why the party system does not easily polarize into left and right is the fact that the Congress split did not, despite Mrs Gandhi's rhetoric, fall along neat ideological lines. There were probably only a few radicals on the Syndicate side but there were plenty of non-radicals on the PM's side. Another reason is the pressure of the secular-communal question which partly cuts across the radical-conservative division. But there is a third reason, one which brings out the last feature of the party system to which attention must be drawn. There is a sense in which it is true to say that as Congress declined the non-Congress parties came increasingly to resemble it. As they came to grips with the exercise of power, for example, they experienced the tensions that Congress had known between what became their ministerial and organizational wings. This was true of both Jan Sangh and the Communist parties. They encountered discipline difficulties of kinds which had not come their way in opposition. But above all they encountered the lively federal realities of India. As the various state units of each of the all-India parties found themselves in quite distinct and peculiar situations, the imposition of a common policy from national party HQ became impossible. If the state unit of Swatantra in Gujarat was to survive as a political force, it had to be allowed to go its own way; likewise with the SSP in Bihar or even the CPI in some other state. As Congress had become regionalized, so also even the more tightly organized and doctrinal parties had to bow to the same compulsions of a federal polity. Thus on top of the great complexities inherent in any one coalitional bargaining system is superimposed the further complication of seventeen such systems, each largely distinct, though also interacting with the centre system. Any simple view of Indian politics is bound to be simply wrong.

Parties and the administration

One of the features of a one-dominant-party system was the special kind of relation which came to exist between that party and the administration. Three aspects of this have already been touched upon: the inner party tensions between ministerialists and organizers, the relations of bureaucrats to ministers, and the electorate's tendency to identify party and *Raj,* Congress and the administration. The fact that Congress was everywhere (or almost everywhere) the government did indeed continuously affect the attitudes of several groups. First, Congressmen themselves were bound to find it difficult to avoid being regarded as valuable channels of influence. The

Gandhi cap became the sign of either belonging to 'the establishment' or wanting to be thought important. Have you a son needing a
job or a nephew wanting to start up in business or would you like
that man who is bringing an action against you in respect of a piece
of land to be dissuaded from doing so? A word with prominent
Congressman X, who is a friend of the deputy minister, would help
you. For these reasons many people wanted to join the party. For
every versatile party member became something of a liaison officer of
government. Men of influence became Congressmen and Congressmen became men of influence. In the second place, administrators
were affected: since their ministerial bosses were always Congressmen it became difficult to retain independence, even more difficult to
to appear to the public to be independent.

   Thirdly, the other parties and their members felt themselves to be
placed at a disadvantage. They could not easily associate themselves
with the beneficent works of the welfare agencies of the state—and
the more government undertook, the more serious did this exclusion appear. The Community Development network had special
significance here. Penetrating to every village, it could hardly fail to
convey a message of Government-cum-Congress generosity. This
has been heightened by the role of bodies like Bharat Sevak Sangh
in which many of the Gandhian 'constructive' social workers are
mobilized. Such agencies, created and sponsored officially, yet not
wholly government and not exactly party either, but poised nicely
between the two, serve further to perfect their identification. Nothing
could in a sense be more natural than that Congressmen should
continue their pre-independence work of social welfare, but the plight
of, say, the PSP in its heyday of the fifties must also be seen. For all
the wishes of Asoka Mehta, its leader at that time, to be constructive
and identified with those government measures which he approved, it
was not easy for PSP men to get in on the welfare administration. The
competition between good works of 'Government-Congress' and
mere faith of 'opposition PSP' was necessarily very uneven, and the
thought that the PSP at least escaped blame for all the unpopular
acts of government was insufficiently consoling. (There has in fact
been some evidence to show that when CD was in process of expanding over the face of India, Congress did relatively worse in districts
where CD had been in force. Did this mean that one voted government to attract the boon and then, having got it with some disil-
lusionment, voted against?) There is also the separate point that other
parties have often felt that they were handicapped by being unable to
attract the open support of men who fear to displease government.
Swatantra in particular has complained that business men—who

certainly might be expected to give some support to that party—do not like to give them donations because they have the idea (which is alleged sometimes to have been put to them as a warning) that this might prejudice their obtaining a variety of necessary permits and licences. It is probably true that many such people do nevertheless contribute to Swatantra—while continuing with payments to Congress also.

With the breaking of the Congress monopoly after 1967, many of these difficulties disappeared—but new ones came in their place. The years of frustration out of power incurred a cost when power came; in some states the new masters threw their weight around with desperate energy. With many promises to keep and every likelihood, in the unstable coalition situations, of limited time at their disposal, incoming ministers made their Congress predecessors look almost gentlemanly by comparison in the matter of rewarding friends and starving enemies. While the administration adjusted as best it could, Congressmen in opposition for a change could try to profit from the disenchantment of the public with their chosen leaders. (There is some evidence that in the 1969 'mini-election' in the northern states, the electorate did swing back in disgust.) All this, however, was as nothing compared with the way in which the CPI(M) ministers in West Bengal and Kerala responded to their powers as masters of the administration. Already under criticism from their own leftists for playing the parliamentary game, they were committed to show how 'the revolutionary struggle' could be effectively furthered from the inside. It would seem, at least from the allegations quickly made against them even by their coalition partners, that they wasted no time in using their portfolios to recruit party members and sympathizers into key branches of the administration including the police and to carry out punitive postings to ensure compliance on the part of those who could not easily be removed. To some extent, however, their leftist critics proved right, for there are limits to how far a constitution can be undermined from within: the falls of the CPI(M)-led ministries in both states in 1969–70 owed something to the fears of their allies that if they were not halted the administration would become a tool that only the communists could use.

Non-party movements

Not the whole of any free country's politics is absorbed within political parties. The proportion which escapes party is small when the state is totalitarian (meaning all-pervading), and in developing countries the state does tend to be totalitarian in this sense even when the rulers are wedded to the idea of a free society. The national movement heritage and the large role undertaken by government alone impose this pattern. Further, a richness of associational life usually comes only when a simple society in which there is an all-embracing unit (family, tribe or village) gives way to various forms of specialization (vocational, religious, cultural). India occupies a mid-way position in this matter and contains several varieties of non-party movements. There is a further consideration: outside observers not particularly familiar with India have found it difficult to believe that in a country with such massive problems political life could be contained within an orderly constitutional framework and channelled through regular political organizations. Such was indeed the position until fairly recent times. The sceptics may derive a perverse satisfaction from the admission that over the last few years there has been a change in this respect. Some attention must therefore be given to those movements which reject the norms of the constitutional system and seek ways outside it of making themselves felt.

First mention must be given to the movements which make their non-party character explicit and insistent. These movements are not easily defined for their organization is, perhaps naturally, extremely loose. Generally, however, they may be described as Gandhian in inspiration and labelled Sarvodayan ('service to all'). The Bhoodan movement, already given prominence in Chapter 2, is one important segment of this whole. The Gandhian inspiration expresses itself not only in the devotion to the characteristically Gandhian 'constructive' or social welfare activities but also in a general attitude to life and to politics in particular—about which a little more will be said in the last chapter. Sarvodaya workers must be regarded as engaged in the kind of activity which they consider Gandhi would have undertaken, had he lived long enough into independent India. Political independence is no more than a by-product of the first stage of the development of human beings; the uplift of man is at once spiritual and social, and political activity as practised in parties and parliaments has little to contribute and much to take away from this task.

Nevertheless, it is not easy for Sarvodaya workers to keep aloof from government and politics. Given a social-engineering government, politics and administration are almost omnipresent. A complete indifference to governmental activities such as Community Development (CD) and the introduction of Panchayat Raj (PR) is impossible. To some extent they have to be criticized from a Sarvodaya viewpoint—as being marred by their emanation from organized power instead of being dependent on voluntary co-operation; to some extent they must be entered into and worked through.

The Bharat Sevak Sangh serves this purpose as a quasi-governmental agency through which the efforts of the social workers can be gently geared into those of official bodies. In the same way, complete alienation from Congress is also unthinkable. Good Gandhians will feel that, apart from the sentiment of tradition and the force of habit and in spite of the base and distasteful struggle for power which corrupts so many in the party, Congress still stands for something noble and is therefore the place where, with reservations, they belong. These links with party and with government permit the ideas of these groups—both their standards of service and sacrifice and their policies of political and economic decentralization and voluntary effort—to exert influence on party officials, on MPs and MLAs, on government officials. to a degree that is difficult to assess but likely to be considerable. It is probably not too much to say that the faith in the idea of CD as well as the criticisms of its governmental implementation—the attitude epitomized and further propagated by the Balwantray Mehta Report, and leading to the great drive to establish PR—has been nourished by the beliefs and ardour of Sarvodaya groups. Anyone who has heard hard-headed, sophisticated bureaucrats speaking the pure doctrine of J. P. Narayan will not readily underestimate the power of these ideas even in the making of immediate policy. It is significant too that the Association of Voluntary Agencies for Rural Development (AVARD) set up under Narayan's guidance in 1960 has been able to enlist the co-operation of senior government officials.

A second category of non-party movements must be looked for in the area of occupational or functional organizations. But here, of course, the non-party element is even less clear and strong than in the case of Sarvodaya movements. The 'pressure groups' of India are only in part the spontaneous and independent results of felt needs among occupational categories. The Chambers of Commerce are in origin probably the most independent of such bodies—in part at least because their rise followed and imitated the fairly independent organizations of British commerce in India. But although the Chambers of Commerce have thus been in no sense creatures of party, links between their members and Congress go back into pre-independence days. Commercial and industrial interests were to some extent supporting Congress from the 1890s though at the same time keeping on speaking terms with government for the purpose of making representations. Since independence made Congress and government one, the links between business and both tended to become stronger. The fact that the Congress government has introduced economic planning has not upset representatives of private enterprise, for the latter have not been opposed to planning. Even the expansion of the public sector has provoked little open distress on the part of business men; the private sector still offers great scope. Private industry and trade is of course subject to much government control, but knowledge of how to use the channels of influence is highly developed in business circles and opportunities for big gains have not been lacking. The pleas uttered on behalf of the business community by the Swatantra Party suggest, however, that there are some frustrated elements and others who have fears for the future. Congress relations with business have also been strained by the blatantly anti-social tax-dodging activities of some interests; the (1963) report of the Commission of Inquiry on the administration of Dalmia-Jain companies high-lighted these activities in such a way as to make Nehru hesitate about giving his annual address to the Federation of Indian Chambers of Commerce and Industry. FICCI meanwhile maintains an efficient office in New Delhi, has its spokesmen in Parliament and access to the ministries. Meanwhile, too, Congress continues to receive massive financial backing from companies and individual business men. When Mundhra revealed (in the course of the Life Insurance Corporation case) that he had paid Rs. 100,000 to the party, and when central minister Malaviya admitted 'asking' a business man to put money into a Congress electoral campaign, a tiny portion of the iceberg of Congress finance came into view. Mutual irritation may frequently occur between business and Congress-and-government, but on the whole each has such great need of the others that the triangle is likely to remain in flourishing existence. The changed position of Congress since 1967–9 no doubt caused some relaxation of the triangular ties; business interests will have found it advisable to position themselves so as to be able to influence government of any party. When the CPI(M)-led government in Kerala sought to attract industry to that state, it did not find big business unwilling to listen. On the other hand, business interests were not disposed to take seriously similar pleas from the CPI(M) ministers in West Bengal who were clearly encouraging conditions of disorder and terror most uncongenial to entrepreneurs.

The origin of trade unions in India was naturally less spontaneous than that of business associations; before the working-class could produce its own leaders, philanthropic motivation had led some middle-class professionals to espouse the cause of the factory labourer. Unions thus organized by white-collar outsiders had come into existence well before the First World War. What is more surprising is that this kind of leadership has tended to persist up to the present. Part of the explanation may be the same as that which explains the large proportion of still unorganized labour —viz., the retention by so many urban workers of rural links (families and possessions still remaining in the village) and 'community' (caste) connections, both of which slow down the process of proletarianization. One consequence at any rate has been that trade unions have from the 1920s been easily led into political affiliation and allegiance. The All-India TUC came into existence as a federation of unions as early as 1920 and was then under Congress influence. Although Gandhi's first successful experiments with *satyagraha* in India were conducted for the rights of indigo plantation workers in Bihar (against British owners) and for a reconciliation of the interests of mill workers and (Indian) owners in Gujarat, Gandhi's own influence and interest in trade union matters remained limited and almost restricted to Ahmedabad, where he had helped to organize the Textile Labour Association. But socialists within Congress were for ever urging the leaders to 'go out' to the workers and peasants, believing partly that only thus could the movement be made truly national, partly that only thus could radicalism penetrate the movement, partly that if Congress didn't others would. Others did; the small but active CPI worked hard in the unions (even they used few men of working-class origins), captured control over certain centres and by 1929 had wrested the AITUC from Congress hands. A similar sequence occurred in the students' organizations.

A doctrinaire sectarianism seems to have led the CPI to form a separate federation in 1931, but after four years they moved back into control of the AITUC. When the CPI isolated itself further from the main stream of nationalist politics by its pro-war policy from 1942 and its pro-Pakistan sympathies from 1945 to 1946, it suffered in student support but held on to its industrial strongpoints. With the advent of independence, Congress had to determine how it was to deal with this labour movement. It resolved, after some careful consideration and in view of the CPI's grip on the AITUC, to create a parallel federation of such unions as it influenced: the Indian National TUC came into being in 1948. The socialists who by now were separating from Congress followed suit: the unions in which their followers had influence were brought together about the same time in the Hind Mazdoor Sabha. While it is therefore correct to speak of three parallel 'TUCs' each aligned with a different political party (four, if the non-CPI Marxist parties' United TUC is included), this may give an impression of greater organizational development than actually exists. The limited proletarianization, amply shown by sociological enquiries into the character of industrial labour, makes that difficult. (Trade union organization, in fact, resembles party in presenting the individual with a 'conflict of norms'.) The federations and the unions themselves are only patchily integrated. On all matters from the basic individual union member-ship to the formulation of a co-ordinated national policy, there is considerable institutional looseness and informality. Coherence depends on personalities of particular union leaders. These men have seldom been able to rise above a local status, but there they may enjoy great sway. Thus independence in the trade union movement is not to be found so much at the top but lower down; the top leaders are not independent of party, but the local bosses are independent of them. That said, however, it must be added that this is far less true of the communist group than of the others. (The communist and Congress splits have confused the situation further but less than might have been expected because of the fact that the splits were uneven regionally—e.g., the Bombay unions remained CPI, the Calcutta ones mainly CPI(M).) It must also be stressed that in spite of the looseness and uncertainty, these union structures do still carry some two-way traffic. The party leaders do have here a channel of influence downwards, while the union leaders do have access to politicians who can put their case.

The organization of the peasantry as an occupational group has, not surprisingly, been even more beset with difficulty. Gandhi and some of his followers had of course led local peasant protest move-ments along *satyagraha* lines in the 1920s; Patel's Bardoli campaign against enhancement of land revenue payments was the best organized and best known of these. Partly in the wake of such campaigns, rudimentary peasant associations developed in some regions and received help from Congress workers. With the rise of Congress radicalism in the 1930s efforts to mobilize the peasantry as an arm of the movement were increased and the All-India Kisan Sabha was set up in 1936. But for a variety of reasons—fundamental-ly, perhaps, because Congress's rural strength lay mainly among men of some substance who were not enthusiastic about such potentially disturbing organizations—the AIKS leaders were not wholly content with their Congress associates, and within a few years the organization had come to be largely dominated by members and sympathizers of the CPI. This domination was reinforced by the withdrawal of many non-communist Kisan leaders from 1942. The AIKS continues to be a loose federation of state bodies, each fluctu-ating in membership and activity according to the energy made available for this 'front' by the regional leaders of the CPI. The core of the matter is that while there are no doubt some rural interests which are as a whole opposed to those of urban areas—and as such tend to get fairly full expression through the more numerous representatives of rural constituencies—it is not easy to find in 'the peasantry' a single simple occupational interest group. The factions of village India—based as they can be on so many things: locality, caste, economic status—cut deep and create fragments.

A third type of movement, non-party but with political significance, is, of course, that based on caste. Sufficient has already been said about the place of caste in politics generally. Here it is only necessary to underline the role of the 'caste *association*'. In the traditional model, caste or *jati* was a unit in a system of complementarity (albeit a system from which some benefited more than others). It has been indicated how modern political parties have had to learn to take caste into account and how in doing so they sometimes emphasize the element of competitiveness as between castes which is already a feature of social change. It has also been pointed out that generally castes have not served separately as bases for new political parties but have rather sought to be 'accommodated' within existing parties and above all within Congress. The intermediate stage between the traditional world and that of parties is partially filled by the caste association—the explicit organization of *jati* groups on a basis wider than a small number of villages in one locality and for the purpose of defending or improving the position of the groups in relation to others.

No nation-wide study of these associations exists but it is possible that the few completed investigations of particular cases are reliable guides to other cases awaiting exploration. It appears that at least in certain areas the formation of caste associations began in the early years of this century. Their creation was sometimes prompted by the usefulness of being able to bring some organized pressure to bear on the decennial operations of the Census Commissioners. Such pressure would be designed—as with the Pallis of certain Madras districts—to get the name of the caste changed (from one implying low status to one indicating, for instance, Kshatriya derivation and connection) or its numbers amply recorded. In the early stages of its awareness of itself as a competing entity which could gain strength by organization and by the throwing out of links beyond immediate locality, caste concentrated on ritual status rather than directly on political or economic rights. The low-caste Pasis of UP were quite recently campaigning, against strong opposition, for recognition as being of high caste, even entitled to wear the sacred thread. (These aspirations, though ritual in character, significantly followed a change of occupation on the part of most of the group from inferior toddy-tapping to general agriculture.) That is, they are now at a stage passed through half a century ago by the Pallis (now Vanniya Kula Kshatryas) of Madras or the Yogi weavers of Bengal. But after a while (and the stages tend probably to be increasingly telescoped with the faster pace of social change) the aspirations take more material form. The 'Sangham' (association) formed by the Vanniyars, for example, began to formulate in the mid-1940s requests for a due number of 'places' in the civil services and a fair proportion of Congress Party candidatures. A similar shift in the concern of the Nair Service Society of Kerala took the organization right into the heart of king-making politics in that state during the late 1950s.

While the Nair organization became an independent political force, it did not attempt to turn itself into a community political party but preferred to work on some of the existing parties, giving its vigorous support to the anti-communist alliance in 1960. The Vanniyars, however, behaved rather differently. Disappointed by the reception given to their requests by Congress in Madras (at that time more Brahmin-led than later), they moved first into 'independent' electoral candidatures and then into the organization of two small political parties. Each of these was restricted in scope to two districts where the caste was strong, but there they did make headway and won several state legislature seats. After this success, and helped by the coming to power of non-Brahmin leaders in the Congress, negotiations with Congress were begun afresh. The major concession of two cabinet places for their members and the promise this contained of better things to come for the whole caste led to the dissolution of the little parties and their absorption in Congress, within which the caste leaders have been able to continue their efforts to lift up the Vanniyars.

The cases mentioned are admittedly 'advanced'. Yet what is significant is that even so, and in both cases, the final (or at least more persistent) pattern is that of the caste association working through existing political parties rather than the caste party. As already stated, caste, even when broadened out into the association form, is still too small to be effective by itself in state politics; it is therefore ready to be accommodated. Lloyd and Suzanne Rudolph, who studied the Vanniyar case, are surely amply justified in insisting that these developments are not simply to be deplored as the corruption of party but, if anything, to be hailed as the adaptation of caste to modern bargaining democracy. For the future it may be less important that India has associations on a caste basis than that these associations are being assimilated into a structure of political parties —and thereby strongly influenced in a modern direction.

Finally, there are the extra- and indeed anti-constitutional organized activities and groups to be considered. Except for perhaps one important body, these are manifestations of the post-1967 period. That possible exception is the RSS. It is not a clear exception because on one view of this organization it is in the nature of a cultural association with local clubs all over the country, devoted simply to the regeneration of Hindu youth. However, since it inculcates a high degree of militancy and produces among its members distrust and sometimes active hatred of Muslims and those who protect them, it operates without question to undermine the secular ideas of the Constitution. Moreover, through its links with the Jan Sangh its trainees are channelled into the political system with something less than full commitment to the maintenance of that system.

The RSS apart, there were also of course in the pre-1967 period particular protest movements which went in varying degrees beyond the use of regular constitutional forms. Broadly these were of three kinds. There were, first, a number of occasions when extremist parties, usually of the left, led demonstrations which culminated in violence; strikes in Calcutta regularly went that way. Secondly, populist agitations on a wide variety of issues—formation of linguistic states, inter-state boundary disputes, southern opposition to Hindi, Portuguese retention of Goa, government agreements with Pakistan —took place, often supposedly modelled on Gandhian *satyagraha* protests, frequently engendering passions which defied control as well as order. The third type may not deserve the term protest and it is always a moot point as to how far deliberate organization is entailed; these are the outbursts, sudden and sporadic, of one group against another—either communal as when Muslims are attacked, or linguistic as when Bengalis are targets for violence in Assam, or social as when an untouchable settlement is raided by a caste group.

There were thus plenty of exceptions to the rule that the pre-1967 period was one of constitutional and peaceful politics—this even after the troubled early years of partition slaughter, communist-led insurrections and breakdowns of order in areas like Hyderabad. Even so, there has been a change since 1967. All the sources of violence just mentioned have remained but to them has been added a new category: movements which are extra- and anti-constitutional by their very design and whose methods, as a matter of 'principle' so to speak, entail violence and terror. They may be inspired by community passion or ideological fervour. The Shiv Sena (Shivaji's Army) in Maharashtra is an example of the former variety, dedicated to the cause of 'Maharashtra for the Maharashtrians' and serving it by making life unpleasant for anyone else. The latter type is exempli-

H

fied by the Naxalite groups of communists in various parts of the country. Named after the Naxalbari area of West Bengal where the movement began, these groups are composed of young zealots drawn mainly out of the ranks of the CPI(M) who believe that their former party by accepting the electoral and coalitional routes to power has betrayed the revolution. Making appeals simultaneously to both the Indian (especially Bengali) terrorist traditions and Maoist teachings concerning rural guerillas, they have concentrated on assassination of substantial farmers and armed attacks on police outposts, the main centres being the northern border areas, parts of Andhra and the Kerala mountain forests.

Despair and desperation are no doubt important elements in the explanation of the attractive power of such movements and it is improbable that conditions will so improve as to remove these causes. It may, however, be possible at least to contain these movements within severe limits. Of the possible limiting factors it may be unwise to rely too heavily on either the efficiency of the police or the revulsion of decent people—though neither is negligible. Perhaps the strongest safeguard is a political one. The Shiv Sena and the Naxalites do more than kill people—they also hurt vested political interests. The interest most damaged by the Naxalites is not the rich farmer's Congress or the business man's Swatantra but the CPI(M) itself. (The Naxalites came formally to be known in 1970 as the CPI(ML), thus bringing Lenin into the foreground; to achieve an effective all-India organization of an underground movement is however very difficult and the evidence pointed rather to only limited cohesion.) The organized communists thus have the greatest incentive to check the Naxalites, though it is true that this may mean at least appearing to go some way to imitate them—as was strikingly done in the party-sponsored 'land-grab' movement of 1970. In a somewhat similar fashion Shiv Sena's most direct political enemies are those state party units in Maharashtra who would otherwise make capital out of issues of regional chauvinism. They will strive hard to keep Shiv Sena in place. It is, alas, true however that the wild boys are not simply a threat to their more respectable political neighbours; they have also a value for them, for it is tempting for the latter to say or imply: if you think we are difficult, look who is waiting to step up if our demands are not met.

Local politics

Although enough has already been said in general terms about the ways in which with the expansion of the political universe the various types of parochial politics have come to be related and integrated with wider district and state systems, a word must be added about the effects on political life of the institutions of Panchayat Raj already briefly mentioned above (pp. 158–9). The hope of at least some of the leading advocates of democratic decentralization was that 'party politics' could be kept out of the new elected local bodies. In order that popular interest and initiative (which had not been effectively roused by the Community Development programme as such) should be enlisted, elected bodies seemed to be necessary. At the same time, there was the fear that election could mean conflict and that this would aggravate the already paralysing faction divisions of village life. To avert 'a trail of bitterness, animosity and feuds', therefore, elections should so far as possible express 'the general consent of the people', and this was taken to imply unanimous choice. It is understandable that small intimate groups as well as perilously divided societies should have a dread of devices which by counting hands make majorities and minorities too explicit. When these two conditions prevail together, as in Indian rural life, the dread is all the greater. This is probably sufficient without any appeal to Indian traditions to account for the ardent desire to have decisions taken not by elections and votes but by 'consensus'.

In so far as this has been encouraged and has come about, it seems very probable that the old village leadership has been able to capture the seats—a situation of apparent no change but with the important difference that the unprivileged or the minorities have the added grievance of electoral hypocrisy. Fortunately, despite encouragement, it has generally not happened. Parties have been drawn in—Congress itself most of all. Existing factions, whether simply caste-based or cutting across caste lines, have certainly shaped village 'party alignments', and it may sometimes even be misleading to use the latter term at all, so decisive is the influence of past divisions. But if faction is to be reduced it will be not by contrived unanimity but by its being transformed through contact with divisions of a wider significance such as party.

More specifically, one may put the probable effects of PR on political life under three headings. The immediate effect of the system was on the whole to increase still further the strength of Congress in the rural areas as against other parties. It had the largest organization, one capable of cultivating this multitude of new bodies; it tended already to have the support of the influential sections of village society; above all, it had as government party a great deal to offer—and at this level tangible material benefits are an even larger part of the purpose of political activity than at ideologically more susceptible levels. The greater identification of Congress, government and local bodies did not necessarily mean that 'Congress candidates' would win elections but rather that candidates who won would tend to become Congress representatives if they were not so already. The decline of Congress has of course opened up this arena more effectively to opposition parties. It has also had the effect, in states of political instability, of making the calculations of village leaders very much more complicated than before.

A second set of effects of PR were those on the internal life of Congress. On the one hand, the new bodies supplied an outlet in terms of governmental power for the local party zealots. These men, if not content to be social welfare workers, had to busy themselves with power contests in the party machine, mainly at the DCC level. This may have been fun, but it was a long way from real power; that was concentrated at the state level where room was restricted. These new avenues did something to absorb unsatisfied party workers and also acted as a training and proving ground for promotion up the party ladder. Above all, perhaps, they did a little to solve Congress's real problem of attracting new blood into the organization; new layers of political talent and ambition in rural areas were tapped by these new tiers of government. On the other hand, this invasion of Congress from below posed fresh problems and created new strains. Village and block factionalism was fed upward into the party.

Finally, there is no doubt that the long-run effect of PR has been to step up mobility and competition in rural politics. Although Congress was the initial beneficiary, this did not permit the dominant party to impede the loosening and opening up of the hitherto tightly held structures of village power. Once that began to happen, Congress, while better placed than most by virtue of being the sitting political tenant, was at the same time more vulnerable. It was too much to expect that all the village *sarpanches* (council chairmen), many of them decked out in Congress labels for the first time, would be scrupulously just—or even reasonably farsighted—in their exercise of the substantial powers of elective office; nor was it easy for state Congress leaders to discipline such men whose need for the party was rather less than the party's need for them. In this way as many enemies were made for Congress as friends and this process had something to do with the party's troubles in 1967. From a wider point of view the question is whether the introduction of elected local bodies with real powers has been assisting the process of peaceful social change in rural India. There was every sign that this was the case. Although the established richer farmers, men of recognized influence in their areas, were by no means thrown out by popular vote, there was change. For one thing many of the older leaders shrank from the indignity of putting up for election and allowed younger and more adaptable men of their families to move in. Moreover, here and there success came to men of slightly lower status, middle-ranking peasants. In general, some greater responsiveness could begin to enter the system. The question then arises whether this responsiveness can keep ahead of a certain restiveness in the lower parts of the rural heap. Outside certain particular areas, it had not proved easy for the left parties to mobilize the village poor; they seemed almost too depressed and too divided to be moved. But as India moved into the seventies the SSP had been able to achieve some success along these lines even in backward Bihar, the 'green revolution' was creating new anger and frustration among those sections who were being relatively left behind, and left parties were evidently believing that there was political capital to be made out of sponsoring a 'land-grab' movement in the name of the landless agricultural labourer.

H*

6

THE ORDERING FRAMEWORK

The length of this chapter is no guide to the significance of its subject matter; it is short partly because the present writer has examined elsewhere the important parliamentary party of the framework, partly because the legal system is well dealt with in other works. By 'ordering framework' is meant those parts of India's political system which make it a constitutional system. By this in turn is meant not necessarily a system equipped with a formal documentary instrument of guidance but rather a system in which the constituent elements, including especially government, operate according to rules which they are not able unilaterally to prescribe. It is at the same time a mediating framework, keeping and holding in relation with each other the two active 'poles' of government and political forces. It requires them to maintain a dialogue and it further imposes the rules and style of their debate. By the same token this framework is at the same time that part of the system which makes government accountable and responsible, imposing on those in authority the obligation to explain and defend their exercise of it, enabling those outside to have channels of representation, criticism and appeal. It is, finally, that part of the system which provides machinery for the rejection of a particular group from the positions of power and their replacement by others. That machinery was little used in independent India's first two decades; it has been exploited to the full since then. But government was not unaccountable even when governments were not being thrown out of office; and by no means all the changes of governments since 1967 have reflected or brought about an enhancement of accountability.

Parliament

There is no doubt a sceptical view about parliamentary institutions in India, even a denigrating attitude, which has to be met. Such views owe a little to examination of the evidence, much more to bits of general reasoning which argue that it is difficult to believe that India can have succeeded where other new states have failed. It is now almost accepted doctrine once again—for it was so in British ruling circles during much of the imperial period—that Western institutions do not export well. So since parliament came from the West, when it is encountered elsewhere it is to be greeted with scepticism. Such an attitude has been backed by mainly two kinds of arguments. The first was mainly heard up to 1967 and held that there was a natural incompatibility between one-dominant-party systems and the functioning of parliamentary institutions. The concentration of power in one party rendered the parliamentary operation otiose and meaningless. The second has been heard mainly since 1967 and sounds a little like the opposite of the first. It holds that when fragmentation produces a multiplicity of parties few of which can command real loyalty and exact effective discipline, parliamentary institutions become a mere playground for the games of defections and government-toppling.

It is easier to answer the first argument because there is available the evidence of a period of twenty years. If that evidence indeed points to the importance of parliament in India, the simple 'incompatibility' view will have to be set aside and reasons given for India's greater success. The study of the role of parliaments has indeed a special significance with reference to 'new states'. The political systems of most of these states are characterized by the dominance of one political party. Yet nothing is clearer than that as between these systems there are large differences. The dominance varies in degree, in form and in cause. Ghana, Tanganyika, Mexico, India, Malaya, Algeria, Egypt—the list of those with such dominance at some stage could be very long indeed—have much in common, but they are, on any close examination, spread over a great range, and any attempt to use a single label is crude and misleading; tests and criteria are wanted which will place these states in meaningful sub-categories. Evidently one set of tests will relate to the nature of the internal organization of the party which counts—and we have already seen some of the features of the Indian Congress Party which would at once serve to distinguish it from other dominant parties. But another test of equal importance is indeed to ask what role is played by the representative assembly or parliament. (The two tests are not unconnected: a certain type of dominant party will fit with a certain type of parliament.) In terms of concepts already used above, a critical question is whether, and if so how far, one can speak of a framework of parliamentary and other institutions which 'mediates' between government and party political forces. In some of these countries party and government have in one way or another become indistinguishable, so that the mediating role disappears and the parliamentary institutions if they exist constitute a meaningless survival or a quaint shop-window which barely hides the different business carried on in the workshop. No accurate account of Indian politics can dismiss her parliamentary institutions in that way.

The Union Parliament consists of two houses—the Lok Sabha (House of the People) and the Rajya Sabha (Council of States). The latter can be briefly dismissed. Whereas the lower house is directly elected on the basis of adult suffrage for five years, the Rajya Sabha (RS) is (except for a few nominated by the President for special knowledge) indirectly elected on a proportional representation basis by the state legislatures. The state quotas for the upper house are proportionate to population, and the justification for the RS has always been in terms of 'second thoughts' rather than 'states rights'. The RS is not dissolved but one-third of its members retire every two years. The powers of the two houses are similar in relation to ordinary legislation, but money bills can be introduced only in the LS, and any changes suggested by the RS must be made within fourteen days and can be rejected by the LS. The machinery for resolving any deadlock between the two houses is a joint sitting in which the RS members constitute less than one-third of the whole. However, this is less important than that the RS is a party-chosen body and conflict with the LS on matters of policy (as distinct from prestige) is scarcely conceivable except in the event of a landslide change in the LS. The upper house is distinct neither in the character of its members nor in the work it does. Yet it cannot be dismissed as merely harmless. On the one hand it does some harm by demanding the too precious attention of ministers who have the right to speak in both houses and therefore are felt to be obliged to do so. On the other hand, it has three outweighing merits: it supplies additional political positions for which there is demand, it provides some additional debating opportunities for which there is occasionally need and it assists in the solution of legislative timetable problems.

Turning mainly to the Lok Sabha, a first question to pose concerns the manner in which the representative body is chosen. Is it elected fairly? Here there are many points to inspect. The territorial constituencies agreed upon by the Constituent Assembly as the basis for elections are left by the constitution to be regulated by ordinary laws of parliament. But the dangers perhaps latent in this provision have been avoided by the provision which Parliament in fact made for a Delimitation Commission presided over by a retired Supreme Court judge. Complaints about gerrymandering have not been absent but have been no more common than in England—and this in spite of areas of great delicacy. Secondly, the electoral system of (since 1962) single-member constituencies with a simple first-past-the-post method of determining the winning candidate was chosen after some discussion of alternative methods. Certainly proportional representation would have favoured all opposition parties, though not so much as they sometimes pretend (see Tables at pp. 184–94 above); proportional representation would not have put Congress generally out of power, it would have complicated its task. Third, the conduct of all elections is placed by a separate chapter of the Constitution in the hands of an Election Commission consisting of the Chief Election Commissioner and Deputy Commissioners. The former is an independent official appointed by the President not for life but under conditions otherwise similar to those of judges, with salary not subject to vote and removal only by a two-thirds vote in both houses. His staff for the preparation of rolls and for the actual conduct of the balloting consists of ordinary state government officers. Complaints of partiality on the part of election administrators have been rare and their substantiation rarer.

Inspection of the legal and administrative framework does not exhaust the question of fairness. It would be absurd to pretend that in India the government party enjoys no special advantages. Ministers may all too easily use their position and facilities and fail during the campaign to draw the lines between government and party. This may often make a mockery of the laws regrading election expenses. The legal limits (Rs. 25,000 for a Lok Sabha constituency) are low and the routes around the provisions are several and well trodden. Moreover, the government party has easier access to large business donations than other parties. Above all, the government party has so much more, legitimately and illegitimately, to offer; and promises to one can so easily become or come to be felt as threats to another. But much of this can reasonably be regarded as the kind of imperfection, aggravated admittedly, familiar to older democracies; an inegalitarian society does place barriers before fairness. It is serious enough, but it is still different in kind from the contrived and unorganized unfairness which handcuffs the opposition Press, inhibits the free activity of opposition politicians and strikes terror into voters. Outside Kashmir (and perhaps at times Punjab) these things do not happen in India. The electoral process has suffered from a small amount of violence, a little attempted bullying and a larger amount of bribery, but if one lumps the unfair means together it is clear that they are the monopoly of no one party. That is something.

If parliament is to be real it must be fairly conducted as well as fairly elected. Here, if more than self-restraint on the part of the governing party is to be looked for, the position of the Speaker and the group of parliamentary officials is central. The Indian Parliament's first decade was guided by the able Mr Mavalankar, sharp and shrewd, patient and determined, faithful Congressman but no tool of the government. He built up his own parliament staff and with them largely shaped the rules and conventions of debate, established the privileges of the house and protected them both from enlargement at the expense of the public and from encroachment for the advantage of government, set up a machinery for determining with adequate opposition participation the allocation of parliamentary time and created a whole system of parliamentary committees to function as watch-dogs over the conduct of administration. That is, he made his position—and through it that of parliament—one of substantial independence of government. It cannot be said that the Speakers of most State Assemblies have been so successful and it cannot be said of all that they even tried very hard. Yet even here the influence of the centre has been felt and by means of the annual Speakers' Conference the spirits of the weaker ones have been rallied. During Kairon's rule in the Punjab, the Speaker of the Assembly, under pressure from the state government to depart from the line of impartiality, made a stand of resistance, and in doing so announced that he would seek support from his fellows at the next conference.

The fair conduct of proceedings is a good test of parliamentary independence, but with a weak opposition more may be required if government policy and its administration are to obtain certain and searching examination. Here the structure and working of parliamentary committees is particularly important. The Public Accounts Committee (PAC) is the senior of them in that the first PACs were constituted at the centre and in the provinces as early as 1923. But they met under the chairmanship of the Finance Member, their secretariat consisted of finance department officials and their role was confined to technicalities. Moreover, the Auditor-General's position was more governmental than independent and he was in no sense a servant of the legislatures. When in 1950 the PAC was made a real parliamentary committee (since 1954, it contains members of the Upper House also) and the Auditor-General's independence spelt out in the Constitution, an effective examiner of the administration was created. Expertise has been acquired and enthusiasm has developed among both the members and the parliament secretariat staff who service the committee. The fact that Congress has, of course, a majority on the PAC is less important than that all members become devoted to the job they have to do. The fact that their scrutiny is *ex-post facto* is less important than that the government has continuously to act in the knowledge that scrutiny of any item may take place and that waste or impropriety may be widely exposed in the House and the Press. The fact that government replies to the PAC are often vague and cool is less important than that behind the reply there has often been embarrassment and some resolve not to let it happen again.

The Estimates Committee, created in 1950, has made up in activity for its later arrival. Indeed, it has gone far to justify the parliamentary joy and the official hostility which attended its establishment. Its thirty (Lok Sabha) members are charged with the examination of departmental estimates. They cannot get far by a perusal of the bare estimates and there is no equivalent of the audit report on which the PAC bases its work. They are therefore empowered to call upon the ministries to furnish material in support of their estimates. Like the PAC they then proceed to the examination of witnesses from the departments under review and by now a good deal has been learnt about the best ways of questioning officials. They are supposed to look for possible economies but they have in fact been happy to rub out the faint line between economy and efficiency. Further, they have not hesitated to recommend in the name of efficiency large administrative reforms and even re-orientations of policy. Their audacity occasioned strong comment and it may be that they have in the last few years been more modest in the scope of their reports. But of their growing competence and effectiveness as a control over ministries there can be no doubt. If they find less to be indignant about it is in part because their influence is now automatically reckoned with.

Similar stories could be told of other committees of the Lok Sabha —including the Committee on Public Undertakings, the extraordinary Committee on Government Assurances which records and chases the most casual ministerial promise to 'enquire into the matter' and the Committee on Subordinate Legislation which scrutinizes the use made by departments of rule-making powers delegated by Parliament. The use of select committees is a stage in the legislative process which has been rather limited to bills of great complexity whose detailed examination would have been difficult in general debate; some such bills have been quite considerably amended in committee. A last kind of committee which must be mentioned is the Consultative Committee. Of these there are now several covering each area of government and corresponding mainly to ministries. They are in a sense a revival of the standing advisory committees of imperial days. Those committees had been effectively dominated by British members of the Executive Council who used them mainly to sound Indian non-official opinion, but this is not to say that their advice was not taken nor that they were otherwise without value. They were in any event done away with in 1952 following the general election—under pressure from ministers, perhaps out of fear that the newly elected opposition members could not respect confidences, ostensibly because the committees blurred and confused ministerial responsibility. Congress back-benchers did not protest loudly for they knew that the party's own committees on transport, agriculture, etc., would achieve the same purpose. To alleviate opposition disappointment, the PM said he would hold informal conferences on different subjects with the opposition. Out of this promise (as well as the desire to meet opposition frustration and perhaps the need in foreign affairs and economic development to associate all with the government) came the Consultative Committees. It is not easy to assess their value but at least some of the advantages hitherto open only to the Congress MP (opportunity to cultivate special interests and enjoy an additional channel for making representations and communicating ideas) must have been made available to the opposition.

To these points must be added others of an even less tangible and measurable kind. Question Hour in India has perhaps gained a certain reputation, not underserved, ever since (then) Sir Anthony Eden was said to have felt more at home during his witnessing of it than he had while attending that of the Australian parliament. While the form of the initial question is firmly disciplined, the freedom given to the putting of supplementaries is fairly large and ministers cannot use escape routes on too many occasions. (In any case, this only gives the Committee on Government Assurances further opportunities for the chase.) Decisions may or may not be affected, but reasons must be given for what is being done.

The same is true of general debates. No doubt the opposition must lose when it comes to the button-pressing and no doubt whips are hardly ever disobeyed. But the opposition is heard by the public and it also addresses itself continuously to the appropriate sections of the Congress Party itself. Further, the currents in the Congress are sensitively judged by the whips and communicated upwards. Concessions may or may not be made there and then, but the point can be taken for next time. Moreover, there have been great occasions when Parliament has 'spoken for India' and surprised the government. Perhaps the reaction to the 'Voice of America' deal in 1963 was a good example.

The outcome of all this is that opposition groups were even before 1967 able to be far more effective in parliament than their proportion of seats might suggest. (They would no doubt have been even more effective if they had not been so diverse in nature and if they had more talent available.) Since 1967 opposition strength has made possible a harassment of government which has called for clear heads and cool temperaments from the ministerial benches. It also addes up to a view of Parliament—and even the State Assemblies though to a much lesser degree—as possessing distinct character and performing a distinct role, an independent institution not to be seen as an extension of government or of party. How has this come about?

A great deal can be attributed to 'legacies' of one kind or another. The pre-1947 experience 'counts'. The legislatures under British rule were not full parliaments but they were not captive and docile durbars. The government could act without the legislature if it could not act with it; it could not be stopped from doing what it liked, but it could not do what it liked with and through the legislature. Within their constitutional limits, the quasi-parliaments preserved their dignity and their independence. Government was massively present in the legislature but the two could never be confused or identified. The legislature was, if anything, its elected element, and that element was largely the permanent opposition to British rule.

A related but different point is that Indian politics has been brought up in a school of distrust. In so far as the distrust is of almost everyone, it is a mark of a deeply divided society. But alien rule added its contribution to this by giving some people, indeed politically leading people, the mission of cultivating distrust in established political authority. This has laid a curse on some aspects of political life, but it has helped to provide a soil for opposition even in the absence (for other reasons and before 1967) of much of an opposition. A particular consequence of this is that India has been able to create a 'separation of powers' atmosphere without any 'separation of powers'. Parliament is far from being the US Congress but very often it speaks of 'government' in the tones that good American legislators use of 'the administration' and the Secretariat is made to seem as far from Parliament House as the White House is from Capitol Hill.

Thirdly, account must be taken of the profundity of the ideological commitment of many of India's rulers to the Westminster model. Even of Nehru himself, headmaster though he was, it makes sense to say that if opposition had not existed he would have found it necessary to invent it. In part, the dedication is determined by the need to prove an old point, to disprove old allegations that India could not be a home for responsible government. But it is also more than that, for attachment to the institution has grown. For one thing it has become easier with time to praise what came from the imperial base, for another it has become easier to forget where it did come from. There is also by now the attachment to the familiar, and habit sets the seal; whether or not 'time and custom give authority to all forms of government', they are at work on behalf of parliament in India, and a quarter of a century is not always a short time. But before habit could do its job it was necessary that in the minds of men at the top there should be some vision of what was proper and some capacity to impose that vision on others.

This capacity to impose brings one to the last but perhaps most vital factor of all: the Congress Party. Without that dominant party there could hardly have been a successful imposition. At least in that sense, then, the one-dominant-party system served not to destroy but to sustain parliamentary institutions. But there are of course specific characteristics of this organization which saved the reality of parliament. In view of the discussions above (Chapters 1 and 5), the three main points can be put briefly. The retentive capacity of Congress—no automatic result of nationalist struggle but rather the work of great skill acquired over a long period—meant the holding together of very many regional sectional interests within the one organization. This not merely ensured governmental stability but also averted the total exclusion of any part of the national community from the channels of power. The Sikhs and the Tamils, the industrial workers and the Harijans have been able to find as much place inside Congress as anywhere else. In this way coherently disaffected segments have not materialized and fear of threats to the integrity of the state has been mostly allayed. DMK has been substantially contained and the CPI has been unable (except in a few areas) to win secure segment bases. The fearlessness which parliament needs has been mainly preserved.

Second, the same retentiveness made a monolithic party very difficult. This has given every opposition group some *point d'appui* (and even point of entry) in the Congress itself, so that its work is not as much in vain as might appear. (The fact that Congress has never at the centre or in the states as a whole had a majority of the country's votes behind it has also given the opposition a boldness and the government a certain caution which could not be understood from the distribution of seats alone.) It has also made a reality of the inescapable federalism of Indian politics, for Congress itself is a highly federal body. Sometimes the High Command has been able to dictate to the party in a state—even shaping the formation of a Congress government. But on other occasions Pradesh Congress Committees have been tails which wagged the dog in Delhi—a tendency sharply increased in recent years. Above all, perhaps, the history of Congress has practically demanded a continuous tension—except at points that were under the immediate control of Nehru—between government and party or between the party's ministerial and organizational 'wings'. (The 1963 Kamaraj plan—and, even more, the choice of Kamaraj as Congress President—permitted the tension to move into Delhi.) This has given state politics an increasingly shabby air in most cases but has also provided a built-in opposition in the form of the party officials.

There is a third sense in which the one-dominant-party has saved parliament. Although Congress was more widely based as a nationalist movement than many, adult franchise nevertheless opened up new worlds to conquer. These new worlds of village politics were in their essential nature alien to the modern political system, worlds of traditional social cleavages and ascriptive political leadership. But Congress, partly by virtue of its hold in the middle layers of the intermediaries, partly because of its power as government party, partly by its willingness to be 'corrupted' by the values and pressure of rural society, has been able to absorb and integrate these realms. Panchayat Raj is now assisting the process. The little loyalties of the 'little community' find room in the party; caste is accommodated. A system of political communication opens up, linking top to bottom. In other words, the men from the alien worlds are not excluded from the system but brought in—and with this, the potential threat to parliament from social change seems to be passing over. If Congress began by being almost the sole integrator and still continues (in its two parts) to be one of the main ones, the non-Congress parties have increasingly taken up the same role, becoming in this respect more and more like Congress itself. The size of what has been called 'the ineffective electorate' is steadily decreasing.

The relation between the one-dominant-party system and parliamentary institutions has been discussed at some length because it is not simply past history (nothing hardly ever is). As already suggested in Chapter 5, the one-dominant-party system has by no means disappeared without trace. Further, even if it had, it would still be important to understand the kind of independent solidity it had managed to allow, and in some respects even encourage, parliamentary institutions to acquire. But there is still a valid question as to how these institutions have fared at the state level where political instability has reigned. In so far as there has been increasing reliance on periods of President's Rule in a number of states, this has of course meant the suspension of the representative assemblies. Few implements improve through non-use. Apart from their periods of suspension, the State Assemblies have, it must be admitted, been passing through a thin time. Useful, critical debate, involving reasoned exposition by governments under the watchful eyes of the oppositions and the latter's presentation of alternative courses, entails a modicum of discipline and order; in many states—though by no means all, let it be said, lest the publicity given to the sensational should mislead us—these have been lacking. Random defections of MLAs from one group to another, neglect of policy questions in almost childish absorption in the games of manœuvre, sheer turbulence and even violence—these widespread features have brought the institution into a degree of discredit. (They do of course keep the Assemblies in the public eye but the interest which they elicit is a perversion.) It may be said that in some states the MLAs are consuming the credit stored up in the name of representative assemblies by their predecessors. It is fortunate that the stock was a large one.

The law, the Constitution and the courts

The second major element in the mediating and constitutional framework is the legal system. No adequate exposition is possible in the space available but its 'framework' character can be somewhat explained and assessed.

The system of law itself in India is basically derived from the 'expansion' or 'migration' of the English common law. This is a rather astonishing fact. The seemingly all-powerful nineteenth-century executive-bureaucracy was neither able nor wholly willing to exclude from its territories a legal system which contained many features unfriendly to autocratic government. The Bentham-inspired law reformers exported to India were not opposed to the transplantation of much that was enshrined in earlier English legal traditions. The result is that with the exception of shrinking areas of family and religious law, the law of India is a codified and modified version of English law. The great codes—Penal (1860), Civil Procedure (1859) and Criminal Procedure (1861)—were supplemented by a series of statutes in the 1870s on succession, contract, evidence and the principles of equity, and in the following decade a further series on property transfer, trusts and negotiable instruments. Large areas of civil wrongs have remained uncovered in this manner and here, as well as in the application of the statutes, the judges have enjoyed powers of interpretation.

Much of this has been unaffected by India's independence; what had been law was to remain law until it received amendment. But two major developments have taken place. First, in the great tradition of the previous century, a Law Commission was set up in 1955, and the examination of substantive law and the administration of justice have been going steadily ahead. In this process, the selective application of English law continues. Recommendations for the abolition of the jury system (which never had more than partial and uneven application in India) have been made as well as for the retention of the system of precedents. Secondly, some of the principles of the common law have been embodied in the Constitution itself—habeas corpus, the independent judiciary and aspects of the rule of law.

Practically any constitution is bound to set limits to the conduct of governments; a constitution as lengthy and detailed as India's does so inescapably. The document does not expressly recognize any doctrine of the separation of powers but it naturally differentiates the various branches and offices of the state machinery and in doing so sets barriers against the assumption by one organ of functions belonging to another. Neat boundaries between executive and legislative are impracticable in a parliamentary system and the balance between the two is a matter of political practice. The position of the judiciary is more evident from the Constitution itself and the key provisions have been already mentioned (see pp. 84–5). The massive report (1960) of the Law Commission on the reform of judicial administration had startling things to say on the degree of independence enjoyed by the judiciary. It found that 'communal and regional considerations and executive influence (exerted from the highest quarters)' had operated to keep the best High Court talent from finding its way into the Supreme Court. It alleged that although the letter of the Constitution had been observed in the consulting of chief justices on the appointment of High Court judges, its spirit had been neglected because chief justices had given in to the wishes of state chief ministers. The quality of the subordinate judiciary also left much to be desired for similar reasons. They recommended an all-India judicial service and a tightening by amendment of the provisions to ensure judicial control of judicial appointments. In assessing the Law Commission Report it must be remembered many of the most severe critics of the working of the judicial system are members of the legal profession. The public respect for judges is exceptionally high and the main public complaint would be that access was costly and process slow. As regards the latter the arrears of cases heaped up in the High Courts is appalling. This itself is in part an indication of the public's trust and confidence in the judicial system; in part it means that to take a dispute to court has become a sign of status which is within the reach of unprecedented numbers of people.

Although that Report strongly suggests that some of the new state-level politicians have not inherited quite the same respect for the impartial judiciary as their predecessors, it is not easy to find obvious signs of government-dominated judges. Judicial review is an essential part of the Indian constitutional system. Apart from being implied in the division of powers between Union and state legislatures and in the inclusion of fundamental rights—both of which deny any simple supremacy to Parliament—judicial review is explicit in the provisions that the Supreme Court has jurisdiction in cases between governments, that it is the court of appeal in cases involving inter-pretation of the Constitution and that the right to move the court for the enforcement of fundamental rights is itself a fundamental right. The weapons given to the judges are also powerful. High Courts have power to issue to any person or any governmental authority any of the established writs or any order for the enforcement of fundamental rights 'and for any other purpose'. The Supreme Court has shown willingness to entertain appeals not only from ordinary Courts but also from industrial courts, election tribunals and other quasi-judicial adjudicating bodies.

In the course of the first dozen years of the Constitution, the courts have had ample work to do in the field of fundamental rights. The group of 'equality' rights (Articles 14–18) produced a quick crop of cases. The provisions are directed, towards securing 'equality before the law' and 'the equal protection of the laws'—the first (British) phrase being usually taken to mean no privileges in law, the latter (American) to indicate similar treatment of similar cases. The dilemma that discrimination on grounds of sex or caste may in fact be necessary in the interests of making special provisions in education and employment opportunities for underdeveloped sections led to the first constitutional amendment making such provisions permis-sible. But difficulties remain: how to square the proper and con-tinuing need for differential treatment with the avoidance of discrimination, and, above all, how to ensure that the really weak and under-privileged are not too timid and poor to be able to reach the courts. Only judicial common sense and political development respectively can meet these.

The 'freedom' rights (Articles 19–22) of speech, assembly,

association, movement, residence, property and occupation, together with those concerning conviction and detention, have naturally occupied an even more prominent place in the interpretation of this part of the Constitution. The framers had sought to protect government by writing in the grounds on which freedom could be restricted but the phrase 'reasonable restrictions' left room for the courts. The original grounds of permitted restriction on speech and expression included libel, slander, defamation, contempt of court, offence against decency or morality and undermining the security of the state. Cases in which the last of these was at issue resulted in bold decisions declaring certain security legislation void and unconstitutional. The 1st Amendment thereupon extended the permissible restriction to cover the 'interests of public order', but the reasonableness of the restriction remains for the courts to judge. This is also the position with the other freedoms, though the 1st Amendment had also to add that freedom of occupation must not preclude the establishment of professional qualifications or state monopolies. The habeas corpus right is expressly declared by the Constitution not to apply to cases of preventive detention. This provoked strong criticism at the time in the Constituent Assembly, and the Preventive Detention Act, first passed in 1950 and subsequently extended, has also been vigorously opposed. The use made of this drastic measure has not been scandalous and the Constitution and the Act provide some checks (e.g. three months' limit unless sanctioned by an independent Advisory Board), but the judges have continued to look askance at this quasi-permanent part of the legal scene.

While the rights against exploitation (forced and child labour) and those of religion and minorities have occasioned less controversy, there remain two further areas where dispute has been great. First, the right to property in its original form led to the invalidation of land reform and nationalization legislation. The 1st and 4th Amendments were required before such legislation—including the amount of compensation for property compulsorily acquired—was removed from judicial attack. Second, the right to move the Supreme Court for the enforcement of fundamental rights was itself suspended as a consequence of the proclamation in 1962 of a state of emergency. In this area the Court 'replied' in 1967 with a decision which astonished the politicians and may yet produce a collision: it ruled that the fundamental rights could not be abrogated or abridged by Parliament even through constitutional amendment. Mention should also be made of cases where courts and state assemblies (e.g., in UP) have got into conflict arising out of the parliamentary power to punish for contempt.

It must be admitted that by constitutional amendments, by the loophole of preventive detention and by the recent use of the emergency provisions, the legal framework has been somewhat bent to the needs of the government. It may also be the case, as some observers allege, that judges have in their still substantial areas of discretion tended of late to be more sympathetic to the point of view of the executive arm of the state. It is very possible that political pressures have influenced some judicial appointments. But when all this is said, it is not enough to make a mockery of the legal and constitutional framework in which the governments are required to move. The political and moral values inherent in a sytem of rule by law have been sufficiently communicated to all parts of the political system to ensure considerable resistance to arbitrary action. Small-town pleader and High Cought judge alike have joined with the parliamentarians to construct, from their different sides, limits within which government and politics and the relations of ruler and citizen must be conducted.

7

TENDENCIES AND IDEAS

Tendencies

The attempt to formulate tendencies is more hazardous in politics than in economics, and necessarily so from the nature of the subject. The propositions of the economist must no doubt be most carefully phrased; he has to define precisely the circumstances in which they hold, and every predictive hypothesis has to be cautiously hedged around with conditions. Nevertheless, he does handle concepts which can be meaningfully quantified and, more important, he is dealing with an aspect of human behaviour which is relatively autonomous and universal in its regularities. Political phenomena are by no means without regularities, but what can be isolated and formulated at present seems likely to be either too general or too trivial when compared with what insists on remaining individual and contingent. However, since even scepticism can become too dogmatic, it is as well to concede that attempts at systematic understanding of politics, though not wholly recent, are yet not so many in the intellectual history of mankind as to warrant disbelief in further advances.

If the preceding pages have done their work, some of the tendencies within the Indian political system will already have been made evident. The main point to be emphasized is that it is in itself a signal achievement of the Indian polity that it has, over a relatively short period, acquired definable shape and form—stability not in the sense of a stationary state but in the sense of regulated movement. It is this which has made possible coherent description and talk of tendencies. This is scarcely true of all new states. In some indeed it is difficult to reduce events to an order and impossible to speak with assurance of any general direction of development; almost anything could happen and an ample variety of things has already happened. India has been given coherence and shape by the character of the three elements in terms of which our account has been given: a machinery of government, a one-dominant-party system and a parliamentary constitutionalism. India, that is, has been able to cultivate institutions. These institutions imply behaviour according to patterns capable of change but not in erratic or wayward fashion. These institutions were in minor measure chosen with deliberation, in major part accepted and acquiesced in. They serve to make development possible by controlling it; they render it real by removing obvious drama. The firmly established nature of the institutions of political life tends to disguise the pace of change, but change is nonetheless taking place. Moreover, the institutions are of a kind which tend to ensure that change is at once about as fast as society can bear and at the same time about as sure (i.e. non-reversible) as man can make it.

Of course, change creates problems, and progress in the life of a society as in that of a person is marked never by the elimination of problems but by the replacement of one set by another. The key problem in India was to make *swaraj* or self-rule genuine rather than formal. This entailed the transformation of huge numbers of people from subjects into citizens, their incorporation into a body politic. The key tendency of the first quarter-century of India's own politics has been precisely thus, the steadily increased participation of almost all levels of society in what is called the political process, by which is meant no more and no less than the business of taking decisions that bind a community. This increased participation is evidenced by the mounting turn-out at elections (1952: 45·7 per cent; 1957: 47·7 per cent; 1962: 56·3 per cent; 1967: 61·3 per cent), by the penetration of the political parties, by the active functioning of so many local elected bodies. The increase is also qualitative; the reports of observers and the reports of surveys alike suggest that a heightened sense of individual responsibility has been developing in the electorate. This is what was implied in the highly significant taunt thrown out by the DMK: 'Congress has the vote-getters; we have the votes'. Tamilnad is not the whole of India and the days of the intermediaries are not yet over; but the direction of change is clear. The main political problems which face India in the 1970s are all, directly or indirectly, consequential on this main development. Since these problems are considerable, some may be tempted to say that the development of participation if deliberate was a mistake and if accidental a misfortune. But of course that needs measuring against the other set of consequences, those of not having citizens.

The changes in the party system are themselves in large part the result of increased participation. Congress, the great highway into politics, became so overcrowded that its managers were unable to control the traffic and impatient or desperate drivers got off the road altogether. Congress, that is to say, lost mainly through its rebels and the reason men rebelled and went out was that there was such a crush to try to get in. Once the internal cohesion of Congress was damaged the rest of the results of 1967 followed. Even the split of 1969 has a direct link with participation, for one of the issues of disagreement was how Congress could recover its appeal to a now more awakened electorate. As to where the party system will get to, it is difficult in detail to say. The move towards coalitional politics arising out of no one party achieving supremacy seems settled, though the revival of some kind of dominance by Mrs Gandhi's Congress is not wholly excluded.

The tendency towards an increase of violence and extra-constitutional action is part of the same pattern: the established avenues cannot cope with the issues which seem to press. More than that, the widening circle of political involvement now brings in sections as yet unpledged to the institutional framework. Here surely there is some danger. But it is not the case that any but a tiny minority are dedicated against that framework. The bulk of those who move outside it do so because they are persuaded that this is an effective way of pressing on those who are within it—where the real power lies. There is this real possibility of hope: the relative incoherence and disorder of the parties as they find themselves in the unfamiliar new world of coalitional politics may diminish as rules of the fresh game come to be established. Further, the making of such rules, the emergence of a new kind of ordered pattern, may well come not from a charismatic leader above as before but by a call to order uttered from the voters below. This, to be sure, is only a possibility. Meanwhile government is continuously faced with the problem of how far and in what way to repress movements which encourage violence. The demand is raised from time to time that all communal organizations should be banned since they foment hatred which then issues in violence when the occasion is ripe. The case against this step is not solely the libertarian argument but also the difficulty of dealing with underground activity and the danger of making martyrs popular.

We have noted tendencies for the two main ideological divisions, communal-secular and left-right to become sharper and more insistent. Both relate to the participation increase in that these divisions are in a sense invited by the process of political mobilization which is the obverse side of increasing political incorporation. As the rival organizers of parties move out in competition with each other to receive the aspiring entrant into political life, the terms of ideology filter down to levels previously less affected. This was less the case when the virtually sole integrator was Congress, for such an 'umbrella', centrist party necessarily muffled the sounds of difference. With the weakening through division of the centre, the at least short-run effect is one of increased stridency and polarization. At the same time there is a check against this: many of the non-Congress parties, emerging from the isolation of despairing opposition, seek to cultivate a wider rather than a narrow range of support and to that extent come somewhat to resemble Congress itself in their style. However, it would be misleading to speak as if ideological divisions were simply carried down into the electorate by the party organizers. With increasing social mobility and a growing ruthlessness of rivalry and competition —paradoxically, a cost of development as well as of development failures—there are also down below a series of social tensions looking, so to say, for justifications. When jobs are few in relation to demand, when licences have to be rationed and fertilizers have to be allocated, men see enemies readily, be they Muslims, the richer farmers or outsiders from another region.

The question of left-right polarization raises another matter. Many mainly outside observers have found it difficult not to look at India in terms of the other large Asian country, China, with its massive problems of development set against a background of an ancient and distinctive civilization. Then, equating Congress with the Kuomintang, they ask when red revolution will reach India, when India's Mao will appear. In so far as they attached great importance to the special restraining influence of Nehru on such development, they confidently expected momentous change following his death. Change there has been, but it falls far short of a communist upsurge and take-over. Part of the trouble about such an approach is that it pays too little attention to history and in particular fails to take seriously enough the legacies inherited by independent India. Such views also fall into the mental trap set by the left-right dichotomy which suggests that either extreme has some sort of stability and that a centre position must be a wobbly balancing point which cannot endure; yet mental trap it is. The Chinese 'model' acquires plausibility too from deterministic notions about the relation between economics and politics; this is very odd since in both countries (in very different ways) the autonomy of politics is striking and it is political compulsions which dictate to the economy rather more than the other way round. In any event, notwithstanding the communists' share of power in West Bengal and Kerala and despite the Naxalite activities, there is precious little evidence of a coming revolution. The communist gains have been very limited and very patchy, and if this is in part due to the division into CPI, CPI(M) and CPI(ML) that itself is an integral part of the scene, not accidental and due to disappear quickly. As indicated earlier, it is true that the 'green revolution' accentuates social cleavages and tensions in rural society, but between that situation and communist revolution there lie barriers galore: deep social cleavages of quite different kinds which cross-cut those of agricultural classes; sets of functioning local bodies more or less responsive to demands; habits and skills of adaptability among those who may be called upon to make concessions; and an army of rival political entrepreneurs eager to cheat the communists of what their doctrine tells them are their dues. No; India is not 'going communist', nor even steadily or uniformly left; it is going both left and right in different respects and on the whole only a little more left than right; it is mainly going Indian.

Finally, there is the tendency for the balance of power to move against the centre and in favour of the states. This has already been referred to not only in the governmental context but also in connection with political parties where we have noted not only the rise of specifically one-state parties such as DMK, Akali Dal and the Congress breakaways, but also the federalizing of the all-India parties as they discover the imposition of discipline from Delhi to be impracticable. This tendency has led several observers to speculate with morbid enthusiasm about a coming disintegration into chaos or balkanization to be halted only by some, perhaps military, form of autocracy. This is heady stuff but there are some calming potions available and the present writer would put his money on a less dramatic future. The undisputed shift in the centre of gravity of the system has to be seen in perspective. This means, first, that India must be judged as a federal state. This should be quite easy for Americans but it is most difficult for Britishers who, while bestowing federal, constitutions on others, have not yet, even with Ulster, had to experience the difficulties inherent in this form of system. The fact is that the DMK in Tamilnad is not running a county council, as any Québecois would readily appreciate. India must, however, not only be put alongside other federal states; it must also be properly put in relation to its own past. Now this entails seeing that neither the period of alien rule nor the first years after independence can be at all reasonably taken as the norm. The degree of central power achieved by the British and sustained for a while by the leadership of the nationalist movement was inconceivable if great expansion of governmental activity was to be joined to a free political system with increasing mass involvement. There is therefore nothing untoward

I

about the observed tendency; it was only to be expected that the generation of ready-made all-India leaders would disappear, that the centre could not take state obedience for granted.

But to say that the trend was to be expected is not yet to prove that it can be halted. Proof in such a matter is indeed difficult. However, one can see that all-India leaders are emerging, not ready-made—Mrs Gandhi is the last of that kind—but at the top end of a ladder starting in the states. Also evident is the development of a difficult but not unmanageable bargaining relationship between the centre and the state governments. The loss of single party control throughout the system has made less difference than was originally feared. The special difficulties with West Bengal derived from the particular frustrations of that state and the strong ideological colour of its government's major component; non-Congress governments in Madras and Orissa were reported to be if anything rather more co-operative than some Congress governments. The managing of all-India parties is perhaps the most difficult of the new exercises that all-India politicians have to master. It must be accepted that the only alternative to the further rise of explicitly regional parties based on single states is a tacit loosening of internal structures in the all-India bodies so that they become themselves thoroughly federal in nature.

The summing-up must be that the trend does not have to proceed to any 'logical' conclusion. There may have to be adjustments in many arrangements of federal finance, in several conventions of centre-state relations, even conceivably in the Constitution itself. Discussion on all these lines has indeed been going on for some time. Regional loyalty and regional distinctiveness are real, so are regional interests. But the cause of preserving India's unity while conceding its diversity does not lack ample support, whether in terms of interests, economic as well as political, or in terms of sentiment. The idea of India as one is no monopoly of the older generation. Nor, among the political parties, is it the exclusive tenet of the Congress parties. The most powerful single non-Congress party, the Jan Sangh, is more determined in its unitary disposition than any; its 'Indianiza-tion' slogan is pernicious in its anti-Muslim implications but it echoes and reinforces a hostility towards disintegration.

Ideas

Thus within this framework of federalist constitutionalism great change now takes place. The speed of change is concealed by the steadiness of its pace and by its being contained within mainly familiar institutions. Politically, the change consists in the permeative absorption of all forms of influence and power in one system—the creation of one political nation, the working out of one 'language' of politics. This happened initially mainly through the dominant party system, calling for skill, flexibility and capaciousness in Congress. Subsequently it has worked through a revised party set-up character-ized by more competition, bargaining and coalitional forms. It takes place mainly in the lower and rural reaches of society, but it involves adjustments and modifications at the higher and more sophisticated political levels. It is a process whereby the many are inducted into the council chambers. Here they come to acquire the ways of speech and thought already in use; at the same time their presence does some-thing to alter the accents and style in which the conversations and debates proceed. The mundane, the local and the traditional, already in a sense announced by Gandhi (which is not to say that Gandhi was either mundane or traditional), make their full appearance but are at the same time guided and contained.

The operation in its first seventeen years was presided over by an outstanding leader who was at once popular idol and aristocrat of aristocrats. But although his qualifications of temperament were perfect for the part to be played, Nehru's intellectual characteristics were less clearly suited. The desire and capacity to reconcile different positions was, of course, eminently present and has proved in-valuable. But the job of meeting the mundane, the local and the traditional was not to his taste, and more often than not these were the very tragets of his abuse. In a polity which if it was to come into being had to be without ideology, he was the natural ideologist. He spoke against 'isms' and he was an eclectic mixer of ideologies, but he could not escape easily from ideological expression. In this he represented urban, educated India, Western-educated at that. In doing so he prevented the complete alienation of that section from the new politics of India.

The educated middle-class citizen of India was the spearhead of the nationalist movement in its early days and was hardly displaced by any of the consequences of Gandhi. (To a large extent, they could be said to have appropriated and used Gandhi—to produce Gandhism.) In the sixties they were in great measure by-passed and left be-hind by the new politics of bread and butter. Yet they remained the commentators, the articulate ones—the journalists, teachers and publicists. Little wonder that the great positive changes in Indian politics took place almost unnoticed, while the air was filled with cries of lamentation and anger from the non-participating intelligentsia. Of course the intelligentsia was not wholly excluded from active politics and its members were in all parties, though fewer in Congress than outside. But their influence seemed to be diminishing and the distaste and frustration which they expressed has influenced greatly the picture of Indian politics obtained by all who stand outside it. If it had not been for Nehru, this would have been worse; if they began long before his death to weary of his leadership it must also be said that without him they would have been even more thoroughly lost and without a man to speak for them.

Lately, of course, and especially since 1969, the scene has changed again. There is the paradox that alongside the omnipresence of the 'wheeler-dealer' politicians, ideology enjoys a fresh lease of life. It is tempting to associate this with Indira Gandhi, child of her father, and to point the contrast with, say, Shastri and Kamaraj. It is certainly very tempting for the intelligentsia to herald the arrival of polarization. These temptations, like most temptations, have to be moderately resisted. There is more than personalities involved and in any case it is not yet ideological harvest-time. But ideas are back in some demand and it is worth asking what is available in the national stock of general ideas about politics. The answer, broadly, is that the stock still consists of ideas Nehru attacked and ideas he put together and propounded. Nehru, that is to say, is still a good starting-point for any exploration of political thinking in India. Of what Nehru attacked the most important single item is Hindu nationalism as expressed in the Jan Sangh. It contains cultural revivalism, hostility towards secularism and non-conformity, an element of xenophobia and a leaning towards autocracy. It merits further study both for the intrinsic fascination of a neo-traditionalist creed as well as for its probable future importance.

The ideologies which Nehru mixed in different proportions during his lengthy political career are many, and they all have their place—separately as well as in Nehru-like combination—in the mind of the intelligentsia. Somewhat over-simplifying, it may be said that the elements are mainly three, two modern and Western, one Indian—marxism, democratic liberalism and Gandhism. Marxism is in some measure present in much anti-colonialist thinking for the simple reason that the exposure and denunciation of imperialism employed some of the key marxist concepts. But the influence of marxist ways of thought, once thus introduced, penetrated further. For example, the presumption that there is a job to be done in the form of an unmasking of the other man's ideology as a cover or 'superstructure' of ideas designed to conceal economic interests is very common. Again, the readiness in developing countries to insist on a major role for the state in economic affairs, together with the drive for greater equality, brings much general sympathy for the marxist position as being one of thoroughgoing socialism. At the same time, marxism has an influence in a diametrically opposite sense: the 'withering away of the state' is an idea which can be used as a support for such decentralization of power as would reduce the state to nothing. The 'ending of power politics' envisaged by ex-marxist Gandhians is as much the result of their old training as it is of their new allegiance.

The messages of Marx are thus by no means confined to the organized marxists of the Communist Parties. Some part of marxism forms an element in the make-up of most members of the Indian intelligentsia. It is in this sense that Laski may be said to have a nation of followers. But this can be said for another good reason: most of these men would also have, as Laski had, a big place in their minds for the tenets and values of liberal democracy. The reconciliation is not easy and may indeed be judged strictly illegitimate, but just as the reply to the view of the American system of government as 'unworkable' is that the Americans work it, so it must be said that the Indian intelligentsia not only manages this reconciliation but feels it to be the most natural and comfortable of all intellectual positions and one requiring no effort or self-deception.

Nor must it be thought that there is anything merely 'borrowed' and 'alien' about these liberal values in the Indian mind. If the British had made a point of preaching them, their conquest of Indian minds would no doubt have been limited and tenuous. But almost the opposite was done—so that it was liberal nationalism which had to do the preaching itself, even to some degree against what has been neatly called the 'guided democracy' of the imperial rulers. That the rulers were ideologically almost defenceless against such attack may be the glory of British imperialism, but it made the Indian take-over of liberalism no less genuine. It is true that Gandhi's leadership swept aside those who called themselves the liberals and it is also true that in Gandhi's teachings and methods there was much that had little to do with liberalism. But in large measure what he did was to add to liberalism while striving to keep many of the liberal values. *Satyagraha,* he might have said, does not abolish liberalism but perfects it. What a large part of all the years of nationalist campaigning could be presented as embodying the gospel of liberalism according to John Stuart Mill and Thomas Hill Green—the protests against police excesses, the protections of liberty of opinion and discussion, the demand for accountable government and proper representation, the freeing of justice from governmental pressures, in a word the opportunity for subjects to become citizens! In this way, through this experience, did liberalism become integral to the Indian way of thought in politics.

As already suggested, Gandhi was nothing if not complex. At the heart of his teaching is a liberalism not unlike that of Green—that is, one which conceives the business of politics to be neither the ardent creation of a social kingdom of heaven nor the austere confining of the state to the avoidance of gross frictions and conflicts, but rather the searching removal by the organized community of all hindrances to the good life to be lived by the individual but not to be chosen by individual whim. The goal towards which Gandhi sought to move was anarchy by self-government through decentralization—the shifting downwards and outwards of decision-making from a centre to smaller communities, and eventually, as a result of example and discipline, to each individual who would by control of self become a citizen without the aid of law. The specifically Indian part of Gandhi's teaching consisted in the mode and language in which this doctrine was expressed, together with the elaboration of the techniques by which the stages towards the goal could be achieved. Thus the unit of initial devolution is the village, the combination of moral persuasion and self-discipline is found in *satyagraha,* the philosophical justifications are given in the language of the Gita, and so on. The end of politics is the ending of politics; the replacement of the government of men by the administration of things can come only through men learning to govern themselves; the process of self-government is one of conquest of violence.

Indian thought of the post-Gandhi period has continued to consist of variations on these three major themes which Nehru combined, together with Hindu nationalism. Of the four, it appears on the surface that marxism and Hindu nationalism may have gained somewhat at the expense of liberalism and Gandhism. This, however, needs more careful examination than can be undertaken here. One needs to beware of facile conclusions in this area. It is frequently asserted that young intellectuals now have no time for Gandhi's teachings. But even among the young intellectuals of a generation earlier there were probably few who were strictly drawn to his ideas; they followed the man and grasped at the opportunities he created for self-dedication but not many were ever real disciples.

If the current thought continues to combine elements drawn from marxism, liberal democracy and Gandhi, this is by no means to say that variety is absent, for the combinations can be in very strongly contrasted proportions and styles. Even within schools of thought which have much in common, clear differences can be seen. The late Sardar K. M. Panikkar, Minoo Masani and A. D. Gorwala all may be described as Western-style thinkers with indifference or hostility towards marxist and Gandhian thought. Panikkar in his *The State and the Citizen* (1956) speaks for all three in his basically liberal democratic views. He sees the problem of reconciling individual rights with welfare state activity; he speaks of the importance of assisting the individual to resist mass opinion and of the need for dispersed leadership rather than the elevation of one man to a unique position; he distinguishes, as the Gandhians fail to do, between the undoubted 'right of each individual, where his conscience is concerned, to decide whether he could submit to the authority of the state' and the impermissible 'right to organize disobedience'. He has only scorn for talk of the spiritual basis of Indian life; this is self-deception and the truth is that 'nowhere do worldliness and the desire for advantage over others have a greater hold on people than in India'. He regards the search for indigenous forms of polity based on simple village units to be 'meaningless'; there must be no attempt to withdraw India from her fortunate and successful marriage with 'the common tradition that civilized humanity has developed during the last 150 years'—the tradition of democratic liberalism. Panikkar was willing to have an interest in 'Indian doctrines of politics' as developed in the ancient and medieval kingdoms but not willing to say that what India now has was built upon those foundations. Masani, founder member of the Congress Socialist Party in the early thirties but now one of the leaders of right-wing Swatantra, would endorse these views, but his main contribution to political debate is a vigorous attack—such as Panikkar did not support—on the expanding state and an equally vigorous (and in a developing country unusual) defence of free enterprise. Also, his dealings with the communists in his earlier career have made him more passionately anti-CPI. A. D. Gorwala occupies a further distnctive position within this trio. A former civil servant, he was one of the few Indians to resign from the ICS after independence. At first he continued not hostile to the government and accepted commissions to report on administrative problems. Subsequently he moved away and in recent years has published privately a weekly *Opinion* which expresses some of the most violent criticism of government. Gorwala is too much of a civil servant to take a Masani view, but he differs from Panikkar in refusing to be on speaking terms with a government which he now regards as simply evil. His concern with clean and efficient administration has widened to become an anxiety about the poisoned atmosphere of public life as a whole, an atmosphere in which Gorwala would say that men of moral standards can scarcely breathe.

Outside men such as these, it might be difficult to find any Indian political thinkers who would not regard themselves as some kind of socialist. But the scope for difference remains. Until his acceptance of the position of Deputy Chairman of the Planning Commission, Asoka Mehta was leader of the PSP and the most intellectual of all the top politicians. In writings such as *Democratic Socialism* (1951) and *Studies in Asian Socialism* (1959) he ranges widely over marxist and non-marxist thought. He readily acknowledges Marx's ideas as 'majestic', but rejects them as illustrating in their determinism a 'lack of faith in social elasticity' and as entailing 'mysticism' about class, and the subordination of the individual to the new servile state by means of the party. He attaches importance to the utopian tradition in socialist thought and speaks of Gandhi and Vinoba Bhave as being in this tradition. In his capacity as party leader, Mehta adumbrated a view of the modifications required in the classical conception of parliamentary democracy before it could fit the circumstances of a developing country; mainly, the role of an opposition should change and become 'constructive' because there was bound to be so much on which men of many parties were really agreed that 'opposition' would tend to be unreal or anti-national. His joining the Planning Commission and Congress was in a sense a consistent conclusion. In these views he tended to part company not only with Lohia (who, while no less distrustful of the communists than Mehta, insists on the theory of 'equidistance' from Congress and CP alike) but also with Kripalani (less socialist but more bitterly anti-Congress than Mehta).

There are various kinds of socialists within Congress as well as outside. Nehru's own brand was the most 'central' and eclectic of all. For him, socialism meant mainly social justice with a movement towards equality, but it frequently connoted efficiency and a modern, scientific approach to the arrangements of society. He always looked back in admiration on the Soviet Revolution as 'a great leap' and 'a bright flame', but marxism was too complete and coherent a doctrine to contain Nehru; he used its concepts when it suited him. He was a marxist without the logic of marxism, a Fabian without the faith in administration, a Gandhian without the acceptance of anarchy for morality's sake.

A leading Congressman who has written on the socialism of his party is Sriman Narayan, Gandhian economist and poet. One of his booklets is entitled *A Plea for Ideological Clarity* (Delhi, 1957)—others are *Towards a Socialist Economy* (Delhi, 1955) and *Socialistic Pattern of Society* (Delhi, 1955)—but he seems not to have achieved any clearly distinctive level of treatment. More interesting is

Sampurnanand, former Chief Minister of Uttar Pradesh, whose views are set out in *The Individual and the State* (Allahabad, 1949) and *Indian Socialism* (Bombay, 1961). Here democratic socialism is presented as a continuation of traditional Indian philosophy. India 'can evolve a new system of political philosophy on the basis of her age-old thought' and an indigenous version of democratic socialism would be no more than the cradle for the philosophers' ideal of self-realization, 'the logical outcome of Shankara's *advaita*'.

What Sampurnanand declares in general terms has not really been worked out in systematic fashion. The nearest attempt was in Professor K. P. Mukerji's *The State* (Madras, 1952). Much more influential has been the rather different development represented by the most vital political thinker in modern India, Jaiprakash Narayan. Here some appeal is made to India's ancient 'village republics' and there is an emphasis on finding a political system suitable to India's own needs. But the ideological arguments used by Narayan have unmistakable Western roots and he makes little attempt to connect with Hindu philosophy. Before the war 'J.P.' was a leading Congress Socialist and one of the more accomplished and ardent marxists of that group. During the Quit India movement of 1942 he was an important organizer of the underground movement. In the course of the first decade after independence his position moved round to one of similarity to Gandhi's. The story is told in his *Socialism to Sarvodaya* (Madras, 1956). But he has not stopped there. About 1959, he prepared for private but quite wide circulation a most stimulating document entitled 'A Plea for Reconstruction of Indian Polity'. In the light of comments received, he published *Swaraj for the People* (Banaras, 1961). Unfortunately, the latter is a version which omits much of the interesting argument of the earlier essay.

J.P. launches an attack on the Western type of democracy which India is attempting to operate. It is not merely unsuitable for India; it is basically deficient, and India will be the world's benefactor if she can show the way to a more true form of democratic polity. J.P. reveals relics of marxist thought when he speaks of his reconstructed policy as 'most rational and scientific' and 'in line with the natural course of social evolution'. The same is true of his persisting vision of a state that will wither away in time, once the 'reconstruction' has been undertaken. The defect which J.P. sees in conventional democracy is that it is still government by a few over the many. It is based, he says, on an atomistic view of society which leaves the individual helplessly at the mercy of power imposed from above. Instead, all legitimate power comes from below and as little as possible should be delegated upwards. The two key adjectives which he uses to describe his kind of democracy are 'communitarian' and 'participating'. A genuine pyramid of politics based on village communities must be created; the 'higher' organs of state power will be derived electorally from the lower bodies and will have only residual co-ordinating functions. In this way all will participate in the making of the decisions. Not only that: by reviving local communities party politics will be slain and the divisive character of party democracy will be overcome; in the real community that is possible in smaller units, consensus is natural and a general will emerges without impediment from the competition for power.

Marx, Rousseau and Gandhi are all discernible as influences here. (So also is M. N. Roy, a communist of the 1920s who moved round to a position which he designated 'radical humanism' and who before his death had captured the attention of many intellectuals even though his political efforts brought little return.) Narayan's gospel was indirectly responsible for the push to introduce Panchayat Raj and, although his teachings may as yet attract no large and active body of followers, his standing is high in many circles. Together with Bhave, he keeps alive the message of purity and idealism already referred to in Chapter 2. He has declared his break with the world of party politics, but what he says still penetrates into that world. Moreover, in any situation that could be presented as one of national crisis and absence of effective leadership, he might still be persuaded to return to the affairs of state. In the meantime, he represents a real and Indian point of view; in his own way he helps to fill the gap left by Gandhi. That gap was so wide that not even a Nehru could fill it; the parts which Nehru could not act are played by J.P. It is true that since the rural masses who now move into the political scene may have less interest in utopias than in irrigation, J.P. may paradoxically find that the receptive audience for his preaching of village democracy will be mainly in the towns.

The most striking confrontation in Indian political thinking is likely to be that between marxism and Hindu nationalism. Yet for two reasons it is not a real confrontation: they scarcely meet because they are not so much opposite poles of one ideological axis as separate poles of separate axes; moreover, they confront with difficulty because there is so much that lies between the two in the grey middle formed from the marxist's red, the sadhu's saffron and even Gandhi's white. Liberalism is there too; it is not so easy to assign to it a colour; it is simply the agent which gets the others to mix.

FURTHER READING

It has been thought worth while to cater for the most serious students by providing a thorough guide to further work. Others can use the Note with varying measures of selection. The sections of this guide have some correspondence with the Chapters: II and III with Chapter 1; IV, Chapter 2; VI, Chapter 4; VII, Chapter 5; VIII, Chapter 6; IX, Chapter 7.

I. The subject of modern Indian politics can be approached by several routes. Much depends on the direction from which one arrives. The reader already familiar with the country's history and culture will enjoy some advantages, the student of comparative politics will enjoy others; each needs ideally to acquire the other's equipment. The following are all in their own way valid routes:

(a) An approach to an unfamiliar country is often successfully made through imaginative literature and biographical writing. English writers who have provided penetrating insights into important aspects of Indian situations and temperament include E. M. Forster (in *Passage to India,* 1924), L. H. Myers and Paul Scott. Many Indian novelists writing in English perform a similar service: R. K. Narayan is outstanding and there are others of interest: Mulk-Raj Anand, Ruth Jhabvala, Khushwant Singh, Kamala Markandaya, V. Madulkar, M. Malgonkar. There are translations of some of the important writers in Indian languages such as Premchand. Some biographical writing illumines social scenes at certain periods: N. C. Chaudhuri, *The Autobiography of an Unknown Indian* (1951) is in a class of its own but there is quality and value in P. Tandon, *Punjabi Century* (1961), D. D. Karve, *The New Brahmans* (1963), Ved Mehta, *Face to Face* (1957) and several books by Sudhin Ghose.

(b) India has always excited visitors in very different ways and continues to do so. Interesting and perceptive personal impressions mainly of shock and distaste are recorded in V. S. Naipaul, *An Area of Darkness* (1964) and R. Segal, *The Crisis of India* (1965). Less coloured but lively reporting is given in Taya Zinkin, *India Changes!* (1958). Indian journalists of

standing have sometimes provided general accounts of political developments; a recent example is Pran Chopra, *Uncertain India* (1968).

(c) India's cultural traditions and her pre-British past are almost
inseparable. They can be studied in histories such as A. L. Basham,
The Wonder That Was India (1954); Romila Thapar, *The History of India*,
vol. 1, (1966); Sir Jadunath Sarkar, *India Through the Ages* (4th ed., 1951);
H. G. Rawlinson, *India, a Short Cultural History* (1952); R. C. Majumdar,
Ancient India (rev. ed., 1960); in rather more popular surveys such as
K. M. Panikkar, *Survey of Indian History* (3rd ed., 1957) and J. Nehru,
Discovery of India (1946); in the appropriate portions of general histories
like T. G. P. Spear, *India* (1952), W. H. Moreland and A. C. Chatterjee,
A Short History of India (1953) and R. C. Majumdar, *An Advanced
History of India* (2nd ed., 1958). W. T. de Bary, *Sources of Indian Tradition*
(1958) is a valuable book of readings. Less historical presentations are
found in classics such as S. Radhakrishnan, *Religion and Society* (1947)
and *The Hindu View of Life* (1928), A. Schweitzer, *Indian Thought and its
Development* (1936), A. K. Coomaraswamy, *Hinduism and Buddhism*
(1943) and Max Weber, *The Religion of India* (1958). Examples of important recent writing are found in two volumes by M. Singer: *Traditional
India* (1959) and *Krishna* (1966).

(d) That part of the pre-British experience which concerns political
institutions and ideas about government may be approached through
D. Mackenzie Brown, *The White Umbrella* (1953), which gives excerpts
from Indian writings and brief commentaries, Kautilya, *Arthasastra*
(Trans. R. Shamasastry, 5th ed., 1956), the medieval classic, U. N.
Ghoshal's general survey, *History of Hindu Political Ideas* (rev. ed., 1959),
A. S. Altekar, *State and Government in Ancient India* (3rd ed., 1958),
C. Drekmeier, *Kingship and Community in Early India* (1962) and J. W.
Spellman, *Political Theory of Ancient India* (1964).

(e) India's politics can also be reached by the different route of comparative politics and in particular the politics of new states and the
problems of political development. Relevant philosophical considerations
are contained in J. Plamenatz, *On Alien Rule and Self-Government* (1960),
E. Kedourie, *Nationalism* (1960) and J. R. Pennock, *Self-Government in
Modernising Nations* (1964). Relatively early general accounts were given
in R. Emerson, *From Empire to Nation* (1960) and Vera Dean, *The
Nature of the Non-Western World* (1957). Seminal contributions to the
systematic study of political development were contained in a number of
articles: Kahin, Pauker and Pye, 'Comparative politics in non-western
countries' in *American Political Science Review*, December 1955; Almond,
'Comparative political systems' in *Journal of Politics*, August 1956;
Rustow, 'New horizons for comparative politics' in *World Politics*, July
1957; Neumann, 'Comparative politics: a half-century appraisal' in *Journal
of Politics*, August 1957; Pye, 'The non-western political process' in *Journal
of Politics*, August 1958; Shils, 'Political development in the new states' in
Comparative Studies in Society and History, July 1960. The most influential
single volume was probably G. Almond and J. Coleman (Eds.), *The Politics*

of Developing Areas (1960), carried forward by G. Almond and G. B. Powell, *Comparative Politics: a development approach* (1966). This was followed by the seven volumes in the Princeton *Studies in Political Development* series including especially those dealing with Bureaucracy (ed. J. La Palombara), Political Parties (eds. M. Weiner and J. La Palombara) and Political Culture (eds. L. W. Pye and S. Verba). Other significant works in this field include C. Geertz, *Old Societies and New States* (1963), K. W. Deutsch, *Nationalism and Social Communication* (1953), D. Apter, *The Politics of Modernization* (1965), R. Bendix, *Nation-building and Citizenship* (1964) which has a perceptive chapter on India, S. N. Eisenstadt, *Modernization—Protest and Change* (1967) and S. P. Huntington, *Political Order in Changing* Societies (1968). A useful set of readings is provided in C. E. Welch (Ed.), *Political Modernization* (1967), while L. W. Pye has put some of his work together in *Aspects of Political Development* (1966).

II. The British period is important for reasons indicated in Chapter 1. The literature is vast but some headings may be useful.

(a) Outline histories include E. Thompson, *Rise and Fulfilment of British Rule in India* (1934), T. G. P. Spear, *India, Pakistan and the West* (3rd ed., 1958) and an Indian 'reply' by K. M. Panikkar, *Asia and Western Dominance* (1953). A. B. Keith, *Speeches and Documents on Indian Policy, 1750–1921* (1922) and, even more, C. H. Philips, *The Evolution of India and Pakistan, 1858–1947* (1962) are useful collections. General features of British rule are discussed in R. P. Masani, *Britain in India* (1960), G. Wint, *The British in Asia* (1954), P. Moon, *Strangers in India* (1945), Sir P. Griffiths, *The British Impact on India* (1952), L. S. S. O'Malley (Ed.), *Modern India and the West* (1941, reprinted 1968) and, most recently, F. Hutchins, *The Illusion of Permanence* (1967). Most evocative portraits are provided in P. Woodruff (pseud.), *The Men who Ruled India* (2 vols., 1953–4) and Lord Beveridge, *India Called Them* (1947). More recent memoirs include J. Halliday, *A Special India* (1968) and J. Beames, *Memoirs of a Bengal Civilian* (1961). A. J. Greenberger, *The British Image of India* (1969) is a study in the literature of imperialism. A. Low, *Lion Rampant: studies in the history of British Imperialism* (1971) uses both Indian and African material in a stimulating series of essays on imperial rule.

(b) The structure of British government in India and its constitutional development are described in A. B. Keith, *Constitutional History of India* (1963) and R. Coupland, *Report on the Constitutional Problem in India* (1942–3). Closer views of the administration are given by L. S. S. O'Malley, *Indian Civil Service* (1931, reprinted 1965) and E. A. H. Blunt, *The ICS* (1937), while H. Tinker, *The Foundations of Local Self-Government in India, Pakistan and Burma* (1954) is the standard work on its aspect of the subject. Some of the earlier accounts, mostly written from the inside, are most illuminating: W. H. Sleeman, *Rambles and Recollections of an Indian Official* (1844); G. O. Trevelyan, *The Competition Wallah* (1864); R. Carstairs, *The Little World of the Indian District Officer* (1912); J. Chailley, *Administrative Problems in British India* (1910). Examples of valuable recent research on the nineteenth century include K. Ballhatchet, *Social Policy and Social Change in Western India, 1817–1830* (1957), R. E. Frykenburg, *Guntur District, 1788–1848* (1965), E. Stokes, *The English Utilitarians and India* (1959), which examines the relation between political ideas and administrative practice. Among the interesting articles are three by B. S. Cohn ('Some notes on law and change in North India', *Economic Development and Cultural Change,* vol. VIII, pp. 79–93, 1959, 'The initial British impact on India; a case study of the Benares region', *Journal of Asian Studies,* August 1960 and 'Political systems in Eighteenth Century India', *Journal of the American Oriental Society,* July–Sept. 1962), which use the insights of social anthropology to illumine administrative history.

(c) The politics of the period leading up to independence is landmarked by the two documents related to the reforms of 1919 and 1935: the (Montagu-Chelmsford) *Report on Indian Constitutional Reforms* (Cmd. 1909 of 1918 and the connected papers Cmd. 103, 141, 176, all of 1919) and the (Simon) *Report of the Indian Statutory Commission* (Cmd. 3568–9 of 1930 with the associated Franchise report, Cmd. 4086 of 1932). Gwyer and Appadorai, *Speeches and Documents on the Indian Constitution, 1921–47* (1957) is an excellent collection. The more useful earlier studies include 'Kerala Putra' (K. M. Panikkar), *The Working of Dyarchy* (1928), A. Appadorai, *Dyarchy in Practice* (1938), G. Schuster and G. Wint, *India and Democracy* (1941) and B. P. Singh Roy, *Parliamentary Government in India* (1943). Important work on the inter-war period now in progress stresses the interaction between rulers and ruled (therefore see Section III also); some of the first fruits are available in A. Low (Ed.), *Soundings in Modern South Asian History* (1967). On the actual transfer of power the basic source will be the series of several volumes of documents from India Office records of which the editor-in-chief is N. Mansergh: the general title is *The Transfer of Power 1942–7* and the first volume to appear deals with the year 1942 and was published by HMSO in 1970. Authoritative accounts based on personal experience and access to papers are V. P. Menon, *The Transfer of Power in India* (1957) and H. V. Hodson, *The Great Divide* (1969) while there are some interesting contributions in C. H. Philips and M. D. Wainwright (Eds.), *The Partition of India* (1970). The aspect of the story concerning the princely states is dealt with in V. P. Menon, *The Integration of the Indian States* (1956) and U. Phadnis, *Towards the Integration of Indian States* (1968). Vivid accounts of events away from the conference tables are contained in F. Tuker, *While Memory Serves* (1950) and P. Moon, *Divide and Quit* (1961).

III. The emergence and development of Indian nationalism is now the subject of substantial historical re-assessment and the literature on Indian politics in the first half of this century is now growing quickly.

(a) The nationalist movement was preceded by social and religious ferment. The religious beginnings are discussed in J. N. Farquhar, *Modern Religious Movements in India* (1915) and D. S. Sarma, *Studies in the Renaissance of Hinduism in the 19th and 20th centuries* (1944). The links between that renaissance and politics were explored in arresting fashion in Lord Ronaldshay, *The Heart of Aryavarta* (1925), and more recently in C. H. Heimsath, *Indian Nationalism and Hindu Social Reform* (1964). Aspects of social change are described in B. B. Misra, *The Indian Middle Classes* (1961), B. T. McCully, *English Education and the Origins of Indian Nationalism* (1940), S. Natarajan, *A Century of Social Reform in India* (1959). An explanation of nationalism in terms of class is attempted in A. R. Desai, *Social Background of Indian Nationalism* (rev. ed., 1954). Some of the best recent work focusses on the distinctive nature in particular regions of the relation between society and politics. Excellent examples are J. H. Broomfield, *Elite Conflict in a Plural Society: 20th Century Bengal* (1968), E. Irschick, *Politics and Social Coniflct in South India* (1969), R. Kumar, *Western India in the 19th Century* (1968) and P. Reeves, 'The Politics of Order' in *Journal of Asian Studies,* XXV, 2. A cross-region comparative view is provided in A. Seal, *The Emergence of Indian Nationalism* (1968), the first of a series of volumes in Political Change in South Asia being prepared under the editorship of J. A. Gallagher and A. Seal. A remarkable study in intellectual history relating nationalism to pan-Asian sentiment is S. N. Hay, *Asian Images of East and West* (1969).

(b) There is still no good history of the Congress movement up to 1947. P. Sitaramayya, *The History of the Indian National Congress* (1946–7) is a chronicle mainly useful for reference on certain points. An early general account is contained in W. R. Smith, *Nationalism and Reform in India* (1938) while C. F. Andrews *The Rise and Growth of the Congress in India* (1938) deals mainly with the early years. The comments of English contemporaries were sometimes illuminating, as in V. Chirol, *Indian Unrest* (1910), J. R. Macdonald, *The Awakening of India* (1910), E. Bevan, *Indian Nationalism* (1913), R. Byron, *Essay on India* (1931), and H. N. Brailsford, *Subject India* (1943). Of recent works, S. R. Mehrotra, *India and the Commonwealth, 1885–1929* (1965) deals in scholarly fashion with certain aspects and further work of relevance can be expected from the same author. Also to be noted are D. Argov, *Moderates and Extremists, 1883–1920* (1968) and forthcoming work by Gopal Krishna of which 'The Development of the Indian National Congress as a Mass Organization', *Journal of Asian Studies,* XXV, 3, is a foretaste.

(c) There is a good deal of interesting writing by and about the leading figures in the movement. D. M. Brown, *Nationalist Movement: Indian Political Thought from Ranade to Bhave* (1961) gives some readings. The following are by or about the main leaders: Dadabhai Naoroji, *Poverty and un-British Rule in India* (1901), R. P. Masani, *Dadabhai Naoroji* (1939), Gokhale, *Speeches and Writings* (Eds. Patwardhan and Ambedkar, vol. I 1962, vol. II 1966), D. V. Tahmankar, *Lokmanya Tilak* (1956), S. A. Wolpert, *Tilak and Gokhale* (1962), W. Wedderburn, *A. O. Hume* (1913), S. K. Ratcliffe, *Sir William Wedderburn and the Indian Reform Movement* (1923), R. Tagore, *Nationalism* (1917), K. Kripalani, *Rabindranath Tagore* (1963), M. Gandhi, *An Autobiography or the Story of my Experiments with Truth* (1927), H. A. Jack (Ed.), *The Gandhi Reader* (1956), R. Duncan

(Ed.), *Selected Writings of Mahatma Gandhi* (1951), B. R. Nanda, *Mahatma Gandhi: a Biography* (1958), L. Fischer, *The Life of Mahatma Gandhi* (1950), S. Banerjea, *A Nation in Making* (1925, reprint 1964), B. R. Nanda, *The Nehrus, Motilal and Jawaharlal* (1962), J. Nehru, *An Autobiography* (new ed., 1949), M. Brecher, *Nehru: a Political Biography* (1959), A. K. Azad, *India Wins Freedom* (1959), S. C. Bose, *The Indian Struggle, 1935–1942* (1952), H. Toye, *The Springing Tiger: a Study of a Revolutionary* (1959), R. Prasad, *Autobiography* (1957), D. V. Tahmankar, Sardar Patel (1970). (The books of Brecher and Nanda are excellent surveys of the period as well as biographies of persons.)

(d) The Muslim movement culminated in the creation of Pakistan but was of course a part of the Indian political scene up to 1947. (For Muslims in India since 1947 see Section IV(c) below, but it must be admitted that there is here some gap in the literature.) The standard work is W. C. Smith, *Modern Islam in India* (2nd ed., 1946), but the following can be useful: A. Husain, *Fazl-i-Husain* (1946), A. H. Albiruni, *Makers of Pakistan* (1950), H. Bolitho, *Jinnah* (1954), K. K. Aziz, *Britain and Muslim India* (1963), R. Gopal, *Indian Muslims, a Political History 1858–1947* (1959), M. Mujeeb, *The Indian Muslims* (1967).

IV. The social setting of Indian politics has become the subject of keen study in recent years. Here it is enough to indicate some of the key works and especially those which have a fairly explicit bearing on political life.

(a) Of earlier studies, two which retain a value are B. H. Baden-Powell, *The Indian Village Community* (1896) and L. S. S. O'Malley, *India's Social Heritage* (1934). Modern studies are usually focussed on particular communities but K. Davis, *The Population of India and Pakistan* (1951), M. B. Singer (Ed.), *Traditional India: Structure and Change* (1959), C. H. Philips (Ed.), *Politics and Society in India* (1963) P. Mason (Ed.), *India and Ceylon: Unity and Diversity* (1967), J. Silverberg (Ed.) *Social, mobility in the caste system in India* (1968), are all general in scope. Perhaps the most important collection of recent papers is M. Singer and B. Cohn (Eds.) *Structure and Change in Indian Society* (1968).

(b) At the centre of recent social research are studies of villages and the significance of caste in rural communities. Some of the more path-breaking contributions have been W. H. and C. V. Wiser, *Behind Mud Walls 1930–1960* (1963), W. H. Wiser, *Hindu Jajmani System* (2nd ed., 1958), M. N. Srinivas (Ed.), *India's Villages* (1955), *Caste in India and Other Essays* (1962) and *Social Change in Modern India* (1966), F. G. Bailey, *Caste and the Economic Frontier* (1957) and *Tribe Caste and Nation* (1960), McKim Marriott (Ed.), *Village India* (1955), S. C. Dube, *Indian Village* (1955), O. Lewis, *Village Life in Northern India* (1958), A. C. Mayer, *Caste and Kinship in Central India* (1960), H. Orenstein, *Gaon* (1965), R. G. Fox, *From Zamindar to Ballot Box* (1969), A. Beals, *Gopalpur* (1963), and A. Beteille, *Caste, Class and Power* (1966). T. Zinkin, *Caste Today* (1962) is a useful booklet summary for the layman; M. N. Srinivas, 'Caste: a trend report and bibliography' in *Current Sociology,* vol. VIII, no. 3, 1959, is the best review of the literature to that date; I. Karve, *The Hindu Society* (Mimeo., Berkeley, 1960) and *Changing India: Aspects of Caste Society* (1961) are more general theoretical re-assessments; M. Carstairs, *The Twice-born* (1957) is a fascinating psychological study.

(c) There have also been valuable studies of particular social groups and religious communities: J. and R. H. Useem, *The Western-Educated Man in India* (1955), E. Shils, *The Intellectual between Tradition and Modernity: the Indian Situation* (1961), R. L. Hardgrave, *The Nadars of Tamilnad* (1969), D. R. Gadgil, *Origins of the Modern Indian Business Class* (1959), M. Cormack, *The Hindu Woman* (1961) and *She Who Rides a Peacock* (1952) and Kushwant Singh, *The Sikhs* (1953). On untouchables some of the best work is by L. Dushkin, 'The Backward Classes', *The Economic Weekly*, Vol. XIII, nos. 43–46 and 'Scheduled Caste Policy in India', *Asian Survey*, VII, 9. Also to be noted are H. R. Isaacs, *India's Ex-untouchables* (1965) and O. M. Lynch, *The Politics of Untouchability* (1969). The Muslim community in India after partition is to some extent a mystery area but some light is thrown by the relevant parts of D. E. Smith, *Religion and Politics in South Asia* (1966) and the articles of T. Wright such as 'Muslim Legislators in India: Profile of a Minority Elite', *The Journal of Asian Studies*, XXIII, 2. Works of unusual interest on the social culture of the Hindus as a whole have appeared in recent years: N. C. Chaudhuri, *The Continent of Circe* (1965), P. Spratt, *Hindu Culture and Personality* (1966), W. K. Kapp, *Hindu Culture Economic Development and Economic Planning* (1963), and on a key segment of the community, B. N. Nair, *The Dynamic Brahmin* (1959) and A. D. Moddie, *Brahminical Culture and Modernity* (1968).

(d) Although several of the works just mentioned touch on political behaviour, this is not their main concern. Political scientists and social anthropologists have, however, fairly successfully closed in on the problem of the politics of caste. Pioneer shots in the campaign included notably S. S. Harrison, 'Caste and the Andhra communists', *American Political Science Review*, June 1956, F. G. Bailey's series of articles in *The Economic Weekly* during August–November 1959, R. Nicholas, 'Village Factions and Political Parties in Rural West Bengal', *Journal of Commonwealth Political Studies*, November 1963, L. Rudolph, 'The political role of India's caste associations', *Pacific Affairs*, March 1960 and M. Weiner, 'Traditional role performance and the development of modern political parties', *Journal of Politics*, November 1964. By now there are a number of important monographs or collections: F. G. Bailey, *Politics and Social Change* (1963), C. H. Philips (Ed.), *Politics and Society in India* (1963), L. and S. Rudolph, *The Modernity of Tradition* (1967), R. Bhaskaran, *Sociology of Politics* (1967), M. Singer and B. Cohn (Eds.), *Structure and Change in Indian Society* (1968), A. Beteille, *Castes Old and New* (1968), R. Kothari, *Caste in Indian Politics* (1970), M. Swartz (Ed.), *Local Level Politics* (1969) and M. Banton (Ed.), *Political systems and the distribution of power* (1965). The programme of community development has focussed attention on the borderlands between sociology and politics: some of the more useful contributions are S. C. Dube, *India's Changing Villages* (1958), Kusum Nair, *Blossoms in the Dust* (1961) H. Tinker, 'Authority and Community in village India' in *Pacific Affairs,* Dec. 1959, A. C. Mayer, 'Some political implications of community development in India, in *European Journal of Sociology,* vol. IV, no. 1, 1963. Several of the chapters in the important volume R. L. Park and I. Tinker (Eds.), *Leadership and Political Institutions in India* (1959) (which is also referred to below) deal with this problem. Relevant also in this area is D. E. Smith (Ed.), *Religion and Politics in S. Asia* (1966), already mentioned above. An article of unusual interest is A. Parel, 'The political symbolism of the cow in India', *Journal of Commonwealth Political Studies,* VII, 3. The student of politics should also note the relevance to his work of some of the explorations in the field where economic and social research meet: valuable examples are R. Braibanti and J. J. Spengler (Eds.), *Tradition, Values and Socio-Economic Development* (1961), T. S. Epstein, *Economic Development and Social Change in South India* (1962), N. V. Sovani and V. M. Dandekar (Eds.), *Changing India* (1961), D. and A. Thorner, *Land and Labour in India* (1962), J. P. Lewis, *Quiet Crisis in India* (1964), G. Rosen, *Democracy and Economic Change* (1967), C. Bettelheim, *India Independent* (1968) and A. H. Hanson, 'Power Shifts and Regional Balances', in P. Streeten and M. Lipton, *The Crisis of Indian Planning* (1968) and W. Ladejinksy, 'Ironies of India's Green Revolution', *Foreign Affairs,* July 1970.

V. There are a few general accounts of Indian politics similar in scope though not in approach to the present volume. The first crop included N. D. Palmer, *Indian Political System* (1961), H. Tinker, *India and Pakistan: a Short Political Guide* (1962), V. Dean, *New Patterns of Democracy* in *India* (1959). Chapters on India have been contributed by M. Weiner in G. Almond and J. Coleman (Eds.), *The Politics of the Developing Areas* (1960), by N. D. Palmer in G. McT. Kahin (Ed.), *Major Governments of Asia* (1958), by R. L. Park in R. E. Ward and R. C. Macridis (Eds.), *Modern Political Systems: Asia* (1963), and, more briefly, by W. H. Morris-Jones in S. Rose (Ed.), *Politics in Southern Asia* (1963). The volume *Leadership and Political Institutions in India* (1959), edited by R. L. Park and I. Tinker, was an early collection of papers but one which retains its value. R. L. Hardgrave, *India: Government and Politics in a Developing Nation* (1970) is a good recent text. R. Kothari, *Politics in India* (1970) excludes government administration but in other respects is most ambitious and valuable.

VI. There is no one full-length account of the machinery of government in India at the levels of centre, state and below. The picture has to be pieced together by taking studies of particular parts and aspects. Much of the most useful material is contained in official publications; with a few exceptions these are not listed here but in section X below.
(a) In the Indian Institute of Public Administration's compilation,

The Organisation of the Government of India (1958), the bare bones of the central administration are exposed (but there have been several changes since the work was completed), while the best critical study is A. Chanda, *Indian Administration* (1958). Most important as a set of documents for the study of administration in India is the series of *Reports* (1968–70) by the Administrative Reforms Commission together with the more detailed Reports of the Study Teams set up by the Commission. B. B. Majumdar (Ed.), *Problems of Public Administration in India* (1954) covers a wide field, though unevenly. Much interesting comment on the administration is found in reports: P. H. Appleby, *Public Administration: Report of a Survey* (1953) and *Re-Examination of India's Administrative System* (1956), A. D. Gorwala, *Report on Public Administration* (1951).

(b) There is nothing adequate on state-level machinery and little enough on the federal relations between central and state administrations. On the former, the student can, however, learn a great deal from a brief analysis by a senior civil servant, E. N. Mangat Rai, *Civil Administration in the Punjab* (1963), also from the reflections of a retired civil servant, S. G. Barve, *With Malice Towards None* (1962) and those of a former minister, K. Santhanam, *Union-State Relations in India* (1960). An important part of federal finance is discussed in the latter book, as also in A. Chanda, *Federalism in India* (1965) and P. P. Agarwal, *System of Grants in Aid in India* (1959). A. Ray, *Inter-governmental relations in India* (1966) is useful. Perhaps only case studies can convey the nature of federal relations; for this reason I. Narain and P. C. Mathur, 'Union-State relations in India: a case study in Rajasthan', *Journal of Commonwealth Political Studies,* II, 2, was valuable and there is now the excellent study by M. F. Franda, *West Bengal and the Federalizing Process in India* (1969) which takes us into the politics of federalism. As these authors make plain, it is impossible to consider federal relations without taking up the whole machinery of planning. H. K. Paranjape provided a useful short descriptive account in *The Planning Commission* (1964) but the main study is A. H. Hanson's *The Process of Planning* (1966). There is some comment of interest to be found in P. Streeten and M. Lipton, *The Crisis of Indian Planning* (1968), K. Santhanam, *Democratic Planning* (1961), V. T. Krishnamachari, *Fundamentals of Planning* (1962), R. Braibanti and J. J. Spengler (Eds.), *Administration and Economic Development in India* (1963), as well as in some of the articles of D. R. Gadgil to be found in his *Economic Policy and Development* (1955) and *Planning and Economic Policy* (1961).

(c) It is no longer easy to separate district (and other local) administration from community development (mentioned above) and democratic decentralization or Panchayat Raj (see below). However, more purely administrative studies are R. Retzlaff, *Village Government in India* (1962), D. C. Potter, *Government in Rural India* (1963), N. B. Desai, *Report of the Administrative Survey of Surat District* (1958), S. S. Khera, *District Administration in India* (1960) and K. S. Desai, *Problems of Administration in Two Indian Villages* (1961).

(d) The bureaucratic structure and personnel are discussed in several of the works listed above (especially Chanda and Braibanti-Spengler). The best general account is D. C. Potter, 'Bureaucratic Change in India' in R. Braibanti (Ed.), *Asian Bureaucratic Systems Emergent from the British Imperial Tradition* (1966). Other studies include N. C. Roy, *The Civil Service in India* (1958), R. Dwarkadas, *The Role of the Higher Civil Service in India* (1958). *Bureaucracy and Political Development* (1963), edited by J. La Palombara, contains no contribution specifically on India but much that is relevant to the Indian situation. A sociological study of great interest is R. P. Taub, *Bureaucrats under Stress* (1969). An enquiry into the public relations of administration is reported in S. J. Eldersveld, A. P. Barnabas and V. Jagannadham, *The Citizen and the Administrator in a Developing Democracy* (1967). On the problem of corruption in administration there is the (Santhanam) *Report of a Committee on Corruption in Public Life* (1964) and J. B. Monteiro, *Corruption* (1966). Police and armed services are arms of administration; on the former there is a useful study, D. H. Bayley, *The Police and Political Development In India* (1969), but on the latter no full-length study pending the publication of S. Cohen, *The Twain Meet,* though interesting articles include L. and S. Rudolph, 'Generals and Politicians in India', *Pacific Affairs,* Spring 1964 and S. Cohen, 'Subhas Chandra Bose and the Indian National Army', *Pacific Affairs,* Winter 1963. An important aspect of modern administration in new states is the management of public enterprise. An early report on this subject was A. D. Gorwala's *On the Efficient Conduct of State Enterprises* (1951), and there is a good deal of India in A. H. Hanson, *Public Enterprise and Economic Development* (1959). Extensive treatments are available in V. V. Ramanadhan, *The Structure of Public Enterprise in India* (1961) and S. S. Khera, *Government in Business* (1963).

VII. The main improvement of recent years in the literature on Indian politics has taken place in the area of political parties and behaviour.

(a) On the general nature of the party system and political behaviour the best early studies were some of the contributions to R. Park and I. Tinker (Eds.), *Leadership and Political Institutions in India* (1959) and M. Weiner, *Party Politics in India* (1967) which focussed on opposition parties' fragmentation. An interesting study and document of the period was A. Mehta, *The Political Mind of India* (1952). Subsequently general accounts appeared in the early editions of the present book as well as in the works mentioned in Section V above. A leading contributor to our understanding of the dominant party system was R. Kothari whose series of articles, 'Form and Substance in Indian Politics', *The Economic Weekly,* April–May 1961 and the later 'The Congress "system" in India', *Asian Survey,* December 1964 were of special importance. Kothari brought together much of his own work and that of his colleagues in *Party Systems and Election Studies* (1967). See also W. H. Morris-Jones, 'Dominance and Dissent', *Government and Opposition,* July–September 1966. On the later developments there are two valuable articles by Paul Brass: 'Coalition politics in North India', *American Political Science Review,* December 1968 and 'Political participation, institutionalization and stability in India', *Government and Opposition,* Winter 1969. S. C. Kashyap, *The Politics of Defection* (1969) gives a detailed narrative of floor-crossing and ministerial instability following 1967.

(b) Excellent studies of particular parties, frequently within particular states, are now available. On Congress: P. Brass, *Factional Politics in an Indian State* (1966), S. A. Kochanek, *The Congress Party of India* (1968), M. Weiner, *Party Building in a New Nation* (1967). See also, for some details on Congress's internal constitution, W. H. Morris-Jones, 'The Indian Congress Party: dilemmas of dominance', *Modern Asian Studies,* April 1967 and for the post-Nehru leadership battles in the party, M. Brecher, *Succession in India* (1966). On the activities of a number of opposition parties in the UP, see Angela Burger's perceptive *Opposition in a Dominant Party System* (1969). On the 'right' parties: H. L. Erdman, *The Swatantra Party and Indian Conservatism* (1967), C. Baxter, *The Jana Sangh* (1969). On the RSS there is the early little study by J. A. Curran, *Militant Hinduism in Indian Politics* (1951) which has not been displaced. B. Graham's forthcoming study of the Jana Sangh will be an important analytical work. While good studies of the socialists are curiously lacking, on the communists the chief work is G. Overstreet and M. Windmiller, *The Communist Party of India* (1959) which now needs to be supplemented by R. Retzlaff, 'Revisionism and dogmatism in the C.P.I.' in R. Scalapino (Ed.), *The Communist Revolution in Asia* (1965) and M. F. Franda, 'India's third communist party', *Asian Survey* (December 1969). R. L. Hardgrave, *The Dravidian Movement* (1965) provides a valuable background on the DMK.

(c) Political activity may be studied by taking not one party but one level or one kind of issue. Some fine studies of the politics of certain states are contained in M. Weiner (Ed.), *State Politics in India* (1968) while there is useful additional data in I. Narain (Ed.), *State Politics in India* (1967). B. R. Nayar, *Minority Politics in the Punjab* (1966) gives a fine detailed account of Sikh politics. The same author's *National Communication and Language Policy* (1970) deals with the politics of the language issue on which there is also J. Das Gupta's *Language Conflict and National Development* (1970). On the politics of particular sections, see P. G. Altbach, *Turmoil and Transition: Higher Education and Student Politics in India* (1968), A. D. Ross, *Student Unrest in India: a comparative approach* (1969), H. Crouch, *Trade Unions and Politics in India* (1967) and H. Erdman, *Political Attitudes of Indian Industry: a case study of the Baroda Business Elite* (1971). M. Weiner, *The Politics of Scarcity* (1962) provided an interesting discussion of the general problem of sectional demands. Earlier studies of the politics of regionalism were Joan Bondurant, *Regionalism versus Provincialism* (1958) and S. S. Harrison, *India: The Dangerous Decades* (1960). M. Brecher, *Political Leadership in India* (1969) reports on élite attitudes. A fascinating study of violent politics is H. Heidenreich, 'The anatomy of a riot', *Journal of Commonwealth Political Studies,* VI, 2.

VIII. The constitutional framework of Indian politics and the working of parliament and courts has had a more adequate treatment than most aspects of the subject.

(a) D. D. Basu, *Commentary on the Constitution of India* (3rd ed., 1955) is the standard full-length lawyer's commentary, but M. V. Pylee, *Constitutional Government in India* (rev. ed., 1965) is comprehensive and less technical, while C. H. Alexandrowicz, *Constitutional Developments in India* (1957) is the most valuable analysis of the main provisions. A detailed account of the workings of the Constituent Assembly is given in G. A. Austin, *The Indian Constitution* (1965); B. Rau, *India's Constitution in the Making* (2nd rev. ed., 1963) hardly attempts that task but does contain some of the papers by the Assembly's Constitutional Adviser. B. Shiva Rao, *The Framing of the Constitution* (5 vols., 1966–8) is useful for reference.

(b) On the executive at the centre, the main study is R. J. Venkateswaran, *Cabinet Government in India* (1967). W. H. Morris-Jones, *Parliament in India* (1957), is the full-scale study of the national legislature. A. B. Lal (Ed.), *The Indian Parliament* (1956), contains some useful essays. The details of procedure are treated in A. R. Mukherjea, *Parliamentary Procedure in India* (1958), and financial aspects in P. K. Wattal, *Parliamentary Financial Control in India* (2nd ed., 1962). On parliamentary committees see B. B. Jena, *Parliamentary Committees in India* (1966) and R. N. Aggarwala, *Financial Committees* (1966). There are interesting aspects of the membership discussed in S. Kochanek, 'The Relation between Social Background and Attitudes of Indian Legislators', *Journal of Commonwealth Political Studies,* VI, 1 and D. Forrester, 'State Legislators in Madras', *Journal of Commonwealth Political Studies,* VII, 1.

(c) The best introduction to law in India is G. C. Rankin, *Background to Indian Law* (1946), and the best brief accounts of the system of law are M. C. Setalvad, *The Common Law in India* (1960) and A. Gledhill, *The Republic of India* (1951). Judicial control is examined in S. R. Sharma, *The Supreme Court in the Indian Constitution* (1958) and A. T. Markose, *Judicial Control of Administrative Action in India* (1956). A crisp treatment of the subject of constitutionally guaranteed rights is in A. Gledhill, *Fundamental Rights* (1955) while V. G. Ramachandran, *Fundamental Rights and Constitutional Remedies* (2nd ed., 1968) is useful for reference. A particular question of interest is analysed in D. H. Bayley, *Preventive Detention in India* (1962). Also relevant though more general in approach is the collection of seminar papers, Congress of Cultural Freedom, *Representative Government and Public Liberties in the New States* (1958). An important aspect of the constitutional framework is its regulation of relations between religious communities and the state; this question is given full-scale examination in the widest context in D. E. Smith, *India as a Secular State* (1963) and on this V. P. Luthera, *The Concept of a Secular State in India* (1964) should also be consulted. A key work on the relation between the framework of law and a religious society is J. D. M. Derrett, *Religion, Law and the State* (1968) while a special issue (Vol. 3, nos. 2–3,

Nov. 1968–Feb. 1969) of *Law and Society* edited by Marc Galanter was full of articles of great interest. See also G. H. Gadbois, 'Indian Judicial Behaviour', *Economic and Political Weekly,* Annual Number January 1970. There are contributions relating to India in J. N. D. Anderson (Ed.), *Changing Law in Developing Countries* (1963). The handling of caste disputes by the courts is excellently treated in M. Galanter, 'Law and caste in modern India' in *Asian Survey,* Nov. 1963.

(d) The electoral part of the framework of politics is less well covered. Apart from the official reports (see below), there are, however, Margaret Fisher and Joan Bondurant, *The Indian Experience with Democratic Elections* (1956), A. H. Somjee, *Voting Behaviour in an Indian Village* (1959), M. Weiner and R. Kothari (Eds.), *Indian Voting Behaviour* (1965) and V. M. Sirsikar, *Political Behaviour in India* (1965). Two books by S. L. Poplai, *National Politics and the 1957 Elections* (1957) and *1962 General Elections* (1962) contain documentary material. Recent work on elections includes the raw material in R. Chandidas (Ed.), *India Votes: a source book* (1968) and C. Baxter, *District Trends in India: a research tool* (1969) and the studies by R. Kothari (Ed.), *Party Systems and Election Studies* (1967) and K. G. N. Murthy and G. L. Rao, *Political Preference in Kerala* (1968). Original approaches to the analysis of election data are found in W. H. Morris-Jones and B. Das Gupta, 'India's Political Areas: Interim Report on an Ecological Electoral Investigation', *Asian Survey,* IX, 6, B. Graham, 'A Report on Some Trends in Indian Elections: The Case of Uttar Pradesh', *Journal of Commonwealth Political Studies,* V, 3 and O. P. Goyal and H. Hahn, 'The Nature of Party Competition in Five Indian States', *Asian Survey,* VI, 10.

(e) There is a large and growing literature on the local framework which has grown out of the community development programme. H. Maddick, *Democracy, Decentralisation and Development* (1963) is a general study but based to a considerable extent on Indian material. His later *Panchayati Raj: Rural Local Government in India* (1970) is now the main work in the field, along with the studies undertaken by the Rajasthan scholars M. V. Mathur and I. Narain, *Panchayati Raj, Planning and Democracy* (1969).

IX. Modern Indian political thinking is of course much influenced by the ideas evolved during the nationalist movement, but a distinctive pattern is emerging.

(a) A good background book of readings is W. T. de Bary and others, *Sources of Indian Tradition* (1958) and a collection of more recent writings is in K. P. Karunakaran (Ed.), *Modern Indian Political Tradition* (1964).

(b) Gandhi's thought (see also III (d) above) is a necessary base line and its quintessence is found more in his *Hind Swaraj* (rev. ed., 1939) than in any other single volume. Among studies of Gandhian ideas are Joan Bondurant's distinguished work *Conquest of Violence* (1958) and Indira Rothermund, *The Philosophy of Restraint* (1963). Reference may also be made to N. K. Bose, *Studies in Gandhism* (rev. ed., 1947), and W. H.

Morris-Jones, 'Mahatma Gandhi—political philosopher?' in *Political Studies,* Feb. 1960. Recent work on Gandhi includes G. Ashe, *Gandhi: a study in revolution* (1968), one of the essays in L. and S. Rudolph, *The Modernity of Tradition* (1967), E. Erikson's notable psychological-historical study *Gandhi's Truth* (1970). The Gandhi Centenary number of *Modern Asian Studies* (Oct. 1969) edited by D. Dalton contains valuable articles by Dalton, Judith Brown and others. Another strong though less original influence was M. N. Roy, whose post-marxist views are found in his *Politics, Power and Parties* (1960).

(c) The most interesting recent writer is J. P. Narayan, whose intellectual journey is indicated by *Towards Struggle* (1946), *Socialism to Sarvodaya* (1956), *Towards a New Society* (1958), *A Plea for the Reconstruction of Indian Polity* (privately circulated paper, 1959), *Swaraj for the People* (1961). A selection of his writings is made in *Socialism, Sarvodaya and Democracy* (1964). A critical note on J.P. was W. H. Morris-Jones, 'The unhappy utopia' in *Economic Weekly* (25 June 1960). Other authors of interest include V. Bhave, *Bhoodan Yajna* (1954), and *Swaraj Sastra: the Principles of a Non-violent Political Order* (1963), K. Santhanam, *Satyagraha and the State* (1960), Sampurnanand, *Individual and State* (2nd ed., 1957) and *Indian Socialism* (1961), S. Narayan, *Socialist Pattern of Society* (1957) and *Gandhian Constitution for Free India* (1946), A. Mehta, *Politics of Planned Economy* (1953) and *Democratic Socialism* (1954), K. Panikkar, *State and the Citizen* (2nd ed., 1960), R. Lohia, *Marx, Gandhi and Socialism* (1963). Worthwhile studies of the Sarvodaya movement include A. H. Doctor, *Sarvodaya* (1968) and a forthcoming book by G. Ostergaard. Accounts of the Bhoodan movement are given in H. Tennyson, *India's Walking Saint* (1955) and J. J. Lanza del Vasto, *Gandhi to Vinoba* (1956). Several socialist tendencies are sketched in Margaret Fisher and Joan Bondurant, *Indian Approaches to a Socialist Society* (1956).

(d) Among the more penetrating early comments on modern Indian thought are F. G. Carnell, 'Political ideas and ideologies in South and South East Asia' in S. Rose (Ed.), *Politics in Southern Asia* (1963), Susanne Rudolph, 'Consensus and conflict in Indian politics' in *World Politics,* April 1961, Phyllis Rolnick, 'Political ideology: reality and myth in India' in *Asian Survey* (Nov. 1962) and 'Charity, trusteeship and social change in India: a study of political ideology' in *World Politics,* (April 1962). The only good treatment at length is K. Damodaran, *Indian Thought* (1967). An important study by D. Dalton, *Ideology in Modern India* is awaited.

X. The Government of India is a great author and Indian official reports and documents are of exceptional value and importance for the student.

(a) Regular or standard publications include: (i) Parliamentary: Lok Sabha *Debates; Reports* of Estimates, Public Accounts and other Committees; *Who's Who; Journal of Parliamentary Affairs;* (ii) Government of India: *Annual Reports* of Ministries; *Descriptive Memoirs* of Ministries; *Allocation of Business Rules; Handbook of Rules and Regu-*

lations for the All-India Services; Administrative Directory of the Government of India; Annual Reports of the Organisation and Methods Division of the Cabinet Secretariat; Annual Reports of the Commissioner for Scheduled Castes and Scheduled Tribes; Annual Reports of the Commissioner for Linguistic Minorities; (iii) Government of India (Planning Commission): *Five Year Plans* (also draft outlines and summaries); *Progress Reports* on the Plans; Annual *Evaluation Reports* and certain special reports of the Programme Evaluation Organization, e.g. *Leadership and Groups in a S. Indian Village* (1955) and *Some Successful Panchayats* (1960).

(b) Special documents and reports include: *The Constitution of India*, as amended; *Report of the Central Pay Commission* (1947); *White Paper on Hyderabad* (1948); *Report of the Linguistic Provinces Commission of the Constituent Assembly* (1948); *White Paper on Communist Violence in India* (1949); *Report on the Reorganisation of the Machinery of Government* (1949); *Report of the Indian States Finances Enquiry Committee* (1949); *White Paper on Indian States* (1950); *Report of the Univeristy Education Commission* (1950); *Report of the Local Finance Enquiry Committee* (1951); *Reports of the Finance Commissions* (1952, 1957, 1961, 1965, 1969); *Report of the Press Commission* (1954); *Report of the States Reorganisation Commission* (1955); *Reports of the Election Commission on the general elections* of 1951–2, 1957, 1962, 1967, on by-elections (periodically) and on mid-term general elections in particular states; *Report of the Railway Corruption Enquiry Committee* (1955); *Report of the Taxation Enquiry Committee* (1955); *Report of the Backward Classes Commission* (1955–6); *Report of the Official Language Commission* (1956); Community Development Ministry, *Local Self-Government Administration in the States of India* (1956) and *Critical Analysis of India's Community Development Programme* (by C. C. Taylor) (1956); Planning Commission Committee on Plan Projects, *Report of the Team for the Study of Community Projects and National Extension Service* (1957); *Report of the Committee of Parliament on the Official Language* (1958); *Report (14th) of the Law Commission on the Reform of Judicial Administration* (1958); *Report of the Commission of Enquiry on Emoluments and Conditions of Service of Central Government Employees* (1957–9); Planning Commission, *Report on Indian and State Administrative Services and the Problems of District Administration* (by V. T. Krishnamachari) (1962); *Report of the Committee on Emotional Integration* (1962); *Report of the Study Team on Nyaya [Judicial] Panchayats* (1962); *Report of the Punjab Commission* (1962); Planning Commission, *Progress of Land Reforms* (1963); Community Development Ministry, *Evolution of the Community Development Programme in India* (1963) and *Report of the Study Team on Panchayati Raj Finances* (1963): *Report of a Committee on Corruption in Public Life* (1964); *Reports of the Administrative Reforms Commission and of its Study Teams* (1967–9); *Report of the Rural Urban Relationship Committee* (3 vols., 1966); *Report of the Banaras Hindu University Inquiry Committee* (1969).

XI. Among other bodies which have produced useful publications may be listed: (a) State Governments: e.g., Government of Maharashtra, *Report of the Committee on Democratic Decentralisation* (1961); Government of Rajasthan, *Report of the Panchayat Elections, 1960* (1961) and *Report on the Working of Panchayati Raj* (1962); also, a few states have published Administration Enquiry Committee Reports: Bengal (1945), Bombay (1948), Kerala (1958); (b) The Center for the Study of Developing Societies: e.g., *Party System and Election Studies* and *The Context of Electoral Change in India;* (c) The Indian Institute of Public Administration: e.g., H. K. Paranjape, *Industrial Management Pool* (1962), V. K. Narasimhan, *The Press, the Public and the Administration* (1961) and several reports of seminars such as *Morale in the Public Services* (1959) and *Recruitment and Training for Public Services* (1957); (d) The Indian Law Institute; (e) The National Institute of Community Development: e.g., H. W. Beers, *Relationship among Workers in C. D. Blocks* (1962); (f) The Association of Voluntary Agencies for Rural Development: e.g., *Report of a Study Team on Democratic Decentralisation in Rajasthan* (1961); (g) The Gokhale Institute of Economics and Politics: e.g., the series of Kale Memorial Lectures; (h) Akhil Bharat Sarva Seva Sangh: e.g., *Report on the Koraput Gramdans* (1960).

The publication activity of the political parties is somewhat uneven but both Congress and the Communist Parties are active in the production of pamphlets. Swatantra has a Newsletter and the PSP publishes Reports of Annual Conventions. The Congress headquarters puts out the *Congress Bulletin* at rather irregular intervals and there is an Annual Report of the General Secretaries. The Congress Constitution is published and there is its official constitutional history, M. V. Ramana Rao, *The Development of the Congress Constitution* (1958). Special organs of the Congress have provided useful reports: e.g. Congress Party in Parliament, *Official Language Controversy Set at Rest* (n.d.); Reports of the Congress Planning Sub-Committee; *Report of the Congress Village Panchayat Committee* (1954); *Report of the Congress Agrarian Reforms Committee* (1949).

XII. As already indicated, much of the more interesting work appears in journals and periodicals.

(a) There is no serious periodical publication outside India exclusively devoted to Indian politics but articles on the subject appear in *Asian Survey, Comparative Studies in Society and History, Economic Development and Cultural Change, European Journal of Sociology, Journal of Asian Studies, Journal of Commonwealth Political Studies, Modern Asian Studies, Pacific Affairs, Parliamentary Affairs, Political Quarterly, Political Studies, South Asian Review, World Politics.*

(b) Indian publications include (i) information summaries: *Asian Recorder* (Delhi, weekly), *Indian Recorder and Digest* (previously *Indian Affairs Record,* Delhi, monthly), *Indian Information* (Delhi, Official, fortnightly), *Journal of Parliamentary Information* (Delhi, half-yearly); (ii) academic journals: *Indian Journal of Political Science, Indian Journal of Public Administration* (which has published useful special issues on particular subjects such as planning administration in July–Sept. 1961), *India Quarterly, International Studies, Journal of the Indian Law Institute, Indian Yearbook of International Affairs, Journal of Constitutional and Parliamentary Studies, Political Science Review*; (iii) general periodicals: *Economic and Political Weekly* (Bombay), which has an outstanding record of achievement in the originality of its contributions and the level of its comment, *Eastern Economist* (Delhi, weekly), *Quest* (Congress for Cultural Freedom organ, quarterly), *Public Opinion Survey* (Indian Institute of Public Opinion organ, monthly), *Seminar* (monthly, Delhi, each issue on a particular topic), *Thought* (Delhi, weekly), *Modern Review* (Calcutta, monthly), *Citizen* (Delhi, weekly), *Link* (Delhi, weekly), *Mainstream* (Delhi, weekly), *Yojana* (Delhi, fortnightly; (iv) political organs: *AICC Economic Review* (Congress), *Socialist India* (New Congress), *Political and Economic Review* ('Syndicate' Congress), *New Age* (CPI), *People's Democracy* (CPI(M)), *Liberation* (CPI(ML)), *Janata, Vigil* and *New Socialist* (Socialist), *Swarajya* (Swatantra), *Organiser* (RSS), *Opinion* (independent conservative); (v) newspapers: *Hindu* (Madras), *Hindu Weekly Review* (Madras) (ceased publication 1969), *Hindustan Times* (Delhi), *Statesman* (Calcutta), each producing also an airmail overseas edition, and *Times of India* (Delhi); (vi) reference volumes: *India: a Reference Annual* (Ministry of Information), *Times of India Directory and Yearbook*.

XIII. Further bibliographical aid can be obtained from: P. Wilson, *The Government and Politics of India and Pakistan, 1885–1955: a bibliography of works in western languages* (1956); J. S. Sharma, four descriptive bibliographies on *Mahatma Gandhi* (1955), *Jawaharlal Nehru* (1955), *Vinoba and Bhoodan* (1956) and *Indian National Congress* (1959); *Indian National Bibliography* 1957–); F. Carnell, *The Politics of the New States: a select annotated bibliography with special reference to the Commonwealth* (1961); B. S. Cohn, *The Development and Impact of British Administration in India: a bibliographical essay* (1961); Maureen Patterson and R. B. Inden, *South Asia: an Introductory Bibliography* (1962); T. J. Leonard, 'Federalism in India', in W. S. Livingstone (Ed.), *Federalism in the Commonwealth: a bibliographical commentary* (1963); J. M. Mahar, *India: a Critical Bibliography* (1965); B. Bloomfield (Ed.) *Theses on Asia accepted by universities in the U.K. and Ireland, 1877–1964* (1967); P. E. Menge, *Government administration in South Asia: a bibliography* (1968); D. A. Low, J. C. Iltis and M. D. Wainwright (Eds.), *Government Archives in South Asia: a guide to national and state archives in Ceylon, India and Pakistan* (1969); *Library of Congress, Southern Asia Accessions List* (monthly); *International Political Science Abstracts*.

INDEX

ACTS: British Parliamentary, 19, 20, 40
Act of 1919, 33
Act of 1935, 21–2, 143
Administration. *See* Civil Service
Administrative Reforms Commission (ARC), 159–65
Akali Dal, 95, 100, 179, 181, 182, 182–4, 188–93, 196, 198, 249. *See also* Punjab, Punjabi Suba, Sikhs
All-India Congress Committee (AICC). *See* Congress
All-Party Hill Leaders Conference (APHLC), 123, 189–93
Ambedkar, Dr. B. R., 33, 79, 86, 105
Andhra, 56, 96–8, 99, 121, 124, 158, 174, 177, 182, 206
Appleby, P., 138
Assam, 54, 99, 101, 123–4, 177
Assembly, *See* State Legislative Assemblies
Avadi Resolution, 109, 201, 208, 209
Ayyangar Gopalaswami, 85–6, 143–4

BANGLA CONGRESS, 190, 193, 199
Bengal, 28, 29, 34, 46, 54, 74, 99, 101, 153, 154–5, 197, 199, 209, 213, 226, 248, 250
Bharat Sevak Sangh, 216, 219
Bharatiya Kranti Dal, 199
Bhave, Vinoba, 59–62, 89, 109, 206, 208, 209, 256
Bhoodan. *See* Bhave
Bihar, 95, 99, 154, 177, 196
Block Development Officer, 113, 157–8. *See also* Community Development

Bombay, 19, 46, 54, 98–100, 196
Bose, Subhas Chander, 34, 172
Brahmin, 51–7, 65, 67, 105, 171, 174, 182, 224
Brass, Paul, 66

CABINET, 79–80, 85–6, 126, 143–4, 146, 162
Committees, 144, 146, 149, 232
Secretariat, 139, 146, 149, 161, 163. *See also* Ministries
Caste, 28, 55–9, 63–4, 65–70, 156, 173–4, 177, 179, 221, 223–7
Central Reserve Police, 155, 164
Central Statistical Organization, 146
Centre-State relations. *See* Federalism
Chambers of Commerce, 219–20
Chandigarh, 123
Chavan, 69, 120, 146, 211, 212
Chief Ministers, 191, 120, 121, 140–1
Christians, 104, 179
Civil Services, 17, 24–7, 54, 86–7, 127–43, 146
Indian (ICS), 25–7, 86, 129, 131–3, 135; Administrative Service (IAS), 86–7, 127–33, 142, 164; Police, 86, 128–34
National Academy of Administration, 130
Organization and Methods Units, 138–9, 146, 149
Pay Commissions, 137
Public Service Commissions, 127–8
Commissions. *See* individual titles
Committee on Plan Projects, 149, 161